Reclaiming Migrant Motherhood

Reclaiming Migrant Motherhood

Identity, Belonging, and Displacement in a Global Context

Edited by Maria D. Lombard

LEXINGTON BOOKS
Lanham • Boulder • New York • London

Cover image credit: "Motherhood" painting. Name: Faiza Nakib. Title: Motherhood. Year: 2017. Materials: Acrylic on canvas. Dimensions : 70cm x 50cm. Photographed by Faiza Nakib. All copyright and reproduction rights are reserved.

Published by Lexington Books
An imprint of The Rowman & Littlefield Publishing Group, Inc.
4501 Forbes Boulevard, Suite 200, Lanham, Maryland 20706
www.rowman.com

86-90 Paul Street, London EC2A 4NE

Copyright © 2022 by The Rowman & Littlefield Publishing Group, Inc.

All rights reserved. No part of this book may be reproduced in any form or by any electronic or mechanical means, including information storage and retrieval systems, without written permission from the publisher, except by a reviewer who may quote passages in a review.

British Library Cataloguing in Publication Information Available

Library of Congress Cataloging-in-Publication Data on File

Names: Lombard, Maria D., 1980- editor.
  Title: Reclaiming migrant motherhood : identity, belonging, and
    displacement in a global context / Maria D. Lombard.
  Description: Lanham : Lexington Books, [2022] | Includes bibliographical
    references and index.
  Identifiers: LCCN 2021055753 (print) | LCCN 2021055754 (ebook) | ISBN
    9781666902051 (cloth) | ISBN 9781666902075 (paperback) | ISBN
9781666902068 (ebook)
  Subjects: LCSH: Motherhood in literature. | Women immigrants in literature.
    | Motherhood in motion pictures. | Women immigrants in motion pictures.
    | Motherhood--Cross-cultural studies. | Women immigrants--Social
    conditions. | Women refugees--Social conditions.
  Classification: LCC PN56.5.M67 R43 2022 (print) | LCC PN56.5.M67 (ebook)
    | DDC 809/.9335252--dc23/eng/20211222
LC record available at https://lccn.loc.gov/2021055753
LC ebook record available at https://lccn.loc.gov/2021055754

Contents

Introduction: Displaced Mothers and the Borders They Must Cross   1
   Maria D. Lombard

PART ONE: REPRESENTATIONS OF DISPLACEMENT   11

Chapter One: "We were born from beauty": Motherly Aesthetics and Poetics of Displacement in Ocean Vuong's *On Earth We're Briefly Gorgeous*   13
   Quynh H. Vo

Chapter Two: Domesticating Displacement, Encounters with Refugee Mothers   31
   Adrianne Kalfopoulou

Chapter Three: Tracing the Impacts of War in Nadifa Mohamed's *The Orchard of Lost Souls*   45
   Alison Graham-Bertolini

Chapter Four: Writing about My Mother: Representations of Alliances between Mothers and Daughters in Young Adult (YA) Refugee Literature   63
   Stella Mililli

Chapter Five: The Ghost Mother in Two Vietnamese American Refugee Novels: A Critical Refugee Analysis   79
   Janet J. Graham

**PART TWO: CONSTRUCTIONS OF IDENTITY AND
BELONGING** 93

Chapter Six: Embroidering Intergenerational Threads of a *Roza*:
Stitching Together Women's Stories and Solidarity in the Fabric
of Diasporic Arab American Fiction 95
Leila Moayeri Pazargadi

Chapter Seven: Mothering on Enemy Land: An Analysis of
Japanese Picture Brides' Motherhood in Julie Otsuka's *The
Buddha in the Attic* 119
Kaori Mori Want

Chapter Eight: Guiding, Shaping, and Resisting: Refugee Mothers'
Educational Strategies as They Navigate "Unsettlement" 131
Lucy Hunt

Chapter Nine: Iraqi Mothers, Diasporic Sons: Narrative Patterns of
Identity and Belonging in *Baghdad Twist* 147
Lamees Al Ethari

Chapter Ten: (Un)inhabitable "homes" for mothers and daughters:
The transmission of memories of "home" in Sri Lankan Tamil
diasporic women's writing 163
Sabreena Niles

Index 183

About the Contributors 193

Introduction

Displaced Mothers and the Borders They Must Cross

Maria D. Lombard

Displaced women who mother traverse complex paths of trauma and hope. *Reclaiming Migrant Motherhood: Identity, Belonging, and Displacement in a Global Context* examines the social and personal impact of displacement on migrant, refugee, or immigrant women who mother around the globe. This transnational and interdisciplinary volume is urgent and timely, as the global refugee crisis continues, and displaced mothers and families endure political, economic, and humanitarian hardships at every border. Particularly with COVID-19 disruptions, displaced mothers have faced even more complexity and this collection can add scholarly insight into the kinds of personal and social challenges they brave. The borders of motherhood examined in this collection are political, geographical, linguistic, and existential. This book deeply analyzes the relationship between identity, belonging, and displacement for mothers who have had to settle elsewhere. Drawing primarily on literary studies and empirical research this volume examines the lives of displaced mothers as they transition into new lives. This volume argues that migrant mothers are themselves sites of knowledge and cultural production, engendering identity and belonging as they move through unfamiliar and transitory spaces.

Questions about the role of society in welcoming and resettling displaced families has long dominated conversations about migrant women, mothers, and their children. This volume reframes these questions by considering the perceptions and labels of the displaced mother along with her own lived experiences as she moves through various borders. Critical refugee scholars have moved away from considering refugee women as only victims to be rescued, and instead look at the ways in which refugee and displaced families reconfigure their identities and fluid situations into lived experience (Abrego,

2014; Chia et al., 2016; Munt, 2012). Similarly, scholars look to both fictional refugee literature and first-hand narrative accounts to answer questions about the complexities of the personal and social identities of refugees (Nguyen, 2018; Pearlman, 2017). Often seen as part of a collective imagination or mythology of the global conscience, migrant motherhood is reclaimed in this volume as it seeks to redefine how migrant mothers construct their identity as members of a community and prioritize their own perceived responsibilities and interests.

This volume builds bridges between literary, refugee, and motherhood studies. Motherhood studies applies feminist, literary, and rhetorical approaches roles to examine the lived experiences of mothers (Buchanan, 2013; Bowers, 1996; DiQuinzio, 2013; Heffernan and Wilgus, 2020). "Motherhood, after all, is formed through reciprocal movements between the experiential and the discursive plane, its transmutations from flesh and action into sign and connotation offering opportunities for reshaping social institutions and cultural codes" (Buchanan 23). For the migrant mother social and cultural perspectives are often extensions of the prevailing beliefs about the place of women and their abilities and (in)abilities to act and cross borders. Tied deeply to the lives of their children and their roles as mothers, displaced women who mother are often inseparable from this perceived identity, from the vulnerability, trauma, and victimhood. Yet, as this volume shows, there are aspects of personal choice and agency that displaced mothers can exhibit, despite the social expectations and walls that may limit them.

THE CONVERSATION: SOCIAL STRUCTURES AND STORYTELLING

Much interdisciplinary research considers displaced mothers a product of their situation and focuses on their dependence on social structures (Schultes and Vallianatos, 2016). Other research looks at aspects of how migrant mothers use the social structures to build new lives for their families. Two books at the intersection of education and anthropology deal with migrant and refugee motherhood. *Motherhood across Borders: Immigrants and Their Children in Mexico and New York* by Gabrielle Oliveira (2018) focuses specifically on Mexican migrant experiences, and is an ethnographic work looking at how Mexican mothers care for and educate their children from afar and negotiate transnational familial identities. This work looks at multigenerational caregiving and the impact of maternal migration on families. Another work focusing on education and migrant mothers is *Motherhood, Education and Migration: Delving into Migrant Mothers' Involvement in Children's Education* by Taghreed Jamal Al-deen (2019). This work is an ethnographic examination of migrant mothers' participation in the education of their children, and the associated social systems of Muslim mothers in Australia. Both studies are culture and place specific, and deal with a particular aspect of identity within the context of displaced mothers, education.

From a literary perspective, contemporary Arab American fiction presents compelling pictures of the displaced mother, as she struggles to move in new directions, build a new home for her family, and traverse complex paths to a life very different from her old one. In *Salt Houses,* Hala Alyan traces the journey of the displaced Palestinian mother, Alia, who has built a life for her children on her own after the death of her husband. Similarly, Zeyn Joukhadar's complex and beautiful novel, *The Map of Salt and Stars*, explores the life of a mother and her young daughters as they become unlikely Syrian refugees. In both of the novels, the father is dead, leaving the mothers to be head of a transitory household. Authors Alyan and Joukhadar both address the complexities of motherhood from a perspective of displacement, giving voice to the thousands of mothers who fade into the dusty routes of (im)migration. This is a pressing topic in Middle Eastern literature and gender studies, as the role of the mother, the caregiver, and the breadwinner are often conflated in refugee and migrant scenarios. Unpacking and giving voice to the countless media stories of mothers at dusty borders is important, but doing so through fiction, as Alyan and Joukhadar do, gives renewed hope that these lives and experiences are meaningful.

For non-fiction accounts, the North American borderlands are filled with complex stories of separation, resettlement, and integration of mothers and their children. With accounts like those from Rosayra Pablo Cruz and Julie Schwietert Collazo (2020), Terese Marie Mailhot (2018) and Dina Nayeri (2019), we find narrative descriptions of the lives of displaced mothers, forming and reforming at every border. Cruz tells first-hand of her journey from Guatemala to the US via detention and separation at the border. She says, "I think about the mothers who are setting off on their journeys north, babies tied to their backs or children's hands in theirs, leading them away from home, probably forever. Then, I fall asleep and dream about the ones who are getting close to the border [. . .]" (Cruz and Collazo 163). Mailhot similarly describes the struggles of her life as a First Nations woman, mother, and author. Her displacements are mental and physical, with the borders not only being about a native reservation or crossing American and Canadian lines, but also about the mother-child relationship, gender roles, and sanity. For Nayeri, displacement happened to her as a child, when she became a refugee from Iran along with her mother and brother. Nayeri describes in great detail her mother's journey and choices, and she is deeply reflective about how that childhood displacement impacts her own experience as a mother. For each of these memoirs, being a refugee, immigrant, or otherwise displaced mother is hard to categorize in simple terms. They have radically different experiences and legal situations determining their belonging to a place. What is common among the narratives is a deep reflection on how the journey, sometimes a multigenerational journey, impacts the mothers and their offspring.

THE COLLECTION: RECLAIMING MIGRANT MOTHERHOOD

While largely situated within literary studies, *Reclaiming Migrant Motherhood* is at the interdisciplinary crossroads of life writing, biography, gender, (im)migration, refugee, and cultural studies. Chapters examine fictional and non-fictional works on migrant motherhood and explore original ethnographic work and personal accounts of displaced mothers. Theoretical frameworks within the collection include postcolonialism, nationalism, feminism, and diaspora studies. The contributors reconsider the displaced mother in relation to identity and belonging in terms of family, community, education, and human rights. The contributors address narrative voice, literature, film, and ethnographic research as they contribute to a contemporary understanding of the displaced mother and disrupt labels like refugee, immigrant, migrant, and diaspora, focusing instead on the lived experiences of displaced mothers. The volume includes voices and stories from Afghanistan, Syria, Vietnam, Japan, Iraq, Canada, Greece, Somalia, Palestine, Sri Lanka, and America.

This volume is organized around two key conversations, "Representations of Displacement" and "Constructions of Identity and Belonging." This volume is an all-women written text, born out of the displacements and deeply personal losses of the COVID-19 pandemic. In Part 1, scholars look at representations of displaced mothers in literary works of authors including Ocean Vuong, Nadifa Mohamed, Terry Farish, Thannha Lai, Bich Minh Nguyen, and Vu Tran. Part 1 also includes a personal essay written by creative writer Adrianne Kalfopoulou that is part ethnography and part critical inquiry into her experiences volunteering with refugees in Greece at the height of the refugee crisis there.

The volume contributors begin to unpack the nature of the refugee mother in Chapter 1 as Quynh Vo examines Ocean Vuong's epistolary novel, *On Earth We're Briefly Gorgeous*. Vo argues that through this lyrical work, Vuong sheds light on the often-invisible lives of refugee mothers who navigate complex realities that impede their hopes for a better life elsewhere. Vo discusses how the protagonist Little Dog wrestles with the violent memories of the Vietnam War that keep haunting his grandmother and mother. Taking the form of a letter to his mother, Rose, Little Dog remarks of his mother and grandmother's resilience in the face of tremendous struggle. Vo notes that throughout the novel, Little Dog and his mother find pleasure together through familial connections and songs. Vo ultimately suggests that *On Earth We're Briefly Gorgeous* allows scholars to envision more livable and ethicopolitical worlds for the displaced in precarious times.

In Chapter 2, Adrianne Kalfopoulou, scholar and creative writer, reflects on the refugee mothers she met during her time as a volunteer in Greece. This chapter is a non-fiction account of the Kalfopoulou's experiences as she volunteered in a once functioning school building in Exarchia neighborhood of Athens where families from Afghanistan, Syria, Iran, and elsewhere had set up living quarters. The chapter explores the kinds of family bonds a refugee mother like Mahilé, in a highly patriarchal culture, nurtures. Kalfopoulou explores some of the ways women like Mahilé express agency within the overt repressions and oppressions of the worlds they have fled, and how the traditions they carry with them shape their relationship to the world. From a theoretical lens, the chapter engages a nuanced view on Western ideas of feminism in discussing this Afghan mother's journey. Kalfopoulou builds on the conversations of Derrida and Dufourmantelle in *Of Hospitality* to frame the everyday experiences of the refugees she worked with.

In Chapter 3, Alison Graham-Bertolini examines the complex identities of mothers ensnared in and displaced by war and political violence in Nadifa Mohamed's novel *The Orchard of Lost Souls*. Through this fictional account of the Somali civil war drawn from Mohamed's memories of childhood in Hargesia, Bertolini draws on nationalistic discourse theories to argue that militarized systems depend on publicly feminizing women. She goes on to argue that such structures maintain and strengthen masculine ideologies of domination. By analyzing the common tropes of the military mother, the modest maiden, and the chaste warrior in Mohamed's work, Bertolini shows that when women challenge these classifications by defying public gendering, they are punished both by their own state, who harms them by asset stripping, as well as from enemies of the state, who threaten them with war violence, including rape, relocation, and death. Bertolini suggests that it is through a female collective, or communal caring and mothering, women find a way to attain freedom and agency in militarized societies.

Stella Mililli examines representations of displaced mothers in young adult literature in Chapter 4. Mililli offers a comparative analysis of the mother figures in two free-verse novels, Terry Farish's *The Good Braider* and Thannha Lai's *Inside Out & Back Again*, and Thi Bui's graphic memoir *The Best We Could Do*. The mothers in these young adult novels are presented through the eyes of their daughters, and the three women experience war as refugees and as women in ethnically marginalized communities in America. Mililli draws on Gloria Anzaldúa's queer and borderland theories and Patricia Hill Collins's Black feminist theory of motherhood to discuss the role of the mothers in a patriarchal society and also as subjects of social change to the benefit of their daughters' lives. Much like the significance of the female collective discussed by Bertolini in Chapter 3, Mililli suggests that in these young adult novels, solidarity between women across different social, cultural, and symbolic borders are necessary for transformation.

As discussed in previous chapters in Part 1, the nature of the displaced, refugee, or migrant mother is complex to say the least, and other-worldly in many ways, almost unknowable for those who have not experienced the ruptures of displacement. In Chapter 5 Janet J. Graham examines a trope that she calls the ghost mother who inhabits Bich Minh Nguyen's *Short Girls* and Vu Tran's *Dragonfish*. With the ghost mother, Graham describes how Nguyen and Tran suggest a need for young adults to critically embrace the refugee experience by troubling the distinction between absence and presence in the figure of the deceased or missing mother who continues to speak through her children's memories of her. Graham builds on theories of memory and intergenerational trauma to show how Tran and Nguyen construct uncanny relationships between the ghost mother and her children. Graham argues that the supernatural ancestral link provides a possibility for forming supportive relationships.

Part 2 of the volume looks at identity development and the significance of belonging for displaced mothers, whether it is through notions of home, the past, or a way forward. Works examined in Part 2 include those by Laila Halaby, Susan Muaddi Darraj, Julie Otsuka, V. V. Ganeshananthan, Shankari Chandran, and Mary Anne Mohanraj. Part 2 also includes an essay by creative writer Lamees Al Ethari looking at the documentary *Baghdad Twist,* as well as an ethnographic study of displaced mother's educational choices and practices in the refugee experience. Part 2 builds on the analysis of what it means to be a displaced mother from Part 1 of the volume.

Part 2 begins with Chapter 6, as scholar Leila Moayeri Pazargadi's discusses the familial bonds between mother and daughter as they relate to the forging of female homosocial networks in Laila Halaby's *West of the Jordan* and Susan Muaddi Darraj's *The Inheritance of Exile*. According to Pazargadi, Halaby's work highlights the significance of cultural and familial identity as the novel examines Palestinian daughters and mothers from the same family. Similarly, as Pazargadi argues, in *The Inheritance of Exile*, Muaddi Darraj shows the diasporic struggles in the lives of four Arab American women and their mothers as they search for a meaningful sense of home while caught in the cultural gap that exists between the Middle East and America. In her chapter, Pazargadi suggests Halaby and Muaddi Darraj's depictions of motherhood reflect the complicated identities of first- and second-generation immigrants who often struggle to reconcile links to home.

In Chapter 7, Kaori Mori Want looks at the ways that Japanese picture brides lived and mothered as the wives of Japanese male laborers in America in the early twentieth century. Want builds her chapter around Julie Otsuka's *The Buddha in the Attic* (2011) which is a work of fiction based on Otsuka's personal interviews with picture brides. Want describes the struggle the picture brides faced mothering in America particularly isolated as they could not speak English and did not understand the social rules. Want brings in historical and theoretical references to give context for the ways that Japanese picture brides struggled, especially at a time when anti-Japanese sentiment among white Americans was very intense. Want examines how migrant women's mothering is affected by a host country when its mainstream population has strong hostility towards them, and she discusses how these mothers develop their own strategies aimed at the survival of their children.

Further examining the strategic nature of migrant motherhood, Chapter 8 by Lucy Hunt explores Hunt's original empirical research on how motherhood is implicated in educational decision-making. In her work, Hunt considers the wider role of motherhood in imagining and constructing pathways towards the futures of displaced and refugee mothers. In her chapter, Hunt explores how young refugees—many of whom have arrived in Greece by crossing the Aegean Sea from Turkey—now find themselves in uncertain situations which they are forced to navigate. Hunt draws from Vigh's concept of "social navigation" and ethnographic fieldwork in Thessaloniki, Greece to address the influence of motherhood on achieving educational goals, while also making the case for including the "spatial" in educational research. Hunt is particularly interested in how young refugee mothers carve out their own educational spaces in the city as an important expression of personal agency.

In a powerful look at storytelling and film, Chapter 9 by scholar and creative writer Lamees Al Ethari examines identity and personal narrative regarding the incidents of *Farhud*, or the violent dispossession, that led to the gradual forced Jewish exile from Iraq. In this chapter, Al Ethari looks at Canadian filmmaker Joe Balass's 33-minute glimpse into the Iraqi Jewish experience through an interview with his mother Valentine Balass. Balass's documentary and visual memoir, *Baghdad Twist* shows Valentine's challenging experiences as a wife and mother as she struggles to hold her family together. Al Ethari analyzes Valentine's retelling of these memories as they establish a historical and personal account for Joe and function as a connection to his Iraqi self. At the same time, Al Ethari argues that through the act of narration, Valentine reclaims her identity as an Iraqi woman and mother, an identity that was challenged and fragmented by oppression, displacement and multiple migrations, as she maintains the authority in (re)presenting herself through the documentary. Al Ethari brilliantly weaves her own story of motherhood and migration into the chapter, as she bookends the chapter with reflections on mothering in Iraq and Canada, sharing her language and culture with her own sons, like Valentine did, as they navigate their own identities.

In the final chapter of the volume, Chapter 10, Sabreena Niles considers her own diasporic identity as she dives deeply into the writings of Sri Lankan Tamil diasporic women writers, V. V. Ganeshananthan, Shankari Chandran, and Mary Anne Mohanraj. Looking at how mothers and daughters displaced by war try to replicate "home" in their new diasporic lives, Niles shows the ways the writers describe Sri Lankan Tamil homes and their homeland. Through a lens of violence and trauma theory, Niles looks at how trauma experienced by mothers ultimately impacts and defines their relationships with their daughters. Niles wrestles with questions of familial inheritance, particularly the ability of a daughter to inherit, inhabit, or recreate her mother's home. Niles shows how intergenerational traumas bond mothers and daughters together. Ultimately, this chapter shows that not only do displaced mothers struggle to reconcile their own identity outside of their homeland, but that this displacement continues to impact the lives, identities, and homes of the next generation of women.

With every border crossing comes a story. The stories of displaced mothers, whether they come to us through novels, second-hand narratives, original research, or films bring real perspective to the journeys and experiences of these women who face complex journeys that don't seem to end once they reach their destinations. As this volume shows, the displaced mother is a significant figure to consider in terms of her identity, agency, and path forward. This volume seeks to frame the conversation around refugee, migrant, and displaced motherhood as interdisciplinary and transborder. The complications and traumas of the lives of refugee and otherwise displaced mothers often mean they are never truly knowable. Vu Tran says about the refugee, "Her identity, her goals and desires and intentions, her place in the world she now inhabits: they are all as hazy as those memories of the world she was once born into" (154). The rich analysis and research in this volume hopefully make her a bit more knowable.

WORKS CITED

Abrego, Leisy. *Sacrificing Families: Navigating Laws, Labor, and Love Across Borders.* Stanford University Press, 2014.

Al-deen, Taghreed Jamal. *Motherhood, Education and Migration: Delving into Migrant Mothers' Involvement in Children's Education.* Palgrave-Macmillan, 2019.

Alyan, Hala. *Salt Houses.* Houghton Mifflin Harcourt, 2017.

Bowers, Toni. *The Politics of Motherhood: British Writing and Culture, 1680-1760.* Cambridge University Press, 1996.

Buchanan, Lindal. *Rhetorics of Motherhood*. Southern Illinois University Press, 2013.

Chia, Youyee, et al. *Claiming Place: On the Agency of Hmong Women*. University of Minnesota Press, 2016.

Cruz, Rosayra Pablo and Julie Schwietert Collazo. *The Book of Rosy: A Mother's Story of Separation at the Border.* HarperOne, 2020.

DiQuinzio, Patrice. *The Impossibility of Motherhood: Feminism, Individualism and the Problem of Mothering*. Routledge, 2013.

Heffernan, Valerie and Gay Wilgus, Eds. *Imagining Motherhood in the 21st Century*. Routledge, 2020.

Joukhadar, Zeyn. *The Map of Salt and Stars*. Atria Books, 2018.

Mailhot, Terese Marie. *Heart Berries: A Memoir*. Counterpoint, 2018.

Munt, Sally. "Journeys of Resilience: The Emotional Geographies of Refugee Women." *Gender, Place & Culture: A Journal of Feminist Geography*, vol. 19, no. 5, 2012, pp. 555–77.

Nayeri, Dina. *The Ungrateful Refugee: What Immigrants Never Tell You.* Catapult, 2019.

Nguyen, Viet Thanh, Ed. *The Displaced: Refugee Writers on Refugee Lives*. Abrams Books, 2018.

Oliveira, Gabrielle. *Motherhood across Borders: Immigrants and Their Children in Mexico and New York*. NYU Press, 2018.

Pearlman, Wendy. *We Crossed a Bridge and It Trembled: Voices From Syria*. Custom House, 2017.

Schultes, Anna Kuroczycka and Helen Vallianatos, Eds. *The Migrant Maternal: 'Birthing' New Lives Abroad*. Demeter Press, 2016.

Tran, Vu. "A Refugee Again." *The Displaced: Refugee Writers on Refugee Lives* edited by Viet Thanh Nguyen. Abrams Books, 2018.

PART ONE

Representations of Displacement

Chapter One

"We were born from beauty"

Motherly Aesthetics and Poetics of Displacement in Ocean Vuong's On Earth We're Briefly Gorgeous

Quynh H. Vo

The atrocities of war and its violent resonance keep ricocheting generation after generation of Vietnamese Americans. As refugees themselves, Vietnamese American authors remind us of their painful genesis and shattered bonds, taking us through lives of the displaced who constantly struggle as outcasts in the margin of their new homeland or are strategically forgotten like specters of history that, ironically, have never ceased to haunt our moral consciousness. In his debut novel, *On Earth We're Briefly Gorgeous: A Novel,* Ocean Vuong offers to us a different prism of war through which Little Dog—the narrator—reconfigures his traumatic memories, sublimating the vulnerability of refugee mothers into power. In Vuong's lyrical imagination, refugees are like monarch butterflies flying away from the burning napalm of history that only their children may desire to revisit one day, because surviving such flight is already harrowing, and the one that survives war is like "the final monarch that lands on a branch already weighted with ghosts" (13). Emerging from brutalities of the Vietnam War, women in *On Earth* manifest their resilience, optimism, and courage. Through his poetic narrative—a poignant paean to the protagonist's grandmother and mother, the women warriors whose names are Lan and Rose—Vuong renames the unsettling existence of refugees like his family from "war" to "beauty," inviting us to imagine an alternative power, a transformative agency beyond war and violence—the creative articulation of, what I term, motherly aesthetics. By depicting illiterate, bruised, scarred, and "monstrous" (grand)mothers whose invincible love for life, art, and family struggle with calamities, in war and in peace, Vuong renders visible precarious lives of refugee mothers who keep navigating multiple constraints and radically uneven realities. In this fashion, *On Earth We're Briefly Gorgeous* allows us to envision more livable and ethicopolitical worlds for the displaced in the age of uncertainty.

Vietnamese American literature, if not including works written in the Vietnamese language, is mostly created by authors of the 1.5 generation who, as scholars fluidly define, came to the United States at a young age with only fragmented memories of the Vietnam war that displaced their families (Chan xiv; Vu 144). What remains in their imagination is as nebulous and adulterated as their mother tongue. Yen Le Espiritu asks in her critical book, *Body Counts:* "How do young Vietnamese Americans, born and/or raised in the United States create 'memories' of a war that preceded their births or their consciousness?" (139). The idea of beauty encapsulates the ways that Vuong represents nation, motherhood and displacement in relation to the history of imperialism and nation-state. As Vuong reveals in an interview with Spencer Quong, this novel is a literary adventure "found in truth but realized by the imagination" (Quong, "Survival as a Creative Force"). This autobiographical novel came shortly after his phenomenal debut, *Night Sky With Exit Wounds*, which Vuong deems not sufficient in answering the question he has been asking for all his life, "What does it mean to be a queer American body, or poor, or a refugee?" (Gonzalé). Like Vuong, Little Dog is weighed with an endless morass. Through his poetic and lyrical reconstruction of memories in his novel, Ocean Vuong seems to respond to Espiritu's question for his generation. By revisiting the history of war and displacement that continues to haunt those who survive, Vuong also reclaims the just memory of Vietnamese refugees whose stories have been overwritten by dominant U.S. narratives in which Vietnamese refugees are portrayed as "ideological figures" to galvanize the U.S. fantasies of rescue and liberation.

On Earth We're Briefly Gorgeous takes the form of a long letter that Little Dog writes to his illiterate, PTSD afflicted mother who could never read it. Why would one desire to write a letter without expecting it to be read? Little Dog does not write it into the vacuum, but "in writing you [his mother] here, I am writing to everyone" (33). Writing to his mother, Little Dog also writes to women warriors like her and their children, to generations before and after him, to victors and victims, to survivors and martyrs of the Vietnam War; inviting us to contemplate his private space, which is "unsafe" and vulnerable like his name, which "can both shield him and turn him into an animal at once" (34). Drawing on his own life experiences of being born on a paddy field outside Saigon in 1988 and growing up in Hartford, Connecticut, during the 1990s, Vuong portrays a poignant saga of Vietnamese refugees running away from their war-savaged homeland. Little Dog lives with his mother and grandmother in the drug-ravaged community of Hartford which is inhospitable to their existence.

For mothers like Rose who are desperately forced to leave their homeland, memories are painful, and anything in the new place may evoke an unspeakable grief. As the novel begins, Little Dog recalled the moment when his mother saw the taxidermy buck, for the first time, mounted above the soda machine in Virginia and was terribly horrified by the "corpse" that got "stuck forever like that" (3). For the first time Little Dog senses how the past as an apparition, like death embodied by taxidermy, is still haunting his mother's life. While a buck of an animal, usually a deer, is ordained to be decapitated and worthy of exhibiting on the wall as an award from a hunting game to fascinate other visitors, this heinous display traumatizes Rose like "a death that won't finish, a death that keeps dying" (3). Instead of suggesting triumph, the mounted taxidermy buck only reminds Rose of the melancholic past of war, violence, and deaths that should be buried forever in her refugee consciousness and replaced with present moments. By depicting Little Dog's painful obsession with the entertaining ornament in an American public place, Vuong also unravels the intersection of power and memory in asymmetrical economies that either enhance hedonistic pleasures of some people or deepen sufferings of financially deprived ones.

As the novel unfurls, the mother, Rose, lost her education as soon as she started it when the Vietnam War exploded and she was then only seven. Years later when her family migrated to the United States, Rose did attempt to practice reading again under her son's tutelage, yet in vain: "After the stutters and false starts, the sentences warped or locked in your throat, after the embarrassment of failure, you slammed the book shut" (5). Like Ocean Vuong who blossoms in a world that excludes his mother, Little Dog finds every word he puts down takes him "further" from his mother who resists reading as it is "too late" for her age. Rose's resistance to another language bespeaks her constant negotiation of home where refugees like her family are treated as perpetual strangers resonates with what Yen Le Espiritu would call "militarized refuge" or a violent in the guise of humanitarian shelter (36). Rose's troubling existence reminds us of her American father who gave her life. Paradoxically, without the war, the encountering between Lan and Paul would have never happened, and Rose never came to life, and Little Dog never existed. But the irony of fate is that Rose's fair skin, "so fair that you would 'pass' for white" (51), makes her an outcast in Vietnam, while her broken English turns her into a misfit in the United States. By portraying Little Dog's refugee mother as an unassimilable woman, Vuong makes visible the inconsistent myth of American multiculturalism that promises equal dignity only to self-sufficient and rational individuals, or what Avery Gordon and Christopher Newfield note as "renewed demands for assimilation in disguise"

(*Multiculturalism* 1) so a war survivor and a linguistically incompetent woman like Rose can never afford.

In Vuong's imaginative cosmos, refugees carry on through their lives not in peace but in the shadow of war that cripples their souls, turning them into monsters. Little Dog struggles to fathom and forgive his violent but caring mother whose haunted memories of war and violence sometimes turns her into a merciless "monster." One time, Rose came home after a long day at work that sapped her energies, leaving herself effete, while Little Dog was scattering his Legos all over the place and messing up the house. She threw the box of Legos at her son's head, leaving "the hardwood dotted with blood" (6). Little Dog neither hates his mother nor does he try to blame her for violently abusing him physically and emotionally. As Vuong shows us pervasively in this novel, Little Dog blames the war for turning his mother into a monster. By linking Rose's monstrosity to war and violence, Vuong reminds us to complicate refugees as people emerging from the war and never recovering "unscarred" from it. Like other refugee parents who soldiered through the brutal war, Little Dog's mother assiduously endures her violent memories in silence to protect her son. This is also observed by Yen Le Espiritu in her studies, that "dangerous stories" of war suffering are usually left untold by Vietnamese refugee parents who never want their children to relive their torture (54). However, this silence also creates an invisible distance between parents and their children that troubles their relationship. The more enigmatic Rose appears to her son, the more lonesome and dejected Little Dog becomes in his quiet struggle to penetrate his mother's turmoil.

On Earth unfolds how the impacts of war on motherhood are intergenerational. Lan herself is traumatized by the war's ramification, so she can empathize with her daughter, fathoming that while Rose beats Little Dog out of her desperate exasperation, she loves him deeply. When Little Dog ran away from home one night, when he was ten, escaping his mother's outrage by climbing up a maple tree in his neighborhood and sitting there until his grandmother finally found him, telling him to excuse his mother's madness because, his grandmother explained, "she loves you, Little Dog, but she sick. Sick like me. In the brains" (122). The sickness or monstrosity that his grandmother and mother undergo resonates with the way other kids see him in his mother's dress and jeer at him ruthlessly, calling him "freak, fairy, fag." Little Dog would learn so much later that those words also bear the same meaning with "monster" (14). In a new world where they take refuge, war survivors like Little Dog's family are doomed to be monstrous.

Little Dog strives to understand himself and the dearest people around him, figuring out one day that "parents suffering from PTSD are more likely to hit their children," only to navigate through his tough childhood and embrace his "monstrous" mother and rationalize her violence, relating it with a motherly care, or "perhaps to lay hands on your child is to prepare him for war" (13). Embracing his mother's pathology as his own living in a cruel world hostile to strangers like them, Little Dog commits an unconditional love to a mother-monster, rationalizing her outrage as "a hybrid signal, a lighthouse: both shelter and warning at once" (p. 13). In her book, *Ingratitude* which explores the irony of second-generation Asian American daughters feeling suffocated with their remarkable upbringings, Erin Khuê Ninh argues that children "trained not to question authority and ideally never to formulate an unapproved thought, are ill-prepared for many arenas beyond the walls of their homes" (Khuê Ninh, "Asian American Like Me"). Little Dog defends his mother's deployment of corporal punishment over him by giving it a very similar reason: preparing him for "war" or imminent danger. So Little Dog, as we can see throughout the narrative, always confronts perilous moments with a stunning calmness.

In *On Earth*, Little Dog takes refuge in philosophical moments of beauty through his quiet journey to grapple with violent memories of atrocities that keep haunting his grandmother and mother. His mother's name is Rose—the name that embraces fragility and heroism; a "flower" and "the past tense of rise"—a rose rising from the bullet-ridden land and blossoming in an exotic place where she struggles to belong. Pervasively in this lyrical novel are revelatory moments when Little Dog and his mother distill ethereal beauty from simple pleasures of familial intimacy, singing their healing songs against the pain of displacement. Vuong's poetic, poignant narrative resists an unjust memory that erases sufferings of refugees like his family—and re-creates beauty out of their endless struggles: soldiering through the war, crossing oceans, grappling with what it means to be alive, and lost, and to carry on. Rose, Lan, and Little Dog propel us forward fearlessly, because beauty is resistance.

Little Dog's narrative of his family frustrates any monolithic representations of ethnic communities by recreating the experiences of a Vietnamese American family who embrace an existence vastly different from that of "good refugees" celebrating the "gift of freedom" with gratitude that has been scripted for them. Mimi Thi Nguyen defines this "precious and poisonous" gift as the liberal empire's promise of "freeing peoples from unenlightened forms of social organization through fields of power and violence" (3). And those who receive this gift is obligated to show their gratitude by becoming free and prosperous agents to justify that intervention. In Little Dog's intimate world of upheavals and unsettlements, Vuong recovers Vietnamese Americans' desires and aspirations larger than U.S. celebratory narratives about them. In *On Earth*, the grandmother "would start to sing any time there was conflict," and "cast a spell over" the family so that they all "could survive our problems" (Rigoberto, "Be Bold") Vuong writes about his world of immigrant people who "lived rich and diverse lives" since he also grew up among blacks, and only learned about white supremacy when he left Hartford, Connecticut, at the age of 12. "I wanted a voice in the conversation about what it means to be a body inhabiting this incredibly complicated, violent, and precarious country," Vuong said that in an interview with Gonzalez. And he redeems this power by retelling the story of his refugee family.

Unlike the desirable fantasy of Vietnamese Americans as a "model minority" whose glossy emergence manifests the righteousness of the war that liberates them, many Vietnamese war survivors still struggle in the dark. Discussing the class stratification among Vietnamese Americans, Nhi T. Lieu observes that some Vietnamese Americans attempt to assimilate into the mainstream economy as a "representational strategy" to counter against the "haunting figure of the destitute refugee" (2). While the first generation of Vietnamese refugees may have thrived economically in a profusion of professions nowadays, the majority of them are still wrestling quietly on the margin without English. In *On Earth*, Rose is not the model minority but the unassimilable refugee. Although she presents as white, without English, she can never pass. For limited, displaced mothers like Rose whose English vocabulary is " fewer than the coins [she] saved from [her] nail salon tips in the milk gallon under the kitchen cabinet," surviving in a strange country is a struggle, if not another war. Rose displays herself both as a burden and a challenge to American rhetoric of multiculturalism that assumes all cultures are equally valued. Her limited and broken English relegates Rose to a powerless individual who cannot afford an equally autonomous and rational life like native speakers. As Little Dog experienced during his childhood in the United States, "One does not 'pass' in America, it seems, without English" (52). Little Dog remembers walking to a store at night with Rose and Lan to buy oxtail for making a Vietnamese beef noodle soup but none of them could explain what they wanted to purchase in English with the men behind the butter counter, ending up being a full circus in public (30). His mother urged Little Dog to interpret the word to the men but he couldn't, watching the men "roar" in "bewilderment" at them. And they finally gave up, walking home with "a loaf of Wonder Bread and a jar of mayonnaise" instead. Little Dog's family did not "pass" as "the freed and reformed Vietnamese refugees" that the American mainstream media want to showcase to justify the American "rescue and liberation" script but as the irony of such myths and memories. By narrating Little Dog's struggle to survive amid a shaky present and an unpredictable future in their adopted homeland, Vuong displays a complex reality that success for everyone is only a promise far beyond reach of unassimilable refugee women like Rose.

The term "unassimilable" is a double-edged sword: Rose transforms the disempowered representation of the unassimilable refugee into a position of insight that enables a critique of American culture. As part of Asian American culture, Vietnamese Americans also remember the past differently, as Lisa Lowe observes in her book, *Immigrant Acts,* "in and through the fragmentation, loss, and dispersal that constitutes that past." This cultural site is "more than critical negation of the U.S. nation; it is a site that shifts and marks alternatives to the national terrain by occupying other spaces, imagining different narratives and critical historiographies, and enacting practices that give rise to new forms of subjectivity and new ways of questioning the government of human life by the national state" (29). Vuong's persistence on historicizing war and refugees through reconstructing stories from his family's experience exemplifies this creative space of resistance and imagination in the face of historical amnesia.

The fashion in which *On Earth* troubles the fantasy of successful refugees prospering in the land of freedom is also sharply represented in other narratives by Vietnamese American authors such as Le Thi Diem Thuy, Andrew Lam, Viet Thanh Nguyen, Amy Pham, Thi Bui, to name a few. In portraying traumatized subjects who perpetually inhabit economically and emotionally insecure lives in the United States, these authors refuse optimist futures imagined for them where they will be successful but will also perpetually be refugees. In their writings, that refugees becoming Americans is forever an unrealizable promise. Their literary work manifests a mosaic of unassimilable, peripheral, and rejected lives whose struggles to survive reclaim the heterogeneous history of Vietnamese refugees larger than war and violence.

Little Dog revitalizes his family history, his genealogy, taking the reader through his memories of war that keeps reverberating, seemingly telling us that they "were born from war"—but Little Dog remembers otherwise—reminding us that they were "born from beauty." In his poetic narrative, Lan and Rose—unlike the flowers that they were named after—never wither away but bloom forever in our consciousness. The beauty of survival is ethereal, since those who survive war become invincible, like "the fruit" that even violence, having passed by, "failed to spoil it" (231). Also in this manner, Ocean Vuong renames the unsettling existence of refugees like his family from "war" to "beauty," inviting us to imagine an alternative power, a transformative agency born out of violence—a creative space of aesthetics, and even more evocative affect in Vuong's narrative is motherly aesthetics.

Beauty, in Vuong's imagination, arises from violence, or perilous moments when one has to fight for survival, something between life and death. That beauty of survival from the war is an invincible power, like the fragile butterflies fleeing from the napalm clouds, flying thousands of miles across the sky and drifting, after all those blazed firestorms, unscathed. Emerging from the war and surviving from its brutality are beautiful, as Little Dog returns time and again, unmoored by the story that his ESL teacher of third grade, Mrs. Callahan, reads for him. The story, *Thunder Cake*, is about a mother and her daughter baking their cake in the eye of a storm. Their spirit of having joy in the face of danger keeps resonating in Little Dog's memory, evoking his recollections of his family surviving in bomb attacks. He remembers that all they had as their refuge was not a house, but a table: "A family sleeping in a bomb crater. A family hiding underneath a table. Do you understand? All I was given was a table. A table in lieu of a house. A table in lieu of history" (232). While trying to grapple with the violent memories of atrocities that keep haunting his grandmother and mother, Little Dog has never ceased to be inspired by their resilience, optimism, and courage (Quong, "Survival as a Creative Force"). The beauty arising from tragedies is a form of resistance, since Little Dog's family refuses to have beauty taken away from them. There is beauty of surviving and power of existence at the proximity to death. *On Earth* evokes nostalgic among war survivors for such a traumatic past because beauty arising from such perilous moment makes struggles in an unequal peace even more ironic.

By creating beauty as the power against violent memories of the war, Vuong, however, does not celebrate a facile oblivion of the violent past but creates a healing space of memories that I term poetics of displacement as an alternative agency. In pages of lyrically allusive narrative, Vuong presents an alternative memory of war and displacement, which is worth preserving in this moment of historical amnesia, when refugees are twice displaced by violence and master narratives that threaten to annihilate their lives the way their homeland was devastated with napalm. It was during this tumultuous wartime the narrator tells us that his grandmother committed a radical act: "a woman gifted herself a new name—Lan—in that naming claimed herself beautiful, then made that beauty into something worth keeping. From that, a daughter was born, and from that daughter, a son" (230). As Vuong depicts the grandmother whose skin has the "color of dirt after a rainstorm, . . . pocked with dark pores," Lan doesn't seem to own an alluring appearance, yet her beauty of struggle—the agency to make choice for her own life—triumphs. In her oblivious moments drifting between past and present, with Little Dog beside her plucking her white hairs, Lan recounts her struggle for surviving during wartime: leaving her daughter to her sisters in the village only to sustain them all by selling her body to American GIs on R&R. It seems that women like her had no choice but embracing social stigma to survive, yet Lan perpetually returns to her past with healing repentance. Lan struggles to forgive her past of being a whore out of poverty that jeopardized her family. Although she knows that through the eyes of her own mother, "a girl who leaves her husband is the rot of a harvest," she rationalizes her choice then as the only one any mother in wartime would do to survive and sustain her family. "Who can judge me, huh? Who?" Lan's searing question reminds us that making choice in the lack of choice is her beauty—the beauty of surviving in the brutal war. It is also this audacity of choice that sustains her family in war and displacement and reincarnates Lan who reclaims her beauty through storytelling: "She rocked from side to side, eyes shut, face lifted toward the ceiling, like she was seventeen again" (46–47). This is also my argument that Lan's reminiscences of beauty and brutalities creates the space for Little Dog to imagine a pain that bonds him to his resilient grandmother's past.

In *On Earth*, Vuong also presents to us a form of beauty budding from uncertainty, or the reality of shakiness that sparks an alternative imagination that resists an unchanged melancholia. Here, we are inspired by what Vuong offers to us: the poetics of displacement through his portrayal of refugee mothers and their shaky, precarious experiences. While speaking English is like hobbling in a mysterious, hostile, and troubling territory with an invisible border that resists refugees like Little Dog's family, it can never thwart their dream for beauty. Rose cannot say the names of "a bird, a flower, or a pair of lace curtains from Walmart," or even after Little Dog taught her those words, she would forget them all the next day, "the syllables slipping right from [her] tongue" (29). What Rose could retain, and she did it naturally, after the ebbs and flows of her tumultuous life, like a hummingbird singing over an orchard in her neighbor's yard: "Đẹp quá,"(It's beautiful,) Rose would smile, "Đẹp quá" (48).

In his flashback memories, Little Dog recalled his mother lifting him away from brutalities, replacing colors of darkness and violence with hues of beauty and love, saving for him a gorgeous imagination. He remembers pushing a cart to the church with his mother and seeing "Red. Red. Red. Red" everywhere, a "trail of blood" of someone who was shot dead the night before on the sidewalk (230). The scene must be too jarring for a little boy like Little Dog who was then too young to understand violence. But holding his little hand in her "hot" and "wet hands," his mother kept asking him to "look up" and pointing her fingers skyward, to imaginary birds: ". . . So many colors. Blue birds. Red birds. Magenta birds. Glittered birds." Little Dog remembers looking at the "twisted branches" that his mother tried to direct his eyes to, and imagining the nest where the mother bird is feeding worms to the yellow chicks. Little Dog kept staring at his mother's fingers until "an emerald blur ripened into realness . . . as [Rose's] mouth opened and closed and the words wouldn't stop coloring the trees" (230–231). Little Dog then forgot the blood and never looked down again. In this poignant episode, the representation of the love and protection of a mother to her son manifests the motherly aesthetics that shelters and reconfigures a child's dark memory to a splendid, humane, and inspiring imagination.

In *On Earth,* Vuong envisioned such beauty as a sanctuary of motherly aesthetics, like Little Dog's mother desiring coloring against her precarious existence. The burning desire for coloring came to Rose one morning when she reached forty-six. Little Dog took his mother to Walmart where Rose bought coloring books and all shades of colors that she couldn't even pronounce: "Magenta, vermilion, marigold, pewter, juniper, cinnamon" (6). Little Dog watched his mother do the coloring passionately for two hours every day and the house turned into an elementary classroom. Little Dog asked his mother why she loved coloring at such moments of her life, and her answer gives us a tingle of revelation, as Vuong depicts vividly: ". . .you put down the sapphire pencil and stared, dreamlike, at a half-finished garden. 'I just go away in it for a while,' you said, "but I feel everything. Like I'm still here, in this room" (6). Rose, who experienced everything of war and displacement, has a resolute longing for a different life, since she understands that leaving or not leaving, she would regret either. She strives to treasure herself because of her worst experiences in the past and her endless struggle in her dark realities for an elusive future. In this manner, Ocean Vuong sublimates the motherly vulnerability into power. Like Rose, we are offered a vision of nascent, an epiphany of beauty beyond the banal world.

In Vuong's novel, beauty and brutality congenitally bind to one another, forging creative adaptability and unflinching hopes against adversities. It is impossible not to view Vuong's novel through the prism of beauty. *On Earth* is, at heart, a poetics of displacement. The world that Little Dog belongs to is rife with displaced lives co-existing that exhibit the vagueness between a promise of American dream and suffocating realities, between freedom and "the cage far widening from you" (216). Freedom, in Little Dog's illumination, is like the calf feeling most free when released from its cage, only to be "led to the truck for slaughter" (216). While the freedom that Little Dog cherishes is only "relative" and seems more like a giant "trap" that ensnares him in a bordered world, he dances in that elusive freedom with "elation" when "fucking" Trevor wildly in the barn. That freedom as a cage vanishes, becoming "invisible." In many episodes of *On Earth*, we see Little Dog is unmoored, displaced from the reality of pain and loss, to claim beauty in an alternative world whether it be in love or in connection with dear and near people. Little Dog is enthralled in his love with Trevor, for example, then he sees it gorgeously as "there were colors" he felt when he was with Trevor (106). And the beauty becomes power when it is shared with his mother, a dearest person that could never access her son's world and imagination, but between them always remains an intimacy that binds and empowers them. Justin Torres observes in his review article on *On Earth* for the *New York Times* that from that intimacy arises the power as if, toward the end of the novel, Vuong takes "the pain of the world home to mother and hold it up to her like a hurt she might kiss." Torres calls it a sort of "talismanic seal, a spell, a gesture that transforms hurt into healing through the shared belief in its power." Here, the beauty of survival, even tattered by the war, becomes indestructible. Although those war survivors like Little Dog's family bear their wounds, as Lan and Rose wrestle with their PTSD, they become beauty. That beauty as power sustains them also in displacement, so that they can march on against all odds.

In *On Earth*, Vuong complicates refugee space through the lens of Little Dog who sees his mother toiling everyday as a beautician in the nail salon. The cost for Rose to become a beautician in the United States, ironically, is the double damage of her own beauty: the first time during the violent war, the second time in brutal peace. Here, we are introduced to a healing but hazardous space for refugee women like Rose: "The salon is also a kitchen where, in the back rooms, our women squat on the floor over huge woks . . . of phở simmer and steam up the cramped spaces with aromas of cloves, cinnamon, ginger, . . . mixing with formaldehyde, toluene, acetone, Pine-Sol, and bleach" (80). The salon represents not only an imagined home space but also the cost any refugees like Rose have to pay for their hopes and dreams in the new country they call home. In her dissertation, *Vietnamese Manicurists: An Intermediary between Cultures,* Hong Kong Tran attributes the tendency of Vietnamese manicurists working together to the Vietnamese traditional value of "a strong familial bond" and the desire to maintain their cultural values in public sphere. Tran observes that nail salons also exist as the space of assimilation where Vietnamese manicurists can absorb American culture and negotiate their sense of belonging. But here Vuong also shows us that within that space, everything articulates "what it means to be awake in American bones—with or without citizenship—aching, toxic, and underpaid" (81). Vuong deepens our understanding of hopes and dreams of those refugee mothers through Little Dog's mixed sentiments when he looks at his mother's battered hands. He loves and hates them since those hands, metaphorically, bear a dream beyond their reach. As Hong Kong Tran observes, many Vietnamese exiles may also assume a nail salon to be an unalloyed haven that promises a healing serenity against some traumatic memories or a capitalist refuge where material success of Vietnamese refugee manicurists is secured by their American acculturation, submission, or professional service. While Rose and those women never desired to bury their lives in such an insecure job where they had to "bend over workbooks at manicure desks, finishing homework for nighttime ESL classes that cost a quarter of our wages" to pursue an elusive dream of getting on their feet one day, they all ended up coming back to that "temporary" place after many futile ventures for better opportunities elsewhere. To those vulnerable women, the nail salon is not only a place they could sustain their families as beauticians, but also a place where they raise their kids, some of whom got asthma after years of inhaling the toxic fumes (79). Without anything to protect them like health care and labor contract, yet refugee mothers like Little Dog's mother could never leave their work for decades until their lungs, livers, and joints wear away because of the chemicals (80). But out of the suffering emerges beauty, as Vuong reminds us of his existence in his another debut of poetry, *Night Sky With Exit Wounds,* in which Vuong imagines war both as a curse and a blessing: "An American fucked a Vietnamese farmgirl. Thus my mother exists. / Thus I exist." Vuong reflects on the irony of the war from which his family had arisen, since had no bombs ravaged his motherland, even Vuong wouldn't have existed: "Thus no bombs = no family = no me." So if there was no labor in a toxic environment, then there would be not Rose as a "boat" that makes Lan and Little Dog happy. So the cost of suffering is rewarding, and like beauty, it's fleeting as the title of the book implies, only "briefly gorgeous."

Vuong offers the new way to read a mother's body, which embodies both the cultural values and the capitalism as a whole. In other words, more than nursing the frail body of his mother after the day's toiling in the nail salon, Little Dog shows us the entire incongruous socioeconomic body that fails to attend equally to immigrant labor like Rose. In retrospection, Little Dog recalls his mother coming home sweaty and frazzled every day, with her skin redolent of "the chemicals from the nail salon" (84). Kneeling down beside his mother, Little Dog would scrape her back until she relaxed and fell into a sound sleep. He had been "kneading out" her tension for "hundreds of times" so his hands just "moved on their own." While scraping and stroking his mother's atrophied body, Little Dog keeps the traditional Vietnamese culture of healing through bruising alive.

The practice of fold therapy and herbal medicine in Vietnamese, according to Long T. Nguyen, has a long history in Vietnam. It is the combination of many traditional medicinal practices garnered through contact with Chinese, European, and American cultures. Many of these traditional Vietnamese medicinal practices are based on the belief that the body is hit by *gió độc* (toxic wind). In their article, "The Use of Traditional Vietnamese Medicine Among Vietnamese Immigrants Attending an Urban Community Health Center in the United States," Nguyen posits that this toxic wind or wind syndrome is "a key culture-bound concept of distress" which is frequently interpreted as the major cause for the failing body among Vietnamese refugees with post-traumatic stress disorder (PTSD) (145). With an acute pain and fainting after being "hit by the wind," Vietnamese usually exercises an immediate counterirritant procedure, such as wind snatching or using fingers to pinch away the skin, wind scraping or using a coin to scrape the skin, and other traditional techniques to expunge the "toxic wind." These procedures are usually practiced by a family member (Nguyen et al. 146). By nursing and healing his physically fragile mother, Little Dog also makes visible an ailing social body that fails to sustain equal wellness for displaced mothers like Rose.

Vuong's focus on refugee mothers like Rose, who subsist on the neoliberal economy that excludes unassimilable subjects, shifts the perception of domestic violence in refugee families. By narrating Rose's arduous journey of "self-care" in conjunction with domestic violence, Vuong shows us how the violent war and neoliberal peace are intimately connected, which destroys powerless refugees like Rose's family, ruining their humanity and kinship. Little Dog's father remains a nameless and shadowy presence in *On Earth*, drifting in and out of his narrative briefly and violently. If anything Little Dog still retains in his fuzzy memory about this father are the wounds on his mother's body. Through the fragmented memory of a toddler, Little Dog reminisces his parents dancing in a kitchen, then blood running from his mother's nose, then his grandmother's screaming, "He's killing my girl!". . . Little Dog did not see the moment of his father cuffed and shoved into the patrol car. The torment that still lingers in Little Dog's mind is his mother's broken face floating past him as she was carried away by paramedics on the stretcher (115). Years later, when Trevor said how he "fucking hate[s]" his father, Little Dog still couldn't imagine a white boy could hate anything about his life so he wanted to fathom that hatred, like crossing a bridge and confront that intense animosity, confessing to Trevor, "I hate my dad, too" (97). If we follow Little Dog to the end of the novel, we see that he chooses a different path from his father, becoming a caring man to his family, proving that violence is not an egress for refugees, but an impasse.

By narrating the caring that Little Dog offers to his mother, Vuong projects women's bodies both as motherly aesthetics and an ideal site for examining uneven material conditions in a neoliberal economy which prioritizes individuals' self-care and economic independence that saps energies of refugee mothers like Rose. Rose's incapability of self-care also relegates her to what Breanne Fahs depicts as "those who lose their moral autonomy as [a] neoliberal subject" (Elias and Scharff 94). Her frazzled and unkempt body after work resists the definition of a good neoliberal female subject who is expected to beautify herself as "an inherently pleasurable aspect of women's lives" (94). Rose's self-care, ironically, reflects an unequal economy or more squarely an economic violence that excludes rather than empowers displaced women like her. The metaphor of self-care, when applied to Rose's condition, is not a pleasure-seeking performance, but a subversive activism, as Audre Lorde deems it: "an act of political warfare" (132) or Rose's failing body itself is a political protest. In this fashion, Vuong's critique of neoliberal economy whose propensity towards exploitation and inequality through the metaphor of "self-care" informs his poetics of displacement.

While Rose's wholeness has been disrupted by violence war and colonial peace, humanity and empathy are resuscitated through her reconnection with wrecked people like her. At the beauty salon where his mother worked, Little Dog would help her take care of a legless customer who came there sometimes for the pedicure service. Little Dog recalls how his mother would tender the old lady's imaginary leg as if there were one there in the void (83). In Rose's hands, the customer would feel her leg again like it had never lost to any misfortune that stole it from her. If Rose had never experienced loss and upheavals in her life, she would have never been able to empathize with her poor customer's situation or would she have attended to her demand, which anyhow ended up bringing Rose $100 as the tip. Here, we also see how Little Dog contemplates beauty through his mother's empathetic submission in her beautifying service, which culminates in an uncanny relationality that augments his power and agency in love with Trevor.

That is also the poetics of displacement, the power of submission that Little Dog contemplates in his wild love with Trevor whose white masculinity both dominates and empowers him from the bottom. "Submission," Little Dog learned by making love with Trevor, "was also a kind of power" (118). This oppositional vision resembles the new framework Nguyen Tan Hoang postulates in his book, *A View from the Bottom,* in which Nguyen challenges Asian American and gay male critics who rely on the strategy of re-masculinization only as "a dense against feminization" by reassessing and rewriting "male effeminacy and its racialization." Nguyen conceptualizes "bottomhood" not only as" a tactic that undermines normative sexual, gender, and racial standards" but also as to offer "a novel model for coalition politics by affirming an ethical mode of relationality" Also in this fashion, Little Dog shows his alliance, empathy, and relationality with Trevor by "lower[ing]" himself "to the base" when Trevor wants to ascend "to be inside of pleasure." It is also in that moment, Little Dog realizes his power, his choice of pleasure, because one cannot rise without something to rise over and "submission does not require elevation in order to control" (118). Putting Trevor's [cock] in his mouth and looking up from the bottom, "as if looking at a kite," Little Dog allows Trevor to "flourish," and it is Trevor who swerves when Little Dog sways after a while. When an animal finds the hunter and offers itself to be eaten, Little Dog fancies talking to his mom, is neither a martyr nor a weakling but "a beast gaining the rare agency to stop" (118). Adopting "a view from the bottom," Nguyen Tan Hoang also reminds us, "reveals an inescapable exposure, vulnerability, and receptiveness in our reaching out to other people" (2). As such, by rewriting "submission" as a power, Ocean Vuong allures us to the poetics of (sexual) displacement as a subversive agenda for queer studies.

Because after they make love, Little Dog experience a sublime transformation, as if he is shedding his own shell, becoming beauty. Little Dog remembers how the beauty unveils itself to him after Trevor loved him, and then Little Dog stepped out from a shower. "The boy before the mirror stunned me. Who was he?" Little Dog traced every edge and curve of his face and his body like a miracle. He desired the boy in the mirror even more, likening him to the sun without shadow, something found again after being lost for a long time in the vast landscape. In that uncanny moment, Little Dog discovered a new philosophy of beauty which is something on the outside, ephemeral. But the boy in the mirror only a few feet away from him seemed to float forward, estranged, like a broken "driftwood," shoreless, oblivious to itself (107–108). In this sense, Little Dog offers to us an awakening truth that beauty is never static, but moving and slippery. The beauty in motion invites us to imagine more beauty blossoming everywhere, like poetics, even the poetics of displacement.

In fact, Little Dog's rejection to be an outcast in love—that is, his realization of a self-empowered position even while at the bottom of life, like his grandmother and mother. They all make their own choice to thrive from the bottom of life. Lan struggled through the war by selling her own body to American GIs. Rose lowers her head everyday on clients' feet to sustain her family in the US. As much as Little Dog realizes beauty in his relationship with Trevor, he also acknowledges that Trevor can only see him through a racist lens as an Asian bottom. Trevor cannot bring himself to be the bottom as he doesn't want to feel like a girl, emasculated: "I'm sorry it's not for me. It's for you. Right?" (120). Little Dog realizes that "The rules, they were already inside us." But he also realizes that people can make their choice to change those rules, making a difference. Little Dog ended up leaving his family by choice, and not long after his departure, Trevor died of overdose in Hartford. Though they are all gorgeous briefly, as Little Dog reminds us, they reveal themselves to us. And we glorify their appearance that remain gorgeous forever in our memory. We will desire to "hunt" that beauty as we desire the sunset which is most beautiful in its afterglow before it entirely vanishes. So "to be gorgeous, you must first be seen, but to be seen allows you to be hunted" (238). Visibility has its cost, Ocean Vuong reminds us, but it's worth pursuing, with optimism.

Little Dog gleans such optimism from his grandmother and mother as a power against cruel vicissitudes of life. Singing, as such a robust mechanism against brutal realities, evokes the poetics of displacement. For his refugee grand/mothers, singing shelters them away from the storm of bullets and its ricocheting memories. For Little Dog himself, singing lifts him up, away from life riddles. And a song is both a bridge and the ground for him to stand on, as Little Dog tells his mother to sing and keep themselves from falling (25). And singing not only keeps Little Dog from falling but also makes him thrive gorgeously from troubles through his relational intimacy with his white teen lover named Trevor—a pain sufferer turned junkie—whom Little Dog met while working on a tobacco farm one summer. A grandson of a farmer, Trevor is far from being a privileged white boy who lives in a mobile home behind the interstate, and from whom Little Dog learned that "want" was even more savage than work (94). With Trevor, Little Dog would sing from the top of his lungs no matter how fierce their lives become, as if nothing can protect them but themselves in their precarious lives, because the boy's body is only single-use, so is his life, which has only one chance (125). Singing, as refugee mothers like Lan and Rose cultivate in their children as an approach of "self-care" falls in sign with what Angela Davis would encourage activists to pursue as a creative praxis of decolonization, because if we all incorporate "self-care" into all our activities, our decolonizing and liberating efforts ". . . will eventually move us along the trajectory that may lead to some victories" (1:46:12).

Through his elegiac imagination, Vuong takes us to the world of refugee lives emerging from the war that displace them, especially women, mothers whose trauma and triumphs reshape their destiny. Motherly aesthetics is conceptualized as a healing space that inspires a past future which embraces tangled memories within moral imagination and illuminates peacemaking endeavors as political dynamics that transform human consciousness. The delicate and dense implication of the theoretical statement enacts visions of freedom outside the fierce market exchange that animates the American society and treats refugee workers as invisible creatures devoid of heart and soul. Reading *On Earth* through the lens of motherly aesthetics invites us to revisit the audacity and poetics of displaced communities and imagine a just future. By suggesting this theoretical framework, I suggest an approach of reading Vietnamese American literature with premonitions into the refugee futurity through narratives of motherly aesthetics and poetics of displacement in the face of historical amnesia and envision a more endurable world for the displaced in this age of neoliberal peace and economic violence.

On Earth, in essence, teaches us about beauty as the power. The displaced women in *On Earth* experienced everything that has ever happened: so there is no end of struggles for surviving. Vuong does not envision a pessimistic future where refugee women's offspring continue to inhabit endless melancholy of race and gender inequality or surrender to destiny. Instead, the novel takes on a prophetic closure; after the first generation complete their journeys, their descendants embrace the past as beauty and power. We eventually discover that the living experiences of Lan and Rose illuminate and empower

Little Dog, guiding him away from refugee's abyss of melancholy, urging him to reimagine it otherwise.

In *On Earth*, refugees like Little Dog's family did not leave their homeland for the American dream, they escaped war violence like hunted animals. "Monkeys, moose, cows, dogs, butterflies, buffaloes," who followed their families to wherever they could be together no matter how perilous it is. Vuong is telling us a human story of "the ruined lives of animals" running away desperately (242). Refugee women like Rose and Lan fled Vietnam when their lives are perilous and unviable, becoming inhuman ever since. They all live traumatic lives in America, torn between past and present, resting on neither temporality. Lan ended up dying a painful death, being consumed by her cancer and war trauma. Only when her body is brought back to Vietnam, can Lan complete her journey in peace and wholeness, because "[i]n the ground, Lan is already Vietnamese," Little Dog tells us (224). *On Earth* is not a narrative of failing refugee women though, they have reclaimed their beauty. While their lives are fraught with violent memories and unsettled present, they embrace that burden and march ahead with audacity and resilience. They set themselves for uncertainty and never shed their hope, since they know without hope, they would risk sinking into the dark abyss. Rose desires coloring, Lan still sings at the top of her lungs, and Little Dog invents happiness from the bottom. The war may forever haunt and and what *On Earth We're Briefly Gorgeous* offers most is the poetics of displacement, or beauty in lieu of violence. It allows us to imagine the "gorgeous" futurity for the displaced communities.

WORKS CITED

Center, Berglund. "Angela Davis - Pacific University 2014." *Vimeo*, 24 Mar. 2020, vimeo.com/94879430.

Chan, Sucheng. *The Vietnamese American 1.5 Generation: Stories of War, Revolution, Flight, and New Beginnings*. Temple University Press, 2006.

Elias, Ana Sofia, et al. *Aesthetic Labour: Rethinking Beauty Politics in Neoliberalism*. Palgrave Macmillan, 2018.

Espiritu, Yen Le. *Body Counts: The Vietnam War and Militarized Refuge(Es)*. University of California Press, 2014.

Gordon, Avery F., and Christopher Newfield. *Mapping Multiculturalism*. University of Minnesota Press, 1997.

González, Rigoberto. "Be Bold: A Profile of Ocean Vuong." Www.Pw.Org, 12 June 2019, https://www.pw.org/content/be_bold_a_profile_of_ocean_vuong.

Lieu, Nhi T. *The American Dream in Vietnamese*. University of Minnesota Press, 2011.

Lorde, Audre. *A Burst of Light: And Other Essays*. Ixia Press., 2017.

Lowe, Lisa. *Immigrant Acts: On Asian American Cultural Politics*. Duke University Press, 2007.

Magazine, Poets & Writers. "Be Bold." *Magzter*, Magzter, 6 Dec. 2019, www.magzter.com/article/Art/Poets-Writers-Magazine/Be-Bold.

Nguyen, Hoang Tan. *A View from the Bottom: Asian American Masculinity and Sexual Representation*. Duke University Press, 2014.

Nguyen, Long T., et al. "The Use of Traditional Vietnamese Medicine Among Vietnamese Immigrants Attending an Urban Community Health Center in the United States." *Mary Ann Liebert, Inc., Publishers*, 3 Feb. 2016, www.liebertpub.com/doi/10.1089/acm.2014.0209.

Nguyen, Mimi Thi. *The Gift of Freedom War, Debt, and Other Refugee Passages*. Duke University Press, 2012.

Ninh Erin Khuê. *Ingratitude: The Debt-Bound Daughter in Asian American Literature*. New York University Press, 2011.

Ninh, Erin Khuê. "Asian American Like Me." *HuffPost*, 26 July 2011, www.huffpost.com/entry/asian-american-like-me_b_866508.

Quong, Spencer. "Survival as a Creative Force: An Interview with Ocean Vuong." *The Paris Review*, 5 June 2019, www.theparisreview.org/blog/2019/06/05/survival-as-a-creative-force-an-interview-with-ocean-vuong/.

Torres, Justin. "Ocean Vuong Makes His Fiction Debut, in the Form of a Letter." *The New York Times*, 03 June 2019, https://www.nytimes.com/2019/06/03/books/review/ocean-vuong-on-earth-were-briefly-gorgeous.html.

Tran, Kong Hong. "Vietnamese Manicurists: An Intermediary between Cultures." *University of California Irvine*, 2008.

Vu, Chi. "The 1.5 Generation Vietnamese-American Writer as Post-Colonial Translator." *Kunapipi*, vol. 32, no. 1, pp. 130–46.

Vuong, Ocean. *Night Sky With Exit Wounds*. Copper Canyon, 2019.

Vuong, Ocean. *On Earth We're Briefly Gorgeous: A Novel*. Penguin Press, 2019.

Chapter Two

Domesticating Displacement, Encounters with Refugee Mothers

Adrianne Kalfopoulou

In March 2016, an abandoned school building in central Athens was transformed into a refugee squat to accommodate what was then a peak in flows from Turkey to the Greek islands. An influx that was exacerbated by the subsequent closure of the borders out of Greece into northern Europe for non-EU peoples as the EU attempted to limit the flows reactively.[1] I joined a clutch of Athens-based volunteers who began to help out. Our sporadic visits to the squat soon developed into a growing relationship with the communities; three Afghan families living in the schoolrooms of the building's first floor, Azize, Saliha, Rakia, Mahilé, Nirgina, the mothers' names, were among those I grew close to. They ranged in age from 21 to 38. After the families had moved on into northern Europe, either officially with relocation papers or with the help of smugglers, Layla, another Afghan mother, arrived in late 2018, the only one of the families I came to know who requested, and was granted, asylum in Greece.

Very early I noticed that the mothers' first names were rarely used. I asked after a name and Maedeh, Saliha's 13-year-old daughter, would say, "You mean Mama Henieh?" When Azize told me her name she smiled. I would playfully say, "Mama Henieh," which she appreciated, and understood I was doing this in a spirit of kinship. All the Afghan mothers I met were referred to by the names of their children, a metaphor and marker of an economy where gender, as in more ancient economies, is tied to specific kinds of labor. Or so I assumed. Then I inquired if this was also true of the men. Mohammad, Rakia's husband, and father of their then 2-year-old Asma, said yes, that it was the first born whose name was referenced. Yet among the mothers in the rooms of the first floor, the children called out to them by the names of the daughters and sons they knew them to be attached to. So Azize was always "Mama Henieh" though Amir Houssein her 11-year-old son was her eldest. When I think of these women I think of their efficiency, their admiration of quality, from fabrics to rice, and I think, especially, of their hospitality. I remember when Azize had her 11-year-old son Amir Hossein bring a plate out to the playground for me on one of the Thursdays we were there to do crafts with the children. Two sliced tomatoes and a cooked potato garnished with a lettuce leaf in thanks for a pair of leggings I had brought her young 3-year-old daughter, Henieh.

I remember how Mahilé, a mother on her own with three of her children, and her own elderly mother Fatima, knotted the bag of raisins I had brought to share, to return it to me after we had had our *chai* and I'd opened the bag onto a plate. I was surprised. We were sitting as we always did on the floor in a circle with Fatima her aged mother and Narghes her 13-year-old daughter who became a friend. I gestured that the rest of the raisins were for her to keep, she treated the offering as a gift, *tashakor*, she said nodding. Of the three families I met in that March, she was the only one without a husband. I learned he had died, and while Narghes spoke of a father who brought her small gifts, Mahilé shook her head and said, in French, "il a tappé a moi" [he hit me]. She had been a child bride at 12. Narghes showed me pictures of a garishly made up girl. I was horrified but smiled. When I visited the family in Switzerland after they were relocated Mahilé showed me her own pictures of herself as a young mother saying, "pas bien" [not good].

I wondered about the conflation of a mother's name with her child's, of its suggestion of an erasure of a self apart from her child, but as I learned more of how gendered spaces were negotiated I learned too of a more collective ethos. Gendered conduct did not necessarily limit agency as much as it channeled it in specific ways. A first name like the idea of self-sufficiency with its suggestion of a Western view (and value) of independence signifies less of the world, more of self and less of what surrounds it; it would diminish the nuanced and myriad expression of these mothers' efficiencies, beginning with how they took care of their children. With Maedeh's help translating, Azize let me know she wanted to have Henieh's rotting teeth fixed. She had an entry paper provided on arrival in Lesvos where Henieh was given a January 1 birth date, a generic date that reflected the day of the month or year of entry at what were known as refugee hotspots.[2] Henieh's birthday was in fact in August, a day we celebrated when Azize gathered mothers and their children in their schoolroom space to share a 3-layered chocolate cake they had made in a portable oven. We gestured across languages, with our *thank yous* and *tashakors*, smiles, and repetitions of "good" and "nice" when the cake was shared. Henieh's hair braided over night so that curls bounced around her face as she led her friends into a circle to dance. Mothers arrived from the other squats, and nearby camps with their own children, and wrapped gifts, where in this room away from the men, chadors came off and Azize wore a sleeveless knee-length dress.

After everyone had eaten, Azize asked the 13-year-old Maedeh, whose English was fast becoming fluent, to ask if there was a way to have a dentist see Henieh's teeth. They smelled, they hurt her; she could not eat anything hard without weeping. I took her to my dentist who said she needed to be seen by someone in the child's hospital in Athens (Παιδων or *Paidon*); an intern in the dentistry school would help. She also needed vaccines before the dental work. This was in the fall of 2016, the then-Syriza government with its socialist platform made it possible for refugees to get an AMKA number, a Greek social security number, which provided for basic health coverage.

Over a period of five months we had appointments outside of the *Paidon* building on Thivon Street. There was a bench next to a kiosk where Azize and Henieh would wait after their ride on the 622 or 815 bus from the squat, and later the Eleonas camp. Henieh was always dressed in colorful outfits, trendy leggings or skirts, her hair in careful bows and pretty barrettes. There was something celebratory about our meetings despite the fact that these were dentist appointments and Henieh was not always happy about them. Olina, the young dentistry intern greeted her with Greek children's songs she played from her cell phone. We had a ritual of getting something afterwards, ice-cream was her favorite choice if she could have one, and I let her know the sample toothbrush and toothpaste, with the sticker Olina asked Henieh to chose after each session, needed to be used. When Henieh was in pain, Azize would opt for a cab back if I couldn't take her, and always refused the fare money I wanted to give her.

In *Of Hospitality* Jacques Derrida and the philosopher Anne Dufourmantelle have a remarkable discussion on the concept and liberating possibilities of hospitality; they remind us that "the subject" must "recognize that he is first of all a guest" (16). A Western construction of subjecthood that aspires to independence and free will is deconstructed as the subject state is rendered more guest than host; we become our own guest within the larger contexts of our existence, which foregrounds our essential interdependence. I felt, for example, as privileged to have been invited to help with getting Henieh's teeth fixed as Azize might have felt to be getting the support. I was also privy to how a lack of resources was negotiated on a daily basis. The preparation of one meal in particular stays with me. It was September and some eight women and children were sharing a meal. Rakia, Azize, Saliha, and others were preparing dumplings they stuffed with ground meat and herbs. Maedeh described several bus rides to a part of town where "a poot" was borrowed, which I realized was the four-tiered pot being used to steam the dumplings. The pot was borrowed from a mosque to be returned in twenty-four hours.

"You a good mama," Narghes said once, though I don't remember the specific context. Perhaps it had to do with something she had asked for, or the emergency trip we took to Kosta, a Greek dentist who was devoting three months of Sundays to provide dental help to the community. Narghes had slipped skateboarding in the hallway and chipped her front tooth. She was 13, and trying not to cry when I asked to see her tooth. Kosta capped the tooth, a gift to Narghes she remembered as one of the most important things that had happened to her in Greece. When I visited the family in Switzerland after they had relocated there, her mother Mahilé introduced me to a neighboring Afghan woman as the person who had fixed Narghes's tooth, when I said it had been a dentist who did this. That I had helped make that possible was for Mahilé was as important as the dentist. Anne Dufourmantelle and Jacques Derrida describe a "giving place to the place" of the unknown as a mainstay of "the question of hospitality" (14–15); that one would, as a refugee, continuously encounter the unknown makes the moments in which needs are acknowledged (rather than treated as burdens), a mainstay of the transformation of the unfamiliar into the potentially hospitable. As much as I was asked to recognize requests for hair dye, antibiotics, diaper cream, shampoos for lice, and so on, I too was being recognized, given a role as someone there to help navigate an unknown, and in that process made familiar. "So to speak of 'the near, the exiled, the foreigner, the visitor, being at home in the other's place' prevents concepts like 'self and other' or 'subject and object' from presenting themselves under a permanently dual law" (51–52), Derrida notes. Therefore, given the porousness of such concepts that include national as much as cultural borders, the constructions of self and other are more interdependent than these divisions will admit.

In a discussion Sara Ruddick and Andrea O'Reilly have regarding maternal thinking, the title of Ruddick's 1989 book *Maternal Thinking: Towards a Politics of Peace*, the authors foreground the prioritizing of particular needs as being specific to the work of mothering. Quoting from Ruddick's 1989 book, attending to a child's needs include questions such as:

> What is your children's shoe size? When was their last immunization shot? Who is their child's best friend? What food don't they like? What is their teacher's name . . . mothers, even with the involved partners, are the ones who do the maternal thinking: the remembering, worrying, planning, anticipating, orchestrating, arranging and co-ordinating of and for the household. (17)

Azize's hope to get Henieh's teeth fixed, and her continued inquiry into how this could be done, or Mahilé's decision after a few months at the squat to move her family to the Malakassa camp because she felt herself, as a woman without a husband, to be the target of prejudice, or a very young Rakia who reminded me to get her diaper rash cream by showing me an empty tin, all suggest the pragmatism Ruddick describes. But as refugees, these women's concerns also emphasize the prioritizing of care within environments that were often hostile to those efforts. An image comes to mind from an early March day in 2016 when the Pireaus port was flooded with tents as borders out of Greece officially closed. I had gone to the E2 gate where a large UNHCR tent was distributing food and supplies, grabbed some things from the supermarket including a broom and packets of sanitary napkins. A woman outside one of the tents was scraping up banana peels and cigarette butts with a sheet of paper. I handed her the broom. She was pleased, using it to clear the concrete around her tent. Another image that comes to mind is of Nirgina, who had just arrived at the squat from Kabul. When I met her she was patiently doing henna designs on the ankles, feet, hands, and arms, of the children and women who wanted them. She had arrived with her 6-year-old daughter Naz from Kabul where she had escaped an abusive husband. She was concentrated on the designs she was making telling me, as I admired her work, that the henna wasn't very good quality, and would fade quickly.

Nirgina was 27, traveling with her daughter Naz. She spoke in clearly annunciated English as she told the story of not wanting to continue with her husband who would not give her a divorce. It had been an arranged marriage, as were so many. I said something to the effect of, "Now you are in Europe, and the world is surprising." She shrugged, admitted she had feelings for him even though he was "not a good person." She had a mother and brother in Sweden and hoped to reach them. Between 2016 and 2018, the borders out of Greece remained porous, and a good many of the families from the squat moved on. There was a steady turn over of incoming families, rooms were vacated and then peopled again, first a good many Syrians, most of whom were granted relocation papers, then the majority of arrivals were Kurds particularly from Iraq. The next time I was at the squat I found Nirgina threading her eyebrows, a car rear view mirror propped up on a stool. It made me laugh. "I'll get you a proper mirror," I told her, and she laughed too. She was getting ready for "an appointment" she said, "with a smuggler." She said it the way someone might say they had a meeting with a potential employer. I said something about being careful realizing as I spoke that I might have sounded ridiculous to her. "I used to teach Oxford English," she said. "You could do that here too," I said, but knew that even certified native-speakers were being paid the bare minimum for private English lessons. In our weekly visits to the squat beyond the things we offered, the time we spent with the children, we had no context to understand any one's full circumstance. In return for the hair dye, food, dentist visits, stuffed animals, shoes and assorted things, we found ourselves invited to share a meal and were included in conversations. Mahilé offered me a black patent leather handbag with large gold-colored links. It was new. I would never use it, but thanked her, moved that she wanted to give me something too. Nirgina told me she had no idea why she still had feelings for the husband who was abusive but she would not tolerate living with him, and had risked her life and Naz's to escape.

One morning in late September the children were all carrying donated Barbie knapsacks. It was the beginning of the school year, and some would be going to the local, neighborhood schools in *Excharhia*. Naz had hers packed and was smiling as she showed it off. Nirgina said she would be trying to get her to Sweden. A few days later a very somber Nirgina said Naz had left with a Pakistani couple on a black passport; the smugglers she had met with had come through. I asked why she had not gone too and she said they had tried several times, and been turned back trying to leave from Rhodes and from Athens. Her brother had put up 4000 euros for the passage. I was speechless. Nirgina was quiet and clearly upset, concentrated on texting a message. I started to cry when she looked at me seriously and said, "Don't." It was not that she didn't understand but that it was an indulgence, and who was I, after all, to indulge in a sentiment she the mother was making every effort to control. "We have never been apart," Nirgina said. I was reminded of Derrida's question when he wonders "is it necessary to start from the certain existence of a dwelling, or is it rather only starting from the dislocation of the shelterless, the homeless, that the authenticity of hospitality can open up?" (56) Is an acknowledgment of a need for shelter what makes it achievable, and who better to understand this than those bereft of it?

In *The Ungrateful Refugee* Dina Nayeri recalls time spent in Hotel Barba, a refugee hostel in the Italian town of Mentana where she and her brother and mother live for some months before being granted asylum in the U.S.; the memoir takes its title from an assumption that refugees are meant to feel grateful for any luck that might come their way. Nayeri describes a scene in which "workers from churches and charities drove up the hill and dumped huge piles of donated clothing in the courtyard" and distributed "coupons that the residents could redeem for tins of snacks if they visited the church." Her mother "never bothered with either offering" (128), Nayeri recalls, and describes the sense of humiliation of sifting through hand-me-downs, the assumption that as refugees they were expected to feel gratitude. I remembered the hairbands in plastic bags that were in the basement of the squat. We had found several bags of brand new colored hair bands on a shelf where some of the French volunteers had made a library, and turned the basement into a schoolroom. The girls always asked for hair bands, Aisha or Iman Noor, and Maia, wanted a "red" or "green" or "pretty" one, instead of the "not pretty" or "no black" choices. When Nayeri speaks of the residents of Barba rushing out to "dig through the piles," of all "the unwanted items strewn around the yard," she calls attention to the reductive aspect of such gestures of charity. Nayeri's mother never participated in these distributions "not because we didn't need the things," she says, "but because you can only accept so much charity before you lose sight of who you are" (128).

We so often left the squat with lists of names, the numbers of shoe sizes next to them, with requests for a color and type of hair dye. Aisha wanted sandals with straps. Iman Noor wanted the color to be white. When the rush of children and mothers would follow us with their refrains of "My friend, for my baby . . . for my sister . . . for my brother," we would sit in a circle or everyone would line up as we distributed items, often wrapped and labeled. It was the attention to specific requests that was appreciated when we managed to fulfill them. Maybe the bags of colored hairbands stayed untouched in the school basement because no person had handed them out to anyone. There was no WhatsApp or Viber message with a picture of a color and type, no comparing of colors. The hairbands were new and packaged and sat there unoffered. Whether a request involved a comb, or more urgent needs for lice shampoo or antibiotics, the fact that any one of us remembered to actually bring a particular item to a particular person built a relationship, for as long or as brief as that might be.

Virginia Held's pioneering work on the ethics of care notes that a primary virtue in society ought to be that of providing for care services. Rather than a notion of sacrificing or conflating care within overriding justice systems, the courts and regulatory bodies need to better integrate an ethics of care: "Justice should not be a concern above all others," she notes. Charity, for example, even when generous, is less of a relational interaction than one that reinforces a power imbalance between the provider and the recipient. Too often the recipient's need for help is viewed as burdensome rather than a reminder of interdependent needs. In her critique of a Western liberal paradigm of self-sufficiency Held argues that society needs to better acknowledge and admit to the shortcomings of views that ignore our having been cared for in order to achieve our self-sufficient agencies.

Held references Sara Ruddick's work on empathetic strategies in *Maternal Thinking*, using the example of a mother's care work to contrast with that of a society "maximizing the interests of the self," within a discourse of "costs and benefits" or "principles of utility"; Held points out such market values feed conflictual paradigms and competitive approaches which overlook more relational paradigms. In the example of a mother who "does not pit her own interests against those of the child" we have a social model that "avoids being domineering." As the political theorist Giorgio Agamben reminds us in *Homo Sacer*, it is the refugee who has "put the originary fiction of modern sovereignty in crisis." It is he or she who constitutes a threshold regarding the rights of the citizen versus those "undocumented" and therefore illegal within a given nation state's judiciary structure (131). More simply, whether one is speaking of the legal parameters of citizenship, the borders of the nation state, or those of the self, how sovereignty, or self-sufficiency, is constructed finds itself in crisis when confronted with a threshold that deconstructs its apparent autonomy.

To return to the example of refugee mothers, Ruddick and O'Reily, and Held too, are suggesting a paradigm shift without suggesting a sacrificial model of motherhood, or a care model that compromises a justice system, but an integration and reassessment: how might society learn from "the often burdensome" work of mothers who manage to attend to "the unique person of a child" alongside their own needs? And to extend this question to one inclusive of the nation state, how would the question of sovereignty redefine itself to more inclusively integrate those bodies that dissemble its "originary fiction" as Agamben puts it. How do refugee mothers, more specially, suggest a fluidity of thresholds that might provide an example of what it means to both care for another and, as Dufourmantelle and Derrida suggest, demonstrate "new powers of communication and information" (57) in our effort to be hospitable to one another, to host (an)other of our selves?

In our interactions with the families from the squat, and my first-hand experiences with Nirgina, Mahilé, and later with Layla, refugee mothers who were without husbands or acted independently of them, and even with Azize, and Rakia who had husbands, there was an agency and consequentiality to their decision-making. Nayeri's mother too whose conversion to Christianity incites the Islamic Republic's moral police who threaten her life, makes the decision to escape Iran with her two children. And when the family arrives at Hotel Barba, finding themselves with other refugees in yet another liminality of possible futures—what country will finally sponsor them, what lives await them—Nayeri recounts her mother's resourcefulness. She finds used English language workbooks, cleans them up, and puts her children to work on their English. They catch up with their grade levels by joining a Catholic Church that offers English lessons that they have to travel to by bus. The vigilance of purpose in Nayeri's mother's determination to provide for her children as they negotiate the uncertainties of circumstance is resonant of Nirgina's determination to get herself and Naz out of Athens, Mahihé's move to the Malakassa camp, and Layla who after the eviction of the squat in 2019, made near-daily trips from the refugee camp in Corinth to settle her asylum papers in Athens. "You must keep living. This is what I learned from her at Hotel Barba," writes Nayeri of her mother, "You can't fall into the waiting space. You must find work, some small gear you can turn—" (354). That "small gear you can turn" whether it was Nirgina plotting her escape or Mahilé's move out of the squat, or Azize's seeking of ways to get Henieh's teeth fixed, or Layla whose mentally challenged husband was one of the reasons she needed to be in Athens for psychological support, underwrite Western stereotypes of Middle Eastern women, particularly practicing Muslims, as dependent on the men in their lives. Western projections of the veiled female body, for example, have read such coverings as an erasure of singularity rather than as another layering to that singularity.

If as Andrea O'Reilly and Susan Ruddick point out, an aspect "of maternal practice" is "the ability to survive in institutions, to negotiate a place within them" the refugee mother is a multivalent example of such negotiations. In a Middle Eastern economy where a woman's place is traditionally dependent on a man's, the fluidity of her own decision-making process can reconfigure that hierarchy as it both works within it, and transgresses it. At a loss of how to categorize Layla's ability to provide for her children, as she simultaneously petitioned for asylum on her own, making ongoing trips into Athens from Corinth to gather the necessary paperwork, Rakia's husband Mohammad, described her as "a man and a woman." His own young wife, Rakia, who had left for Germany five months pregnant with their second daughter, had rejected possibilities of sending Asma, their 2 year old, with any other family. She would leave her husband behind, but not their daughter. She would be willing to travel with their 2 year old, alone and pregnant, to an unknown country and future that might not, for an indefinite amount of time, include him. As Mahilé waited for the Swiss government's decision to reconsider their petition for relocation, she let them know her family would not accept the government's offer to move to Switzerland without her elderly mother Fatima. They would move together, or they would remain in Greece.

Naz made it to Sweden some days after she left Athens, and was with her grandmother, given, in Nirgina's words, "Good food and clothes, but she wants me." Some weeks later I received a VIBER message from Nirgina, "Pray for me my friend, I am going to Naz tonight." And she did. I carried around a pocket mirror I had bought for her in my knapsack after seeing Nirgina thread her eyebrows with a rearview car mirror. I'd forgotten to give it to her, and kept it as a reminder. Nayeri asks, "How can one be self-reliant in the Emersonian way . . . always transitioning, taking control of the change in oneself, if one is taught to hate the very self that is supposed to do all the work?" (354). Where is the will to survive meant to come from if the society one lives in rejects and undermines any sense of self? Within the network of women at the squat, community building was an exercise in living within, as much as between, multiple cultural, gendered, and religious sites, "We need each other to make a community," writes Nayeri, "—the immigrant can't transform by sheer will" (354). Whenever I looked at the pocket mirror in my knapsack I also remembered that I had offered to give Nirgina money for the henna designs she was doing, and she had shaken her head and said quietly, "It's for free."

Narghes sent a text message that she had "two rooms" at the Malakassa camp and wanted me to visit. Her mother, Mahilé, was cooking "rice you like." I had seen Mahilé lugging bags with Fatima, her elderly mother, down Harilaou Trikoupi Street; I didn't make anything of it as families regularly cleaned out rooms or helped someone who was moving on. Narghes texted "The camp is good." They had just heard from Switzerland about Fatima, Fatima who loved to draw elaborately colored butterflies. It was hard to gauge Fatima's age, her skin was deeply lined and her eyes rheumy, maybe she was in her 60s, maybe she was closer to 80, she took great joy in any of the activities we did with the children when we were at the squat, sitting in a corner of the blanket or sheet we spread over the playground's concrete with a crayon or marker or sheet of paper drawing and coloring in butterflies.

At the Malakassa camp Narghes and her twin brother Unés met me at the gate; Mahilé made a spinach dish with potato paddies we took on a picnic into the surrounding green. Mahilé had waited to show me how to cook the rice. She poured boiling water onto the dry grains then sifted and wrapped the steaming pot in a towel. I met her sister Oulié who had her young son with her, her other four children in four different countries, Canada, Austria, Iran, and Germany, as a result of each having left Kabul at different times. As we ate in the midst of that April's green I asked Oulié if she was upset that she would soon be losing Mahilé who did finally get an endorsement to go to Switzerland with the whole family including Fatima, at the end of May. Oulié shook her head, she was happy she said in Farsi as Narghes translated, that Mahilé and the family could "continue their lives." Fatima was smiling. I wondered aloud, "Your grandmother must have been beautiful when she was young." Narghes shrugged, "I don't know," and Oulié who must have understood my English, said again in Farsi "We are all beautiful when we are young" which Narghes repeated for me in English.

In the world of the refugee, mother countries so often become the faces on their cell phones, of sons and daughters, spouses, relatives, an extended family that transgress and connect borders. There is a reconfiguring of scale and geography in this. "Germany is better for my future," Azize's 11-year-old Amir Hossein said as he showed me the passport he would be carrying, he too about to go with a family that was not his own as if they were his own, to meet that future. He was happy in Athens; he could buy a SIM card, and "be free" which had not been the family's experience in Iran where Afghans were discriminated against.[3] He adored soccer and had asked if we knew of any teams that he could join in. Some months after he had arrived in Germany and was living with a host family, Amir posted photographs of himself on Facebook clothed in the German soccer team's uniform that he had joined. He looked pleased, and serious. "Do you miss him?" I asked Azize, and her response surprised me. Through Maedeh she said she thinks about what he's doing all the time, but did not say she missed him. I understood the distinction between missing him and being preoccupied with him, adding again through Maedeh "our family's hopes are with him." In these displacements were invested hopes, a way to imagine what the future might or might not promise; it domesticated the uncertainties by personalizing them, and giving their dreams the faces of their children. Once Maedeh's family moved to Sweden, she would still help me confirm the dentist appointments Henieh had by texting Azize in Athens of the time, and day I would send her to pass on in Farsi; we managed to continue our ongoing meetings, and I learned to feel that geography didn't always separate us.

"People think of the refugee camp as a purgatory, a liminal space without shape or color. And it is that. But we kept our instinct for joy" (142) says Nayeri, referring again to the time spent at Hotel Barba. And I am again reminded of the attention mothers at the squat gave to their children, the images of Henieh's hair decorated in ladybug clips and bright fuchsia ribbons, of how Azize would emphasize that a gift was especially for her on her birthday, of how Azize would tell Henieh that her teeth would be able to bite on carrots and apples when she complained about the dentist visits. There was Judi, "the water lady" on hot July days, using the hose and large plastic pans the children loved to play in, a father who brought his very young daughter to the basement classroom to make cutout collages. These were reminders of how parents, and the mothers in particular, individuated their children's needs, and by extension a sense of their own desires.

Under the previous Greek Syriza government whose socialist agenda made basic health care available, the squats were tolerated, considered a temporary housing solution for these displaced communities. One of the first things the right-wing New Democracy government elected in July 2019 did was to evict the squats. Under Syriza, I was able to get Henieh's teeth fixed and her immunity vaccines at minimal cost. Under New Democracy, the required AMKA numbers for health coverage are no longer available to refugees. To go back to Virginia Held's point that one cannot insist on the ethics of a justice system without integrating an ethics of care, if basic human needs are neglected, as Giorgio Agamben argues in *Homo Sacer*, "bare life" becomes abject in the politicized body of the state. As such, "The refugee must be considered for what he is: nothing less than a limit concept that radically calls into question the fundamental categories of the nation-state, from the birth-nation to the man-citizen . . . to clear the way for a long–overdue renewal of categories in the service of politics . . ." (134). As with Derrida and Dufourmantelle, Agamben is arguing for the recognition of how we might better define ourselves in respect to the other, to understand those interdependences. "For if I practice hospitality '*out of* duty' [and not only '*in conforming with* duty']" writes Derrida, "this hospitality of paying up is no longer an absolute hospitality, it is no longer graciously offered beyond debt and economy, offered to the other" (83).

I think of Maedeh telling me that on the evening before they left for Sweden she and her family with Azize and Henieh and Nirgina decided to walk up the Lykabettus hill in Athens, she described the moon of that September night, that they returned to the school room, and danced. I saw Athens imbued with Maedeh's description of that last night before their move to yet another country, climate, and language where they would learn to again adapt themselves. From Sweden I received pictures of their faces under the duvets, the white of snow-covered landscapes and empty snow-covered roads of the town of Porjus in northern Sweden with its 328 inhabitants. It was October 2017. Some months later, in 2018, Maedeh called on WhatsApp and showed me Saliha cooking. She waved to me. There were later voice messages from Saliha that said, "I miss you," and "cold . . . very very very cold." Eventually Maedeh started school and said she was happy. Over the next year I would get more voice messages, "I miss you very very" Saliha said, and I replied that I missed her too. She sent a picture of us together at a café near the squat: Nirgina and Naz, Azize and Henieh, Maedeh and her older daughter Mina. It brought those days back. They felt close again despite how much had changed in Athens and in the world in general.

WORKS CITED

Agamben, Giorgio. *Homo Sacer, Sovereign Power and Bare Life*, translated by Daniel Heller-Roazen, Stanford, 1998.

"Care practices: towards a recasting of Ethics." University of Oxford, lecture by Virginia Held, 4 October 2014, ethicsofcare.org/lecture-care-and-justice-in-society/. Accessed 4 May 2020.

Derrida, Jacques, and Anne Dufourmantelle. *Anne Dufourmantelle Invites Jacques Derrida to Respond*, translated by Rachel Bowlby, Stanford, 2000.

Held, Virginia. *The Ethics of Care: Personal, Political and Global*. Oxford, 2006.

Nayeri, Dina. *The Ungrateful Refugee: What Immigrants Never Tell You*. Catapult, 2019.

O'Reilly, Andrea, and Sara Ruddick. "A Conversation on Maternal Thinking," www.academia.edu/30133669/A_Conversation_on_Maternal_Thinking_Andrea_O_Reilly_and_Sara_Ruddick. Accessed 17 March 2020.

Ruddick, Sara. *Maternal Thinking, Toward a Politics of Peace*. Beacon, 1989.

NOTES

1. See *The Guardian*. https://www.theguardian.com/world/2016/mar/09/balkans-refugee-route-closed-say-european-leaders

2. For more on the European Union hotspot approach, see https://ec.europa.eu/home-affairs/what-we-do/networks/european_migration_network/glossary_search/hotspot-approach_en

3. See Human Rights Watch. https://www.hrw.org/news/2013/11/20/iran-afghan-refugees-and-migrants-face-abuse

Chapter Three

Tracing the Impacts of War in Nadifa Mohamed's *The Orchard of Lost Souls*

Alison Graham-Bertolini

Using Nadifa Mohamed's novel *The Orchard of Lost Souls* (2013) to provide representative examples,[1] I argue that militarized systems across the world depend on feminizing women so that masculine ideologies of domination are maintained. My argument hinges on establishing that during times of war, women and children are expected to assume artificial, *hyperfeminine* gender roles that work to support public wartime ideologies. I assert that when women choose to disobey the weak and restrictive roles assigned to them, they are in danger from their own state, which rejects or abandons them for undermining their nationalistic cause, as well as from those considered to be enemies of the state. I conclude by demonstrating that in militarized societies, where both men and women are gendered to extreme degrees, it is the female collective that offers women agency and a way to attain freedom and full personhood.

Mohamed's fictional account of the dawning of the Somali civil war is drawn from her memories of childhood in Hargesia. She explains in an interview from 2013,

> The whole book is informed by the distant memories I have of the neighborhood we lived in, and by the stories my mother and female relatives have told me of that time. My own grandmother was already paralyzed when I left the country in '86 and was one of the many disabled or elderly people abandoned when the war broke out. (Wilson)

The Orchard of Lost Souls depicts a fictional community of Somalians who exist on the verge of civil war. President Oodweyne has been in power for 18 years (7), but the Somalian people have not truly celebrated their freedom since British forces left the country in June, 1960 (11). The Oodweyne regime controls all aspects of public life in Hargesia to maintain extensive nationalized, militarized order. The militarized government determines how citizens dress, how they behave in public, their civil liberties, and it controls large social organizations such as the health care system and the public orphanage. Before I undertake a close reading of the female characters in *The Orchard of Lost Souls* and how they are expected to conform to hyperfeminine gender expectations, I briefly explain how increased militarization in domestic communities leads to the intensification of gendered expectations for both men and women.

Militarization, writes gender and militarism scholar Cynthia Enloe, is "A step by step process by which a person or thing gradually comes to be controlled by the military or comes to depend on the military or militaristic ideas" (3). Similarly, Meridith Turshen, Professor of Planning and Public Policy at Rutgers University, defines militarization as "mobilization for war through the penetration of the military, its power, and influence, into more and more social arenas, until the military have a primacy in state and society" (7). In both definitions, militaristic ideas infiltrate the public mindset until they become predominant. Militaristic societies are damaging to all citizens, but have been shown to be especially physically and psychologically harmful to women and children. As Turshen observes, "Militarization is disenfranchising; it is politically, as well as economically and physically debilitating. In militarized societies, violence becomes a crisis of everyday life, especially when dirty war strategies are used by contenders for power" (7). Indeed, armed conflict kills and injures thousands of people each year, and damages the livelihood systems and communities of hundreds of thousands more (Raven-Roberts 36). The violence of militarized societies puts civilians at increased physical and psychological risk for extended times, and women and children are especially subject to danger (Plumper & Neumayer quoted in Raven-Roberts 36).

Scholar Angela Raven-Roberts explains that during wartime "women die at higher rates than men from the indirect effects of war on health and social services" (36). Moreover, Janet Lee and Susan M. Shaw document in *Women Worldwide* (2010) that women and children constitute the most civilian casualties during home front invasions: they constitute 80 percent of refugees displaced by war; they experience increased domestic and sexual violence during conflict (leading to an increase in STIs and health-related expenses);

and they suffer the most from cutbacks in state provisions, including cutbacks in health, education, and social welfare (564).

One consequence of the entrenchment of violence on the home front is that gender-based categories and expectations are magnified. This can be explained by the fact that to thrive, militarized systems require the hyperfeminization of women and the hypermasculinization of soldiers (even female soldiers), because in times of crisis, people tend to fall back on stabilizing structures that provide order and directive in the face of a changing unstable environment. Sjoberg explains, "In times of war, men . . . are expected to be able to be transformed into people willing to go through the torture and terror of soldiering, war-fighting, and killing. The practice of war-fighting requires, then, the military control of masculinity/ies . . . asking them to behave as *men*—as soldiers, protectors, and providers—not only for their family or their city or their town but for state and nation, at the risk of all else, including death" (171). Sjoberg builds on the work of Cynthia Enloe when she writes, "militarized femininity . . . is the development of militarization being reliant on the control of femininity . . . for the purposes of extending and succeeding in the war effort" (171). Public artificial hypergendering during wartime is thus used as a way to establish support for nationalistic war efforts.

In Chapter One of *The Orchard of Lost Souls* readers are introduced to three female protagonists who, in turns, narrate the story: Kawsar Ilami Bootaan, a widow in her 50s who has lost her daughter to political violence; 9-year-old Deqowareego, a refugee who has never known her parents; and Corporal Filsan Adan Ali, a female soldier who fights for the Somalian government under the reigning president. Mohamed entwines the stories of these three women in the initial chapter, and their stories reconverge in the final chapter when the women regroup to offer one another support and ultimately a tentative means of escape from the conflicts of the war zone. In the meantime, readers are privy to each woman's account of the gendering and gendered violence she experiences as the result of the military takeover in Hargesia.

According to Nira Yuval-Davis and Flora Anthias, there are five major (although not exclusive) ways in which women are gendered within nationalist discourses (7):

1. As biological reproducers;
2. As reproducers of the boundaries of ethnic/national groups;
3. As reproducers of the ideological collective and as transmitters of culture;
4. As signifiers of ethnic/national differences;
5. As participants in national, economic, political and military struggles.

(7)

Women are seen as socially valuable for their ability to reproduce, and for their ability to teach nationalistic scripts to the next generation. They are also valuable as symbols of ethnic categories who participate in nationalistic discourse. In *The Orchard of Lost Souls* Mohamed restores the agency of her three female protagonists by allowing them to cast off the confining roles of the militarized female subject and assume self-sovereignty. As I demonstrate, this transition is not without its risks.

The first narrator of *The Orchard of Lost Souls,* Kawsar Ilami Bootaan is initially valued by the state as a *reproducer*, a woman who can reproduce Somalian children whom she will presumably teach to fight for Oodweyne's regime. I refer to Kawsar's iconic place as that of the "military mother." She is a *signifier* of culture because her position as wife/mother makes her a subject of nationalist representation.

The second narrator in *The Orchard of Lost Souls,* 9-year-old Deqowareego, is a *public symbol* for "ideological discourses used in the construction, reproduction and transformation of ethnic categories." Deqo is a virgin/innocent maiden who represents the purity of the nation state and the possible tainting of that purity by an invader. She is a symbol of all that the Oodweyne regime posits it is fighting for. She is positioned as vulnerable and weak (along with countless other women, children, elderly, and sick) and thus must be protected by the strong and brave warriors of the nation.

The third and final narrator of the novel is Corporal Filsan Adan Ali, a female soldier who fights in the Somalian army. Filsan is an icon of national identity who adheres to and enforces a troubling set of gender assumptions—she is a model of virtuous behavior but despite her commitment to her career finds herself routinely having to place the wants and needs of her male colleagues ahead of her own. Her role in the military thus models both the necessity for women to present themselves as masculine to achieve any real state power, as well as the valorization of the feminine as a signifier of national virtue.

In Chapter One, for the first time in over a decade, the current Somalian regime is threatened by dissenters from the National Freedom Movement who "persist in nipping at the government's tail" (8). Suddenly then, the threat of war stemming from an outside rebel force exists in Hargesia. This threat is the impetus for the sudden amplification of the army's militarized conflicts with civilians and the reason for the extended encroachment of the militia into spaces typically reserved for civilian activity. As the threat of outside forces grows more imminent, the highly structured militarized government, in place in Hargesia for over ten years, breaks down. This social insecurity means that the prescribed roles for "militarized women" obtain even more symbolic significance, women in the community are scrutinized even more carefully, and those that flout gender norms are harshly punished.

THE TROPE OF THE MILITARY MOTHER

The trope of the "military mother" attempts to feminize women in a very particular way. Carol Cohn describes this type of wartime feminization as follows:

> They raise sons they willingly sacrifice for their country, support their men, and mourn the dead. Sometimes they have to step in and take up the load their men put down when they went off to fight; they pick up the hoe, or work in a factory producing goods crucial to the war effort—but only as long as the men are away. To the men in battle, they symbolize the alternative—a place of love, caring, and domesticity. (1)

The "military mother" represents a nostalgic version of home, "a place of love, caring, and domesticity," something for which those doing the fighting might risk their lives.

At the novel's outset, Kawsar and her female neighbors walk to the stadium in Hargesia, where they have been summoned to show public support for the reigning presidential regime at the October Twenty-first Festival (4). Despite their clear dislike of the regime, their presence at the event is mandatory. The women are considered "mothers of the revolution" (5), and are expected "to show foreign dignitaries how loved the regime is, [and] how grateful they are for the milk and peace it has brought them" (5). Although the narrator uses the term "mothers of the revolution" ironically, the phrase helps readers grasp the extent of the gendering that middle-aged, middle-class Somalian women such as Kawsar undergo. Both literally and symbolically, women such as Kawsar are expected to "mother" a new generation of soldiers and patriots who are loyal to the regime.

Kawsar is a widowed, middle-aged, home owner who has raised a respectable, educated daughter. Yet Kawsar blames President Oodweyne and his regime for the violence in her life, including the death of her husband, and especially the death of her teenage daughter. The contempt that she feels for Oodweyne and his regime positions Kawsar in opposition to the Somalian military system instead of as an agent who works in support. Kawsar feels no loyalty to President Oodweyne; she attends the October Twenty-First Festival only because she must. This lack of nationalistic pride soon leads Kawsar to experience discrimination and violence that put her very life at risk. Because she dares to question the regime she is jailed, beaten, and sustains life-threatening injuries that leave her permanently disabled and dependent on others to care for her basic needs.

At the Festival, Kawsar flouts convention, and intervenes on behalf of an orphaned child (Deqo) whom the *Guddi* is mistreating. Kawsar is then arrested and punished. The irony is that Kawsar's action *is* in fact motherly, she is seeking to protect a child from violence. Yet, in taking this public action, she challenges a decision made by the regime, and suddenly Kawsar is perceived as a problem, a threat, and a rebel who portends trouble. Thus, as the result of a seemingly harmless intervention, Kawsar is taken to jail and beaten so severely that she is left unable to walk and without access to adequate health care or social services.

Kawsar's story highlights the gendered vulnerabilities faced by civilian women on the militarized home front. First, readers see what frequently happens when a civilian missteps; that is, takes action beyond what is expected of them within their gendered role. Second, readers are privy to a believable concrete example of the physical and emotional trauma faced by women and children and the lack of resources available to address such problems in communities where all resources are going to support war.

Following this scene, Kawsar's experience at the hospital in Hargesia depicts the inadequacy of hospital care during military occupation. The hospital is "falling into ruin, the inside walls are cracked, the plaster peeling, creepers snaking their way through the windows" (125). The care, too, is inadequate. She lies in a bed with "a mattress so thin she can feel the bars of the base against her back" (121). The doctor, after a three-minute exam, explains that the hospital is too short of equipment to operate, and that the best they can hope for, as far as recovery, is to manage her pain (122).

Importantly, the death of Kawsar's daughter, Hodan, exposes the frequency and consequences of rape in a militarized zone. Hodan, a university student, is raped while temporarily jailed for taking part in a political protest opposing the impending war conflict. This scene, while fictional, pinpoints a very real problem for Somali women in militarized communities. Mugo Mugo's 2014 article "Rape in Somalia: Women and 'Double Victimisation,'" is based on findings from a 2014 report by the Human Rights Watch Organization. The article provides a clear account of the double victimization experienced by Somalian women who are raped by men in authority, and then left without effective justice or medical and social support (1).

The violence Hodan experiences is perpetrated by a police officer employed to protect civilians. He experiences no repercussions for raping Hodan; in fact, Hodan finds it impossible to even discuss the rape because of her great shame. The fact of the rape essentially excludes her from the possibility of a good marriage in the future, for she will be seen as polluted and unclean. Even her own mother, Kawsar, cannot bring herself to discuss the rape or the consequence of the rape with her daughter. She thinks, "If she said the word they both left unspoken it seemed as if everything would break, that the presence of calm would be eternally lost, that shame would replace everything else in their lives" (176). With no way to psychologically process what has happened to her or to find justice for the crime, Hodan grows increasingly more unstable, until she takes her own life. Mohamed thus unflinchingly exposes the consequences of wartime sexual violence on the mental and physical health of victims.

Mohamed also makes note of Kawsar's multiple pregnancies and lost children, calling them "the children that had passed through her . . . harsh womb" (165). The lost pregnancies suggest something important about Kawsar's character, that she is perhaps not the "military mother" that the regime would like her to embody, but that her value lies elsewhere. She buries her "lost children" in the field behind her home, where an orchard grows: "in her orchard the trees had been born from the deaths; they marked and grew from the remains of the children that had passed through her" (165). This "orchard of lost souls" suggests that beauty and good can come from loss: "out of those soft, unshaped figures had grown tall, strong, tough-barked trees that blossomed and called birds to their branches and clambered out over the orchard walls to the world beyond" (165). That the novel is titled *The Orchard of Lost Souls* further highlights the tragedy of lost innocence and the importance of regeneration.

Thus, when Kawsar rejects her public role of military mother, she is essentially cast out of the social system and left to die. First, she is widowed and loses her daughter. Then, when she literally steps out of line and stops behaving as expected, she is hurt by officials, abandoned by the medical system, and left to die at the hands of the invading force. The lack of state-sanctioned resources to address the physical and psychological consequences of war force Kawsar to rely on a handful of close female friends for support and care. These women not only help her understand her conflicting emotions but later nurse her when she is beaten and disabled. Because Kawsar is left unable to walk, her dependence on her female friends is total. She requires assistance with feeding, bathing, even using a bedpan. The women who rally around Kawsar give us the first glimpse of how female community is a salvation and answer to militarized violence. This is a theme that recurs and to which I will return.

THE MODEST MAIDEN

Nine-year-old Deqowareego is the second protagonist of the novel, the child of a refugee woman who abandons her when she is just days old, to camp officials. Deqo's experience as an orphan living in a refugee camp is illustrative of the dire circumstances faced by the many people in contemporary society who find themselves displaced by war. Like these individuals, Deqo is a survivor. She thinks, "In the camp it was as if each day brought a new threat—maybe a fire, or flooding, a new outbreak of illness, or someone would die inexplicably; life was a tightrope to be walked pigeon-toed" (95). In surviving such conditions, Mohamed depicts Deqo's strength and resiliency as well as acknowledging the strength of those who survive such conditions in real life.

Deqo's public role is that of a young girl who is expected to show her gratitude to the regime who supports her by performing a nationalistic dance. At her young age, she is capable of contributing little to the nationalistic cause, other than being a form of entertainment and a visual reminder of how the regime protects and supports its children. She thus serves as a symbol of hope and future prosperity. When the orphanage officials begin physically abusing her, she flees. This act, although brave, shifts her role in society to that of vulnerable female without a protector (read, man), and leaves the reader anticipating all of the horrible things that might befall her. Her seemingly unavoidable fate is postponed, ironically, when a prostitute takes pity on her and employs her as a servant in a brothel. Here then, for the third time in the novel, we see women supporting and helping each other survive. Unfortunately, Deqo is ultimately unable to trust this woman despite the woman's good intentions.

Deqo's story provides specific insight into the refugee experiences of displaced people during wartime, especially those of women and children. Women and children comprise 80 percent of the refugees displaced by war (Hawkesworth 555). These refugees lose their homes, their communities, and even their family members, and for the most part, writes Wenona Giles, they are fleeing from very poor developing regions to other very poor developing regions, where there are few social programs and little humanitarian aid to support them (84–85). For example, as a result of the war in Somalia alone there are more than three million displaced citizens, many of whom were women. These women crossed into Kenya between 1991–1993 to escape political violence and wartime rape, "only to face rape in the camps in which they sought shelter" (Turshen, *Women's War Stories*, 14). Because there is little to no infrastructure in the refugee camps, women and girls are at sustained risk of sexual assault.

Mohamed employs Deqo's character to demonstrate some of the material and emotional consequences of refugee life. Deqo for example, grows up knowing nothing of her parents; "She has no knowledge at all of where the rest of her family are; there are no stories passed on by cousins, no villages to return to, no genealogy to pass on if she ever has children of her own" (92). Because she has no knowledge of her family, she has no family name or clan (68) to provide her with aid. Deqo survives on her own, selling pilfered fruit at the Hargesia marketplace, where "most of the other sellers are middle-aged women, with hefty arms and feet overflowing the edges of their sandles . . . one of them . . . is always kind to her" (72). It is important to recognize that in Somalia, the marketplace is one of the few public places occupied by women. Because she is helpful and does not make trouble, Deqo is accepted into the female community of the Marketplace, which provides her a modicum of safety. The women recognize her and look out for her—they prevent her from being hassled by men and boys, buy her pilfered fruit, and assign her odd jobs for pay. Deqo then, for a second time, finds support in a community of women.

The loss of the marketplace in Hargesia because of invasion is an example of what happens when the "livelihood systems" of a community are disrupted by war. Raven-Roberts defines "livelihood systems' as "the various ways in which people 'earn a living'" (42) and explains that such systems can be "subject to inadvertent damage from conflict or, more commonly, can also be the target of deliberate destruction and 'asset stripping'" (42). In this case, the destruction of the market has dire repercussions, especially for women, who are more affected by such a loss than they would be from an attack on any government building, simply because the marketplace is largely a female-occupied space. Specifically, Deqo loses the care of a community of women who recognize and accept her, and where she is relatively safe from physical harm, because of the market's public nature and the protection that the women offer her against unlawful men. The closing of the marketplace thus becomes the final indicator that Hargesia in no longer habitable. The remaining civilians must evacuate because there is no longer a source for food and provisions.

The civilian population flees Hargesia, and a once-settled community of people is cast adrift. The result is that their security becomes more tenuous as their existing social structures disappear, as is the case in real life. For example, in actual cases of displacement because of war, local languages, cultural traditions, and even physical property can be lost. So too, survivors of wartime displacement suffer myriad psychological consequences such as fear, pain, grief, guilt, and anguish, conditions that necessitate access to health clinics with adequate medical supplies, equipment, and trained health care professionals. Unfortunately, the chances of securing such resources in most poor war-torn countries are slim to none (65), leaving entire populations without emotional support or recourse. Thus we can see that forcing a community to flee for their lives is a strategy of warfare designed to make a people permanently unstable.

Deqo is also a fictional example of how the risk of sexual violence increases exponentially for displaced peoples. In this novel Deqo successfully fights off the attacker who attempts to rape her, but in reality, sexual violence in militarized communities occurs with alarming frequency. The high incidence of wartime sexual violence is attributed to increased aggression, patriarchal attitudes, militarization of a community, rape as a war strategy, rape as a tactic for ethnic cleansing, or as a reward (DeLargy 60–64). Further, while authorities may try to regulate prostitution during peacetime, during times of military strife authorities are more likely to ignore prostitution because of the increased demand for sex in occupied areas.

Nine-year-old Deqo thus ultimately moves from her public role as child/maiden-in-need-of-protection to that of social outcast when she refuses to submit to rape and a life of prostitution. When the powerful militarized social forces of the Oodweyne regime fail her, Deqo turns to other marginalized women for help and protection.

THE CHASTE WARRIOR

The third and final narrator/protagonist of the novel is Corporal Filsan Adan Ali, a female soldier who is assigned to oversee the events at the stadium, and who is subsequently responsible for breaking Kawsar's hip and pelvis during a violent beating, leaving Kawsar permanently unable to walk. Mohamed seems to be asking how a woman might perpetrate such violence upon another, yet she provides us with no easy answers. To come closer to answering this question we must first consider how infrequently women are placed in positions of power in the first place, and why this might be. Laura Sjoberg writes,

> The continued presence of gendered subordination . . . is particularly visible in two areas. First, . . . women often lead either when selectors express an interest in characteristics traditionally associated with femininity or when a woman leader can adequately prove her masculinity over assumptions of her incapability. Second, . . . women's opportunities to lead and the integration of feminine values into war decision making will remain limited until our understandings of war decision making come to see and deconstruct gendered assumptions about leaders and their decisions. (161)

Sjoberg identifies two important reasons that hinder women from attaining influential leadership positions during wartime. First, that women are *expected* to lead using "feminine" qualities in very specific public situations where the feminine might be useful, such as negotiating with villagers, or gaining access to female heads of households; second, women are allowed to lead after they have somehow proven that they are appropriately masculine.

In Filsan's case she chooses the second route; that is, she does her best to prove her masculinity so as to attain the respect of her peers. Filsan believes that to enter and remain within the masculinized realm of the military she must renounce both her femininity and her sexuality altogether. She does her best to ensure that she will not be sexualized and/or perceived as weak by the male soldiers with whom she interacts. However, despite her extreme attempts to neutralize any traces of the feminine that might give her away, Filsan is repeatedly demeaned by her male peers who sexualize and prey on her. The first example of this comes on the eve of the October Twenty-First Festival when a superior officer accosts her for sex. Filsan refuses his advances, jumps from his car, walks to the jail, and soon after proceeds to beat Kawsar, presumably taking her frustrations out on the other woman and attempting to regain some authority for herself. The reasons behind her actions in no way legitimize or make them right, but readers do at least have a glimpse of the psychology surrounding her heinous decision-making. The horrifying scene during which Filsan beats Kawsar provides readers with an example of the way that women in wartime can "collude in their own oppression and are even complicit in the oppression of other women" (Turshen 10). Moreover, violent women reveal women's ability to act in a "masculine" manner, "thus exploding gender myths of what constitutes 'masculine' and 'feminine' conduct" (Graham-Bertolini 6).

Enlisting in the military does nothing to protect Filsan from sexual objectification by her male counterparts. It garners her no additional respect, despite what she has hoped. For example, although Filsan at first believes that she has been noticed by General Haaruun for "the sharpness of her uniform, the straightness of her back, the smartness of her salute" (28–29), she quickly realizes that "Even in her uniform they [male soldiers] see nothing more than breasts and a hole" (34). Her physical body is publicly gazed upon and commented on, with the expectation that she will succumb to any man who shows interest; yet ironically, Filsan is called "whore" when she rejects the unwanted advances of her peers. Filsan quickly learns that being in uniform does not prevent pervasive sexism and subordination; in fact, it often amplifies and makes such treatment worse. In constant anticipation of judgment, she "lives the celibate, sterile, quiet existence of a nun" (213), a lifestyle that situates her as entirely asexual; in fact, as we see when she first inflicts violence upon Kawsar and see again when she needlessly murders two village elders, she even occasionally takes on masculine aggression and behaviors to gain favor from her superior officers.

Jennifer Mathers writes, "Some of the most powerful and effective barriers which women face in state militaries are the ones that are informal and invisible. These range from the gendered assumptions that can prevent soldiers and officers from even perceiving (much less rewarding) the competencies demonstrated by women, to undermining slander and innuendo, to violent sexual assault and abuse by fellow soldiers" (140). In the United States, one of the few countries that collects and records statistics on sexual assault within the armed forces (Mathers 143), an average of one in three military women has experienced sexual assault (142). Moreover, it is important to keep in mind that recorded statistics of sexual assault in the US military are estimated to be conservative, because so many women do not report abuse for fear of internal consequences (143). During wartime, the threat of rape and sexual assault increases even more so. In the words of an American infantryman interviewed in the 1990s, "In a situation where times are hard—less food, no showers, road marching, with 70–100 lbs ruck on your back, and [you] don't know when the next supply shipment with be in, the male soldier will start thinking of sex and the female soldier may be raped or something" (quoted in Bourke 370).

Filsan, working a desk job, is passed over multiple times for promotion despite her qualifications. Mathers writes that women in the military "almost always find they are limited to a relatively narrow range of positions in areas such as administration, communications, logistics, and medicine. Not coincidentally, these are the roles within militaries that most closely resemble the roles that women play in families and in civilian employment" (136). This seems exactly the case for Filsan, about whom the narrator observes, "She is an office worker within the military, neither noticed nor commended by the gold-braided men above her, and it galls her that despite two years of enlistment in the Women's Auxiliary Corps and five years working for the green-uniformed enforcers of the regime, the Victory Pioneers, her chief tasks are still those of a secretary" (Mohamed 214). After two years, and only when a male officer develops a crush on her, Filsan is promoted to serve in a combat unit. This promotion is what she has hoped for, yet is a questionable reward. Serving in a combat unit still does not give her the status required to formulate policy; Filsan is a cog in the machine and as such is unable to implement lasting positive change.

Filsan's first assignment in her new position is to destroy the water supply of the small town of Salahley, because the water is believed to be used by rebels (217–218; 224–225). The military hopes to control the villagers' access to water as a way to ensure their allegiance. When Filsan accidentally and needlessly shoots two village elders during a preliminary investigation, she is lauded by higher-ups and exploited by the media who fawn over the existence of a female combat soldier. She is introduced by the radio commentator as "A Mogadishu girl who is serving her country in the armed forces, a remarkable young lady, in fact, who has put aside the usual desire to settle down with a family of her own . . . and has taken up arms to defend her country" (242). The media places emphasis on how Filsan is a good girl who is sacrificing her own happiness (establishing a family and becoming a wife and mother) for the nationalistic cause. What is telling, however, is the way that the interviewer manages to depict Filsan as a masculinized soldier who is just as strong and qualified as her male counterparts, while also situating her as a future wife/mother who has simply "put aside," her desire for family until a later date. She is thus publicly constructed as masculine warrior and feminine caretaker—an image that comes across as acceptable and desirable to Somalian listeners, and a perfect representation of the nationalist myth that the Oodweyne regime is promoting.

Despite the way the incident is "spun" by the military propaganda office and the media, the unnecessary murder of civilians is a catalyst for Filsan, who finally recognizes that life in the patriarchal military system leads to false reward. She acknowledges to herself that she has been seeking the approval of others rather than living a life that is self-directed. Unable to reconcile her personal ethics with her needlessly violent actions (229), she blames her weak sense of self on "listen[ing] to the rules" (230), and being "desperate for a pat on the head" (230). Thus, one positive conclusion to the novel is that Filsan learns that unnecessary violence demeans her own sense of morality, instead of making her "stronger."

A short time later, Filsan's love interest, Robul, is killed during a surprise attack by rebel forces (297). The needless loss of Robul, combined with the realization that the military for whom she works is a corrupt institution, drive Filsun to question everything in which she has believed. In a particularly graphic scene, Filsan learns that the authorities have authorized the bleeding to death of children, essentially using them as a source of blood donation for those they consider more important, with no regard for the children's lives (305). In response she rants, "Follow orders. Follow orders. Follow orders. That is the code they have been brought up under and it endures until the burden of guilt cracks the spine. Her father would probably explain their actions as the necessities of war, but to her they seem like the cannibals of old tales: totally ordinary yet irrevocably depraved" (308). Soon after Filsan deserts her position—she exchanges clothing with a dead woman and literally walks away from her job, thinking, "she cannot remain, whatever the cost" (317). She walks away knowing she might be killed as a traitor. Yet, ironically, the moment that Filsan decides to risk her life for what she believes is the moment that she finally acquires her strength.

Corporal Filsan Adan Ali finally realizes that she will never be free from public gendering within the military system, no matter how she tries to erase important parts of herself. She will never be embraced by a military system that valorizes and privileges masculinity, violence, and aggression. Instead of continuing to harm herself and/or innocent victims of the insurgency, Filsan decides to abandon her post, an action punishable by death.

CONCLUSIONS

In the early chapters of *The Orchard of Lost Souls*, the threat to the women's survival comes directly from the Somalian military/government itself, not from an outside enemy force, as one might expect. The militarization of Hargesia requires citizens to curtail their normal day-to-day activities like visiting friends and shopping at the market, as well as sacrifice their own personal freedoms for the sake of security and nationalism. Mohamed demonstrates how women put themselves in great danger when they transgress hyperfeminine categories of wartime. Yet, we see, transgression is necessary because the gendered categories are oppressive and do not protect women from harm of a different sort.

The military takeover of Hargesia causes Kawsar to lose her home and her social support system of female friends and neighbors. The takeover forces Deqo to flee her female-centric sanctuary at the brothel with nowhere to go, because the local market place has been abandoned. Militarization destabilizes the lives of both women to such a degree that they find they must leave the city to survive. But even after forming an alliance, they still lack the physical strength to travel. Kawsar's broken hip and pelvis render her bedridden, and Deqo is simply too small to lift her. Their situation sheds light on some of the many difficulties that women face in the real world as they grapple with wartime disability, displacement, and lack of support. Wenona Giles writes, "Women the world over are generally less mobile and monied than men. Their gendered responsibilities of caring for children and other dependents tend to hamper their ability to flee" (86). Certainly, traveling with dependents makes movement much more difficult for anyone. For Kawsar, who has resourcefully stashed money away, it is still only with the help of Deqo and Filsan that she is eventually able to leave. After Filsan pledges loyalty to Deqo and Kawsar, she places Kawsar in a wheelbarrow, and the three set out on foot for the Ethiopian border.

In reality, when civilians must flee from their homes because of militarization, they often move to the unsafe and unsanitary conditions of refugee camps. Approximately "6 million people . . . are living outside their homelands in what are called 'protracted refugee situations.' These refuges have been living in exile inside and outside of camps for at least five years or more" (89). Such refugees are stuck in long-term exile, unable to return to their dangerous homelands, unable to remain in the country of their exile where resources are scarce, and unable to relocate to wealthier nations that bar them for financial and political reasons (89–90). In *The Orchard of Lost Souls*, Kawsar, Deqo, and Filsan pay a truck driver to carry them to the Ethiopian border, where they arrive at the relative safety of a refugee camp established by the United Nations (Mohamed 333). The camp "is too new to have any water, standpipes, clinics, or latrines, and there is still vegetation . . . for people to raid for firewood and construction" (333). Despite the lack of running water and nonexistent latrines, it is a sanctuary for the three Somalian women who pledge to protect one another from whatever is to come.

Is there a positive side to the upheaval and destruction experienced by war-torn communities? Turshen argues, yes, that "In the very breakdown of morals, traditions, customs, and community, war also opens up and creates new beginnings" (20). For example, she continues, "war and displacement in the Sudan have changed women's status from housewives to breadwinners . . . women have vowed never to give up this change and never to revert to the status of being owned or inherited or of being revered only as mothers and wives without having any property or freedom of movement" (20). Women's choices may remain limited, but they negotiate their circumstances with the few options they have. Likewise, in *The Orchard of Lost Souls* the three protagonists claim agency and independence when they band together. Their friendship is mutually beneficial, allowing them to travel successfully to the Ethiopian refugee camp and to survive as a unit. Filsan relies on Kawsar's determination, strength of character, and cash. She finds Kawsar to be the resourceful, accepting, parental figure she has lacked. In Deqo, Filsan finds a generosity of spirit that inspires her to be a better person. Deqo relishes the companionship, guidance, and protection of Kawsar and Filsan. They offer her protection, acceptance, and love. Kawsar benefits from the alliance most clearly in terms of receiving help for her physical incapacity; but additionally, the two young woman help her to overcome her grief for her daughter, and to realize that life must go on. Kawsar's strength, resilience, intelligence, and her money (which she contributes to ensure the escape of the trio) confirms that she, on the other hand, is key to the survival of the younger women. It is within these moments of communal change, risk, and impermanence that hope emerges for the first time for all three of the characters. These moments of community inspire the three women to reject their prescribed public roles. The women are "in transit" both literally and metaphorically. Although they are still at great risk of violence, their powerful will to survive has emerged and promises to save them.

Mohamed suggests with this conclusion that a feasible way for women to protect themselves and achieve agency during wartime is for women to band together and help one another. In fact, she suggests that this is the ONLY way that women will survive, for none of her three protagonists could survive without the help of the others. Forming a collective provides them with concrete protection against forces that conspire to disempower and harm them. We suspect for the first time that in sticking together, the women will survive and find happiness.

As *The Orchard of Lost Souls* portrays, when home front spaces break down as the result of military invasion, a corresponding breakdown of social life takes place for civilian residents who find themselves in precarious, dangerous circumstances. Women and girls in militarized communities are often forced to conform to artificial, hyperfeminine gender expectations that relegate them to restrictive gendered categories during wartime. The "militarized mother" is responsible for raising the next generation of nationalistic soldiers/citizens; the virgin or innocent maiden represents the so-called purity of the nation state that can be invaded and polluted by outside forces that wish to inflict harm; the chaste warrior must model virtuous behavior while never flagging in her commitment to her military career—she is expected to sacrifice not only her femininity but also her feminist morality for the sake of the nation. The importance of these public roles is amplified during wartime and enforced to extreme degrees. Those who refuse to conform risk physical and mental violence, even death.

Mohamed's characters all eventually transgress their public roles and work together to escape Hargesia. In doing so, they risk their lives to challenge dominant wartime representations of women with individual narratives of their own. In forming a collective, the women commit to helping and supporting one another, which creates an avenue of escape for all of them, something that would not otherwise be possible. In militarized societies, where both men and women are publicly gendered to extreme degrees, it is the female collective that offers women a way to attain freedom for self-definition. The stories of the three protagonists in *The Orchard of Lost Souls* (an old lady, a young orphan, a soldier), crystallize the violence experienced both within the Somalian military and by the civilian population and demonstrate the way that home fronts and war zones interconnect and overlap in contemporary warfare.

WORKS CITED

Bourke, Joanna. *Rape: Sex, Violence, History*. UK: Virago Press, 2007.
Cohn, Carol, Ed. Malden MA: Polity Press, 2013. 54–79. Print.
DeLargy, Pamela. "Sexual Violence and Women's Health in War." *Women & Wars.*
Enloe, Cynthia. *Bananas Beaches and Bases: Making Feminist Sense of International Politics*. Los Angeles: University of California Press, 1989.
Giles, Wenona. "Women Forced to Flee: Refugees and Internally Displaced Persons." *Women & Wars.* Carol Cohn, Ed. Malden MA: Polity Press, 2013. 36–53. Print.
Graham-Bertolini, Alison. *Vigilante Women in Contemporary American Fiction*. New York: Palgrave, 2011. Print.

Hawkesworth, Mary. "Women, War, and Peace." *Women Worldwide: Transnational Feminist Perspectives on Women.* Janet Lee and Susan M. Shaw, Eds. New York: McGraw Hill, 2011. 553–578.

Mathers, Jennifer G. "Women and State Military Forces." *Women & Wars.* Carol Cohn, Ed. Malden MA: Polity Press, 2013. 124–145. Print.

Mohaned, Nadifa. *The Orchard of Lost Souls.* New York: Farrar, Straus, and Giroux. 2013.

Mugo, Mugo. "Rape in Somalia: Women and 'Double Victimisation.'" *Global Education Magazine. March 2014. 1–11. Web.*

Raven-Roberts, Angela. "Women and the Political Economy of War." *Women & Wars.* Carol Cohn, Ed. Malden MA: Polity Press, 2013. 36–53. Print.

Sjoberg, Laura. *Gendering Global Conflict: Toward a Feminist Theory of War.* New York: Columbia University Press. 2013.

Turshen, Meridith and Clotilde Twagiramariya. *What Women Do in Wartime.* New York: Zed Books, 1998.

Wilson, Annasue McCleave. "The Only Seeds Being Sown Were Bullets: PW Talks with Nadifa Mohamed." *Publishers Weekly.* Dec 9, 2013. Web.

Yuval-Davis, Nira and Flora Anthias. *Women, Nation, State.* New York: Palgrave, 1989. Print.

NOTE

1. These examples are used to exemplify social problems that are experienced in various, unique ways by women exposed to war across the world, as borne out by statistical evidence and individual testimony. I use these examples with the awareness that all wars, all militaries, and all individuals, are different, with different specific experiences.

Chapter Four

Writing about My Mother

Representations of Alliances between Mothers and Daughters in Young Adult (YA) Refugee Literature

Stella Mililli

The interest in the representation of mother-daughter relationship in young adult literature (often abbreviated as YA) has increased in the last thirty years (Crew). Black American Feminist sociologist, Patricia Hill Collins and American Feminist poet and essayist Adrienne Rich, for example, developed new florid traditions in Black feminist studies and feminist literature, respectively, greatly influencing the narrations of the entangled relation between teen daughters and their mothers in the genre of the Bildüngsroman. According to Hilary Crew, the absent parent and the conflicts between teen children and their parents, perceived as a constitutional and necessary part of their individual development (2), have been conventional elements in literature for YA, and for this reason, the focus on the daughter-mother kinship has been under-represented and under-investigated.

In discussing the representation of displaced motherhood in contemporary refugee literature for young adults, I provide a comparative analysis of the mothers in two novels in free verse, Terry Farish's *The Good Braider* (2012) and Thannha Lai's *Inside Out & Back Again* (2011). *The Good Braider* offers insights into the generational and cultural conflicts between children and parents in refugee families. In particular, this book of fiction follows the poetic narration of Viola, refugee teenager, and her mother Tereza from Sudan to Portland, Maine. Farish is not a refugee herself, but her literary ouvre has been informed by an interest in narrating characters who are usually put at the margins of the so-called multicultural society in the US. *Inside Out*

& Back Again is the first novel by Vietnamese-born American writer, Lai. Gleaning from her personal family history of flight during the Vietnam war, Lai gives poetic voice to the emotions, the memories, and the struggles of Hà, a young refugee who fled Saigon to Alabama with her mother, who she calls "Mother," and her brothers in 1975.

As previous studies have pointed out, the verse novel has gained noticeable popularity in the field of YA literature in the last twenty years (Abate; Cadden; Campbell). Having its origin in the ancient poetic oral tradition, the genre offers the young readers a narrative site where the poetic words encounter empty "silent" spaces on the page and between the characters' words, thus stimulating reflections and imagination. Withing this "relatively" new literary tradition, the verse novel has been a prominent choice of authors of refugee literature. In the case of *The Good Braider* and *Inside Out & Back Again*, while Farish's choice of writing a novel in free verse seems to be dictated mostly by her sense of respect and homage to the community she is representing in the novel, Lai turns to the novel in verse in order to be able to convey the musicality of Vietnamese, her mother tongue.

These are texts that are targeted for young adults, so it is important that the narrative voice is the one of a young character as this enables the identification between young readers and narrator, and possibly helps readers empathize with young refugees in their schools or social groups. My analysis follows these lines of enquiry to discuss the voices of the daughters talking about their mothers and their connections with them. In focusing my analysis of the voices of the daughters I bear in mind Elizabeth Podnieks and Andrea O'Reilly reminder that stories of mothers have been dominated by the perspective of the daughters, thus preventing expressions of maternal voices and subjectivities. In the introduction to their edited collection *Textual Mothers/Maternal Texts: Motherhood in Contemporary Women's Literature* (2010), they insist on inviting scholars and researchers to keep investigating maternal subjectivity even though the mother's voice has become more present in maternal narratives and studies in the last few decades (2). Podnieks and O'Reilly also argue that in the last two decades, literature about minority women has been characterized by narratives about rebel daughters giving "voice to their often silenced mothers" (8) and celebrating their bond.

According to Natalie Rosinsky, published author of children's books and young adult books, analyzing the mother-daughter kinship in minority literature is "disheartening and encouraging," because of the pain portrayed in this literature, but also because it shows the depth of this tie. She continues defining this literature "political as well as aesthetic[al]" (290). The triad gender, class and race has often defined the study of the mother-daughter relationship (Crew, 4). For this reason, and because the mothers portrayed in the books are members of minoritized groups, such as Black African and Vietnamese communities in the US, I heavily draw on Gloria Anzaldúa's queer and Chicana theory of the borderland (1987) and Collins's Black feminist theory of motherhood (1994) as they both theorize about the lives of marginalized subjects in the society. I am indebted to these scholars in the way I consider the position occupied by the mothers and their role of "silent guardians of the tradition" (Anzaldúa) in the patriarchal societies they occupy but also as subjects of social change to the benefit of their daughters' lives in society.

I suggest that these YA refugee literary texts can enrich ethical discussion about social power dynamics and gender stereotypes, while proposing a counter-narrative where emotions and affect, such as pain, love, and compassion, are fundamental to define the subjectivity of the refugee character and contrast "dehumanizing" mainstream discourses. Ultimately, this essay fleshes out daughter-mother relationship as portrayed in situations of displacement as sites of care, compassion, knowledge production, and empowerment between generations of women. I maintain that these texts tell stories where characters are able to show compassion towards their mothers, which is key for the representation of the refugee character as a "feeling" subject and of the familiar bond as a site where compassion circulates. Kathrine Ibbett, who explores the affect of compassion in texts from early modern France, provides a precise historical investigation that can be applied to contemporary texts as well, concluding that compassion is a "a mode of thinking about difference" and a tool to find new forms of relation (228).

In this chapter, I argue that *The Good Braider* and *Inside Out and Back Again* texts not only broaden the definition of maternal power by offering an insight into the complex daughter-mother relationship in contexts of displacement, but also show the strategies the mothers adopt to fight different forms of oppression. This contributes to the call from transnational feminist scholars, to "be inclusive, and look at mothering from a different perspective taking into consideration the cultural, social and spatial location of the people instead of using western middle class definitions and concepts of family and mothering" (Kyomugisha, 84).

MATRICENTRIC FEMINISM

In contrast to stereotyped and reductionist depictions of minoritized and refugee mothers in other media, the refugee mothers in these YA books are portrayed as complex and unique individuals. Following the intention of both Farish and Lai as authors, this essay wants to bring up and focus on their differences and unique traits as transnational women and mothers. The recognition of the importance of the different ways of being a mother and experiencing motherhood is one of the main focuses of matricentric feminism, together with finding strategies to deconstruct the oppressive structures and dynamics that affect motherhood (Porter et al., xii). O'Reilly aptly explains the concept of matricentric feminism as a "particular form of feminist enquiry, politics and theory which is consistent with and receptive to feminist frameworks of care and equal rights" (25) with a clear understanding and determination to respect "situated realities" of motherhood (xii). Matricentric feminism speaks to me and my analysis because it ties together the maternal experience and bond with the feminist perspective about ethics of care and equality, that are vital elements I address in this chapter. Furthermore, more correctly, the notion of transnational feminism constitutes a base to my enquiry in that it explores feminist strategies of resistance and care in two literary examples of transnational and displaced mothers located in two different geographical and sociocultural contexts—Tereza from South Sudan, and "Mother" from Vietnam.

BRAIDING AS FEMINIST GENEALOGY RESISTANCE IN *THE GOOD BRAIDER*

As Crew aptly states, Black feminist theorists and writers, such as Collins and Toni Morrison, have recognized the necessity of contextualizing the mother-daughter relationship in a racial, social, and cultural context, because "white Western psychological interpretations and analysis are inappropriate to studying the black daughter-mother relationship" (191). Bearing this in mind, I have approached my literary research being aware of my position as a white Western researcher and how my positionality could influence my interpretation and discussion of the book. Therefore, I have decided to rely, as explained in the introduction to the chapter, on Black feminist theories as a methodological framework.

The Bond "Grandmother-Mother-Daughter"

In his essay "A Genealogy of Refugee Writing," Arthur Rose claims that "Genealogies are conventionally understood as a subversive form of history, whereby a subterranean continuity underwrites 'normal' patterns of historical events" (53). This genealogical bond with the women in her family allows Viola, the narrator and protagonist in *The Good Braider*, to think about her own history and identity through processes of association, comparison, identification, and differentiation with the other women. I argue that the influence of her mother, Tereza, and her grandmother, Habuba, their behavior and words towards Viola are elements that affect Viola's life and identity definition process. I maintain that it is crucial to refer to the concepts of genealogies, and thus place the mother-daughter relationship in the broader genealogy that connects Viola to her mother and her grandmother.

Slam poet and Sudanese refugee, Emi Mahmoud, describes her writing experience of her poem "Mama" ("Emi Mahmoud-Mama") about her mother, grandmother, godmother, and other women in her family, as if she is writing a genealogy of the matriarchal figures of her life, "every symbol of strength that I knew" ("Slam Poet and Sudanese Refugee Emi Mahmoud Shares Her Story"). Mahmoud's work is relevant in connection to the analysis of portrayals of feminist genealogies because she offers a refugee perspective on the importance that mothers and other older women have in the life of their children in contexts of war and displacement. I observe an example of the strength Mahmoud refers to in *The Good Braider*, when Tereza gives Viola a piece of elephant bone while saying: "No animal can kill the elephant" (Farish, "Elephant Bone," 23). Viola will keep her mother's gift with herself throughout her journey and her life in Portland, and the symbol of the elephant will become a trope in her narrative of identity development. I see here a resonance also with Lynn Z. Bloom's definition of motherhood as "a heritage is a gift from the past and a hope for the continuity of the future; as such, mother-daughter relationships are vital, important linking of the generation, as varied as the women who comprise them" (291).

In *Zami: A New Spelling of My Name* (1982), Audre Lorde coined the expression "grandmother-mother-daughter triad" as a strong bond, where the subject at the center is constantly moving, in opposition to the "triangle of mother father and child, with the 'I' at its eternal core" (7). As I understand Lorde, the matriarchal triad is an inclusive and equal familiar structure where the different subjects are respected and valued. Lorde's perspective is applicable when considering the representation of motherhood and the grandmother-mother-daughter tie in *The Good Braider*, because, in my view, the three women are intimately connected, interdependent and necessary to each other. According to Crew,

> A story about a teen daughter and her mother is frequently told in the context of a generational story. The interrelationships between grandmother, mother and adolescent daughter form a significant element of the daughter-mother narrative in different racial and cultural contexts . . . the grandmother daughter-mother narrative serves to provide a more extensive description and explanation of the daughter-mother relationship . . . into a "historical" context. (169)

In *The Good Braider*, communication suffers when Habuba has to stay in Juba and cannot flee together with Viola and Tereza. In Cairo, for instance, where she is alone with her mother, Viola suffers the trauma of the distance from her beloved grandmother. Thus, the girl stops braiding her hair:

> I am not who I used to be
> We were three, like three strands
> We lay, three of us, on the steamer, warming each other.
> Without the third, I don't know what to do. (Farish, "Sahara," 82)

Viola not only seems to be missing her grandmother but also a part of herself that is now lost. The loss and the trauma of war make Viola experience and understand her vulnerability as an individual and a social being. In Viola's story, the character of Habuba, the grandmother, is also essential for Viola's identity development. As Crew contends,

> The special bond between grandmothers and granddaughters is a frequent element of story in grandmother daughter-mother narratives in young adult novels . . . by suturing the differences and/or absences of a daughter's mother . . . also serve to connect a granddaughter to a beneficent grandmother who empowers her granddaughter in a way that her own mother cannot. (182–183)

I recognize the beneficial role that Crew talks about in Habuba who empowers and comforts Viola when her mother is behaving in a stricter and distant way. The grandmother in the narrative supports her granddaughter by telling her about her capacities, her quick mind, and a bright future in front of her: "I have made all Habuba's memories my own" (Farish, 27). Viola interrogates her grandmother about her future, as to find confirmation about what her life will be.

Together with Viola's struggle to define her identity, her relationship with her mother also suffers increasingly, until a tragic fight in Portland, where Tereza punishes Viola for disobeying her orders against seeing her male friend, Andrew, with a corporal punishment. After that, the mother-daughter relation becomes colder and silent, because Tereza refuses to talk to Viola. Tereza's pain and her way of processing it seems to bring her to close in herself and avoid sharing her feelings with her daughter. Tereza appears to be withdrawing from communicating with Viola and she is unable or refusing to speak also in Cairo, when mourning the sudden death of her young son who was escaping Sudan with them. In *Black Feminist Thought* (2000), Collins points out that Black mothers are often described as strong disciplinarians and overly protective; yet, these same women manage to raise daughters who are self-reliant and assertive (454). Viola's mother appears as a strong and overly protective parent both in Juba and in Portland. Authority and discipline are some dominant traits of the mother-daughter kinship between Tereza and Viola, and several times, Viola writes about her wish that her mother would comfort her instead: "[. . .] *Comfort me,/* I want to say./ I want her to tell me I am still her child" (Farish, 35). However, the mother will be able to interrupt a social and culture rule of shame that negatively discriminates and isolates women who are victim of rape in Sudan when she decides to let Viola stay with the family. Later, in Portland, Tereza will break the shame circle around women for having boyfriends before marriage and allow Viola to see her new friend Andrew. However, her words "the elders say we must—she pauses— educate ourselves in American ways" (203), also contain, in my opinion, a bittersweet taste connected to the idea that to fit in a new society, the refugee mother (and daughter) must assimilate into the new society's culture and values. In this sense, Tereza's behavior is similar to Mother's in *Inside Out and Back Again*, as I will explain later.

Braiding Hair: Creating Feminist Knowledge and Resistance

After having analyzed the relations between Viola and Habuba, and Viola and Tereza, I will now present the act of braiding as the ritual act through which the knowledge between generations of women is transmitted in the novel. According to Rich, "Mothers and daughters have always exchanged with each other—beyond the verbally transmitted lore of female survival—a knowledge that is subliminal, subversive, preverbal [. . .]" (220). Rich further defines the knowledge originated from this maternal tie as "transitory, fragmented, perhaps, but original and crucial" (225). Her words resonate with my discussion of *The Good Braider* in that the knowledge that is created and passed between grandmother-mother-daughter is one of tradition and resistance in a context of displacement. Grandmother and mother pass to Viola, and create with her, knowledge about the ritual of braiding hair as a form of matriarchal alliance to tackle problems and strengthen bonds. They also create knowledge about the feminist resistance against devaluating gender roles that deprive women of personal freedom, subjectivity, and agency. Following Evelyn Nakano Glenn, "The everyday activities of the mothers in maintaining tradition and in keeping kin ties alive can be seen as resistance" (18). I claim that the act of braiding each other's hair symbolizes the resistance of Viola and Tereza as daughter and mother facing the challenges of living in displacement, while just having each other and their strong tie. I find a similarity between the act of braiding hair and Naomi Ruth Lowinsky's analysis of weaving threads given how in both situations the matrilineal conversation takes place and ties are created. In *Stories from the Motherline: Reclaiming the Mother-Daughter Bond, Finding Our Feminine Souls* (1992), Lowinsky reflects on the generational bonds involved in the act of weaving: "The weaving of tapestry whose threads are tied to different generations and as the spinning goes on, a more complicated network of relationships is thus developed" (68). I find a parallelism between the activities of weaving tapestry and of braiding hair, in that both involve generations of women who sit together, pass generational knowledge through their hands and the act of being together, and build kinships that are as strong, entangled, and indissoluble as their handworks.

Podnieks and O'Reilly describe mothering "as much a lived action as it is a narrated dialogue" (21). I distinguish these ideas in Tereza's act of mothering Viola and in their kinship. The act of braiding, which, in my view, symbolizes the daughter-mother tie in the novel, is both lived and narrated. Viola experiences braiding and reflects on its meaning, as well as she experiences being a daughter, observing her mother and reflecting on their tie.

Braiding establishes this lived and physical connection between bodies through the act of touching the mother's and the daughter's bodies.

INSIDE OUT & BACK AGAIN: **VULNERABLE ALLIANCES IN DISPLACEMENT**

If the importance of the act of touching is central in the creation of the mother-daughter bond in *The Good Braider*, the voice and the oral communication is the key element in Hà's relationship with her mother. Motherhood as site of transmission of oral knowledge and the voice of the mother as form of resistance to racism will be the focus of this part of my chapter.

Inside Out & Back Again, as well as *The Good Braider*, offer a complex description of motherhood in displacement. As in *The Good Braider*, the mother in Lai's novel is represented both challenging gender roles, while, at the same time, reproducing gender stereotypical discourses. Furthermore, the daughter-mother kinship is marked by silences and struggles, but also by great compassion and care. In my analysis, I discuss the mother-daughter kinship in *Inside Out & Back Again* as a site of solidarity and alliance in constant state of transformation, and in a delicate balance due to the vulnerable condition of being a displaced refugee.

The Mother as a Vocal Subject

The novel opens with a representation of motherhood as a site of struggle for Mother, who, because of the Vietnam war, cannot provide enough resources and food to feed her children. Collins aptly remarks the underprivileged conditions in which children of women of color must live: "Physical survival is assumed for children who are white and middle-class" (49). Collins further discusses the disadvantaged situations that mothers of color have to face when bringing up their children in the US. I argue that Lai's novel provides an example of how appropriate it is to extend to other ethnicities Collin's assertion that focuses primarily on Black mothers. For example, during the sea crossing in *Inside Out & Back Again*, Hà is hungry, and the mother cuddles her. Mother exhibits painful awareness and consciousness of her children's struggles, and at the same time, attempts to comfort them, and also inspire social justice and just values in order for them to survive and become, paraphrasing Judith Butler's words, "responsible members of the society" (37).

Mother is also portrayed in the novel as a vocal subject who functions as a compass in her daughter's life: *at times you have to fight, but preferably not with your fists* (215). Later the mother will give an example of what she means; when met with hostility at the local butchery, she firmly and steadily speaks to her interlocutor in Vietnamese but ends her sentence with "a clear NOW" (218). As Bunkong Tuon, who considers the concepts of accommodation and resistance in *Inside Out & Back Again*, aptly contends, words play an important role in the novel (547). According to Tuon, Lai's description of her mother as an educated, non-violent Vietnamese woman disrupts the stereotype of "the South as a place of uneducated, ignorant, and racist 'rednecks'" (547). It is worth reminding the reader that Mother and her family were settled in Alabama, and as I read Tuon, Mother, with her presence there, contributes to disrupting the negative stereotypes of people living in Alabama. In my view, the capitalization of the adverb NOW is used not only to dismantle stereotypical discourses, but also, most importantly, to emphasize Mother's strength and determination in being "heard" and respected. The mother is here as a subject resisting silencing and discriminatory social attitudes, that would want her silent instead. Furthermore, the adverb comes after her speech in Vietnamese, that she knows the butcher does not understand. I see in Mother's use of language and words her strong, but peaceful fight rejecting to communicate in the language of the "host," which she has encouraged her children to learn, but that has brought to them also much pain because of many racist attacks. In this way, Mother gives Hà an example of how to resist racism and discrimination without violence.

However, in her resistance to racism, Mother is well aware of the differences between herself and the rest of the Southern American community, although she both hides and renounces to some aspects of her culture in order to receive asylum in the US. In my view, Mother symbolizes the struggle and fragmentation of personal and cultural identity that many refugees must often undergo under the "request" of assimilation in the "hosting" country.

Tuon aptly explains that "the mother's story serves as a type of family inheritance to be passed down to younger generation, it also gives [. . .] readers an insight into Viet Nam's complicated history" (540). Thus, I maintain that the mother, by accommodating Hà's wish to hear a story from her, not only transmits family and historical knowledge, but also, by doing do, she creates the premises for alliance and solidarity with her daughter based on sharing of emotions and personal history:

> It's not easy
> to persuade Mother
> to tell of her girlhood
> in the North,
> where her grandmother's land
> stretched farther than doves could fly,
> where looking pretty
> and writing poetry
> were her only duties.
> She was promised to father
> at five.
> They married at sixteen,
> earlier than expected.
> Everyone's future changed
> upon learning the name
> Hô Chí Minh.
> [. . .]
> I always wish for her eyes,
> but Mother says no.
> Eyes like hers can't help
> but carry sadness [. . .]. (27–29)

In this passage, Mother's personal history and the national history of Vietnam are intertwined, and together with the history of war, Mother's voice carries personal pain and sadness. In her act of sharing her stories, although sometimes the grief and sorrow silence her, Mother is portrayed as the subject who does an act of deconstruction and reconstruction of narratives of national and international displacement.

Compassionate Alliances

Jean-Luc Nancy reminds us that compassion is not "a pity that feels sorry for itself and feeds on itself. Compassion is the contagion, the contact of being with one another in this turmoil. Compassion is not altruism, nor is it identification; it is the disturbance of violent relatedness" (xiii). In my view, Nancy uses "com-passion" to underline the aspect of being together, close and in proximity. As I understand his words, being "infected," touched and disturbed by the feeling of relating to someone else's situation, being with the suffering of the other is a necessary personal, social, and political tool for a change. *Inside Out & Back Again* offers several examples of daughter-mother compassion that touches, disturbs, and provokes a change for more just social connections. When Mother becomes silent, Hà shows empathy and compassion towards her feelings and pain. In Alabama, the daughter's uncertainty is met with cold words, sighs, and disappearances: "I wish . . . that Mother wouldn't hide her bleeding finger" (158). Just as the relationship between Viola and Tereza changes once they arrive in Portland and their conflicts become stronger and causing more distance between the two, also the relationship between the Hà and Mother changes once they relocate in the US. Initially, Mother does not show empathy and stops comforting her daughter, while also trying to hide her own weaknesses. Her behavior is not appreciated nor understood by the daughter, who seeks, instead, empathy and a mirror in her mother: "I wish she wouldn't try/ to make something bad better" (Lai, 116). Furthermore, Hà shows empathy with her mother for hiding her feelings and her pain, but she wishes she did not.

In her study on representations of Vietnamese (and Hmong) women in public spaces and in in literature written by Vietnamese America and (Hmong American) women, Lisa Long talks about "the first-and-a-half generation of refugees who become not literal but figurative mothers to their parents, creating a 'transmaternalism' of sorts" (16). As I understand Long, transmaternalism is a concept that characterizes an affective bond defined by care and love, but that crosses the normative and ordinary association of motherhood to the mother. I claim that Hà is not portrayed in the novel as a figurative mother to her own mother, but as a daughter who shows understanding, care, compassion and empathy towards her parent, together with making her a central figure in her poems.

Motherhood as Site of Negotiating Gender Roles

When the moment to leave Vietnam comes, the mother discusses with her children the possibility of leaving their home. She will listen to what they have to say and only afterwards she speaks and shares her worries: "You deserve to grow up where you don't worry about saving half a bite of sweet potato" (47). It will be the mother who will make the decision to leave Vietnam, but she will first discuss with her children and hear their opinions about fleeing. Sandra Cox has analyzed this critical moment when the mother decides to leave Vietnam as a moment of reflection for the readers about the consequences war has on individuals and families (26). Analyzing this episode by focusing on the mother certainly allows the readers to consider how difficult, extreme and painful the choice to leave and still risk her children to die in a context of war and displacement. I agree with Cox and I continue her analysis, underlining that this moment brings up power dynamics where the mother has authority over her children (she already witnessed war and imperialist consequences), but she still shows understanding, respect and desire to dialogue. I recognize here a positive model of matriarchal organization of the family, where the authority is not associated with domination, but care and love. Together with Mother's incarnation of alternative family roles, another aspect of Mother's decision to leave Vietnam without waiting for her husband to return from the war is worth reflection. I read Mother's action as a feminist act of resistance against patriarchal expectations about gender roles, thus subverting the "Penelope" model of the woman waiting, in pain and devoutly, for her man to come back home and take again his leading role of the house. Moreover, Mother becomes an example for Ha, of a woman with strong will and agency.

Lai provides a depiction of Mother's personality, but also of her physical aspect. Hà uses a simile to describe her mother's body: "Who can go against/ a mother/ who has become gaunt like bark/ from raising four children alone?" (54). The simile "gaunt like a bark" offers a cause for reflection on the corporeality of motherhood, and in general opens to the line of enquiry into the representations of the body of the refugee mother.

Inside Out & Back Again engages with rendering the displaced mother a subject who not only crosses national boundaries, but also engages in a feminist resistance of gender stereotypes. However, after having explored the ways motherhood can teach to resist and change gender stereotypes, I will now discuss how the mother can also become a "silent guardian of the patriarchal tradition." In the second poem *1975: Year of the Cat*, Hà reveals that she has broken a rule during Tet, the first day of the lunar year:

> But last night I pouted
> when Mother insisted
> one of my brothers
> must rise first
> this morning
> to bless our house
> because only male feet can bring luck.
> (Lai, 2)

According to Anzaldúa (1987), women can play an important role in the formation, establishment and transmission of culture in a male-dominated society:

> Culture forms our beliefs. We perceive the version of reality that it communicates. Dominant paradigms, predefined concepts that exist as unquestionable, unchallengeable, are transmitted to us through culture. Culture is made by those in power—men. Males make the rules and laws; women transmit them. (16)

Following Anzaldúa, I suggest that Mother in *Inside Out & Back Again* is reproducing traditional gender stereotypes that undervalue the young Hà. If it were easy for the readers to "ally with the autobiographers against mothers who transmit values which their daughters reject" (Bloom, 297), I think this episode would be particularly explicative of how subtly transmission of patriarchal values can be transmitted within the mother-daughter bond, and how difficult it is to change that culture, mostly in the context of social vulnerability caused by displacement.

To conclude my analysis of the relationship between daughter and mother in *Inside Out & Back Again*, I will discuss Hà's reaction to Mother's prohibition to bless their house back in Vietnam:

> An old, angry knot
> expanded in my throat.
> I decided
> to wake before dawn
> and tap my big toe
> to the tile floor
> first. (Lai, 2)

Hà's challenging reaction to Mother's prohibition reminds me of the rebel Anzaldúa describes in *La mestiza:*

> There is a rebel in me—the Shadow-Beast. It is a part of me that refuses to take orders from outside authorities. It refuses to take orders from my conscious will, it threatens the sovereignty of my rulership. It is that part of me that hates constraints of any kind, even those self-imposed. At the least hint of limitations on my time or space by others, it kicks out with both feet. Bolts. (16)

As well Anzaldúa refuses constraints and limitations coming from the patriarchal Chicana dimension that she critiques and against which she uses her physical strength, also Hà, using the strength of her toe, rebels and rejects gender roles stereotypes. I see a great symbol of resistance in the 10-year-old Hà's toe, that although silent and unseen, breaks patriarchal rules, and, as Mother will say later to her in Alabama, "If anything,/ you gave us luck/ because we got out/ and we're here" (Lai, 215). However, after discussing Hà's brave reaction to limitations, it is important to consider her emotional reaction to them. The girl's emotion of anger, an emotion that she often feels throughout her story, is described by the metaphor of the knot that "expands" in her throat, that, I claim, well portrays the feeling of being silenced, suffocated, and, consequently unheard, by discrimination and inequality. In a way that brings to my mind Lorde's words about the ways to use anger against racism, Hà's anger seems to have found a brave form of expression and resistance against gender discrimination perpetrated by her own mother, and that will allow later on in the novel honest and brave conversations between daughter and mother.

CONCLUSIONS

This chapter has been an exercise of "weaving" the poetic representations of the daughter-mother relations in context of displacement with transnational feminist questions about motherhood. The representations of the maternal relationship through the daughters' eyes in *The Good Braider* and *Inside Out & Back Again* has allowed the exploration of the maternal kinship as a site where painful silences meet caring words, and where the mothers appear as resilient subjects and voices of feminist resistance, but also as silent guardians of the patriarchal values at the same time. Furthermore, motherhood is portrayed as the relational site where alliances within vulnerability are forged between refugee mothers and daughters.

WORKS CITED

Abate, Michelle Ann. "Verse-ality: The Novel in Verse and the Revival of Poetry." *The Lion and the Unicorn*, vol. 42, 2018, pp. v–viii.

Anzaldúa, Gloria. *Borderlands/La Frontera: The New Mestiza*. Aunt Lute Books, 1987.

Bassin, Donna, et al., editors. *Representations of Motherhood*. Yale University Press, 1994.

Bauer Maglin, Nan. "Don't Never Forget the Bridge that You Crossed over on: The Literature of Matrilineage." *The Lost Tradition: Mother and Daughters in Literature*, edited by Cathy Davidson and E. M. Broner. Frederick Ungar Publishing Co., 1980, pp. 257–267.

Berlant, Lauren. *Compassion: The Culture and Politics of an Emotion*. Routledge, 2004.

Bloom, Lynn. (1980). "Heritages: Dimensions of Mother-Daughter Relationships in Women's Autobiographies." *The Lost Tradition: Mother and Daughters in Literature*, edited by Cathy Davidson and E. M. Broner. Frederick Ungar Publishing Co., pp. 291–303.

Brandt, Di. *Wild Mother Dancing: Maternal Narrative in Canadian Literature*. University of Manitoba Press, 1993.

Butler, Judith. *Frames of War: When is Life Grievable?* Verso, 2009.

Cadden, Mike. "Rhetorical Technique in the Young Adult Verse Novel." *The Lion and the Unicorn*, vol. 42, no. 2, 2018, pp. 129–144.

———. "The Verse Novel and the Question of Genre." *The ALAN Review*, vol. 39, no. 1, 2011, pp. 21–27.
Campbell, Patty. "Vetting the Verse Novel." *The Horn Book Magazine*, vol. 80, no. 5, 2004, p. 611+.
Collins, Patricia H. *Intersectionality as Critical Social Theory*. Duke University Press, 2019.
———. *Black Feminist Thought. Knowledge, Consciousness, and the Politics of Empowerment*. Routledge, 2000.
———. "Shifting the Center: Race, Class and Feminist Theorizing about Motherhood." *Mothering: Ideology, Experience and Agency*, edited by Glenn Evelyn Nakano, et al. Routledge, 1994, pp. 45–65.
———. "The Social Construction of Black Feminist Thought." *Signs,* vol. 14, no. 4, 1989, pp. 745–773.
Cox, Sandra. "Broken Up and Inside Out: Theorizing Subjectivity in Children's Seeking Asylum through Close Reading of Two Novels-in-Verse about the Vietnam War." *Red Feather Journal*, vol. 6, no. 2, 2015, pp. 22–38.
Craddock, T. Katrine, editor. *Black Motherhood(s). Contours, Contexts and Considerations*. Demeter Press, 2015.
Crew, S. Hilary, editor. *Is It Really Mommy Dearest? Daughter-Mother Narratives in Young Adult Fictions*. Scarecrow, 2000.
Davidson, Cathy, and E.M. Broner, editors. *The Lost Tradition: Mother and Daughters in Literature*. Frederick Ungar Publishing Co., 1980.
"Emi Mahmoud-Mama." *YouTube*, uploaded by Button Poetry, 3 June 2018. https://www.youtube.com/watch?v=kpnEXcA-Dgs.
Farish, Terry. *The Good Braider*. Marshall Cavendish, 2012.
Fraustino, Lisa Rowe, and Karen Coats, editors. *Mothers in Children's and Young Adult Literature: From the Eighteenth Century to Postfeminism*. University Press of Mississippi, 2016.
Glenn, Evelyn Nakano. "Social Constructions of Mothering: A Thematic Overview," *Mothering: Ideology, Experience and Agency*, edited by Glenn Evelyn Nakano, et al. Routledge, 1994, pp. 1–29.
Ibbett, Katherine. *Compassion's Edge: Fellow-Feeling and its Limits in Early Modern France*. University of Pennsylvania Press, 2018.
Kyomugisha, Florence. "Transnational Mothering. The Meaning of African Immigrant Lives." *Black Motherhood(s). Contours, Contexts and Considerations*, edited by Karen T. Craddock. Demeter Press, 2015, pp. 71–86.
Lai, Thanhha. *Inside Out & Back Again*. Harper Collins, 2011.
Long, Lisa. "Contemporary Women's Roles through Hmong, Vietnamese, and American Eyes." *Frontiers: A Journal of Women Studies*, vol. 29, no. 1, 2008, pp. 1–36.
Lorde, Audre. "The Uses of Anger." *Women's Studies Quarterly*, vol. 25, No. 1/2, Looking Back, Moving Forward: 25 Years of Women's Studies History (Spring - Summer, 1997), pp. 278–285.
———. *Zami: A New Spelling of My Name*. The Crossing Press, 1982.

Lowinsky, Naomi Ruth. *Stories from the Motherline: Reclaiming the Mother-Daughter Bond, Finding Our Feminine Souls*. Jeremy P. Tarcher Inc., 1992.

Nancy, Jean-Luc. *Being Singular Plural*. Translated by Robert D. Richardson and Anne E. O'Byrne. Stanford University Press, 2000.

O'Brien Hallstein, et al., editors. *The Routledge Companion to Motherhood*. Routledge, 2020.

O'Reilly, Andrea. *Matricentric Feminism. Theory, Activism, Practice*. Demeter Press, 2016.

———. "Introduction: Maternal Activism as Matricentric Feminism: The History, Ideological Frameworks, Political Strategies and Activist Practices of the 21st Century Motherhood Movement," *The 21st Century Motherhood Movement: Mothers Speak Out on Why We Need to Change the World and How to Do It*, edited by Andrea O'Reilly. Demeter Press, 2011, pp. 1–33.

Podnieks, Elizabeth and Andrea O'Reilly. *Textual Mothers/Maternal Texts: Motherhood in Contemporary Women's Literature*. Wilfred Laurier University Press, 2010.

Porter, Marie, et al.. *Mothers at the Margins: Stories of Challenge Resistance and Love*. Cambridge Scholars Publishing, 2015.

Rich, Adrienne. *Of Woman Born. Motherhood as Experience and Institution*. Norton & Company, 1985.

Rickard Rebellino, Rachel. "'I'll Write What Needs to Be Remembered': The Use of Verse in Children's and Young Adult Historical Fiction about the Vietnam War." *The Lion and the Unicorn*, vol. 42, 2018, pp. 162–179.

Rose, Arthur. "A Genealogy of Refugee Writing." *Refugee Imaginaries*, edited by Emma Cox et al. Edinburgh University Press, 2020, pp. 50–64.

Rosinsky, Natalie M. "Mothers and Daughters: Another Minority Group." *The Lost Tradition: Mother and Daughters in Literature*, edited by Cathy Davidson and E.M Broner. Frederick Ungar Publishing Co., 1980, pp. 280–290.

"Slam Poet and Sudanese Refugee Emi Mahmoud Shares Her Story." *YouTube*, uploaded by Now This, 30 December 2018. https://www.youtube.com/watch?v=yVwZG1I1UvQ.

Tuon, Bunkong. "'Not the Same, But Not Bad': Accommodation and Resistance in Thanhha Lai's *Inside Out and Back Again*." *Children's Literature Association Quarterly*, vol. 38, no. 4, 2014, pp. 533–550.

Chapter Five

The Ghost Mother in Two Vietnamese American Refugee Novels
A Critical Refugee Analysis

Janet J. Graham

In Vu Tran's *Dragonfish*, Hong Pham meets a ghost one night at a refugee camp in Malaysia with "long tangled hair, her white blouse drenched and clinging to her skin" (Tran 107). As Hong watches the ghost slowly wade through the sea "with her head bowed, searching for something in the shallows," she recognizes her as the single mother who she witnessed jumping off the boat and drowning when she mistakenly assumed her son was lost at sea (Tran 107). The ghost asks Hong if she has seen her son. Hong does not admit he is alive but asks the ghost what she will do if she finds him. The ghost replies "I'm taking him with me. What else?" (Tran 108). This "strange tragedy" (Tran 88), which involves a ghost who seeks her son's death so he can be with her, depicts family separation and the yearning for uncanny connections that outlive death across generations for survivors of trauma. The refugee mother is a displaced mother who has experienced trauma in the midst of motherhood. She has lost her home and may have lost family members, including children. She is also a mother of the displaced, whether or not her children accompany her on the voyage.

Literary representations of mother-daughter relationships that center displacement and disappearance are sites of critical refugee inquiry that further the work of Yến Lê Espiritu who envisions Critical Refugee Studies as an interdisciplinary field that centers refugee voices to critique the structural conditions that create displacement and explore the ramifications of its affective afterlife. For Espiritu, critical refugee narratives are also ghost stories. In *Body Counts* Espiritu writes, "As tellers of ghost stories, it is imperative that we always look for the 'something more' in order to see and bring into being what is usually neglected or made invisible or thought by most to be dead and gone—that is, to always see the living effects of what seems to be over and done with" (187–188). That something more she refers to includes the challenges refugees face after they find refuge as well as the bonds that remain between those who survive and those who are no longer present. Through an analysis of the bonds between parents and children that exceed death, this chapter will show how to "read trauma productively as a disruption of the US myth of 'rescue and liberation' that enunciates violence *and* recovery simultaneously" (Espiritu, "Toward" 422).

This critical refugee analysis of *Short Girls* by Bich Minh (Beth) Nguyen and *Dragonfish* by Vu Tran, two Vietnamese American refugee novels, describes the figure of the ghost mother and her beneficial presence in the lives of her daughters in contrast to the drowned mother whose unearthly desire for her lost child makes her a menacing presence. According to the *Oxford English Dictionary*, a "ghost" denotes "the soul of a deceased person, spoken of as appearing in a visible form, or otherwise manifesting its presence to the living," while earlier senses of the word include good and evil spirits. Figuratively, a "ghost" may also refer to "a shadowy outline or semblance, an unsubstantial image, a slight trace or vestige" (*Oxford English Dictionary*). For the purposes of this analysis, a ghost mother is a good spirit who, though physically absent, continues to function as a mother in a shadowy or unsubstantial form.

The authors of both novels relate to the disappeared by highlighting the uncanny bonds between absent mothers and their daughters, and this characterization relates to Marianne Hirsh's concept of postmemory as a fuzzy understanding of past events as well as a sense of hauntedness that the children of refugees and survivors of trauma inherit from their parents' experience. From her study of art that children of survivors and victims of collective trauma create, Hirsch uses postmemory to describe "the relationship of the second generation to powerful, often traumatic, experiences that preceded their births but that were nevertheless transmitted to them so deeply as to seem to constitute memories in their own right" ("Generation" 103). Hirsch claims that postmemory "seeks connection. It creates where it cannot recover. It imagines where it cannot recall" ("Past" 664). In this sense of creating incomplete links to the past and to earlier generations' traumas, the ghostly aspect of the absent mother in this chapter represents the post in postmemory. In the context of the Vietnamese American refugee novel, postmemory informs how the daughters tell or understand their own story of loss embedded in the body rather than in conscious memory, one they cannot tell without the knowledge, memory and consciousness of their parents. Nguyen and Tran portray children employing the ghost mother's benevolent presence to construct creative relationships to trauma that reprogram affective pathways away from filial debt and gendered structures that define the refugee mother's experience.

Yến Lê Espiritu argues that refugees' complex stories begin with the conflicts and traumas that impelled them to leave their homes under difficult conditions and introduces the concept of militarized refuge(es) to "hold the United States accountable for the epistemic or symbolic violence of its wars *and* for the actual physical violence" that continues to effect refugees in the aftermath of displacement (176). As a critical refugee studies project, this chapter examines the affective structures inherent in capitalism and patriarchy in the United States that shape relationships across generations, specifically between mothers and daughters. Refugees experience trauma before they leave their homes as well as on their journeys to safety, which often involve loss or separation from loved ones. Receiving nations separate family members when their policies result in dividing multigenerational families into nuclear families or placing children in foster care. For example, Viet Thanh Nguyen describes his family's traumatic experience with separation and wonders how it affected his mother: "One sponsor took my parents, another took my brother, a third took me. . . I remember being reunited with my parents after a few months and the snow and the cold and my mother disappearing from our lives for a period of time" (Nguyen 8). His mother's brief and mysterious absence after forced separation from her children clarifies the stakes involved in a critical refugee analysis of the ghost mother.

Upon arrival in the United States, refugee parents process trauma and loss as they raise children and manage a household while trying to live under liberal capitalism, often lacking facility in English or recognized qualifications with limited or no financial or educational support through US government programs, and this is especially difficult for women and new arrivals. Katharya Um, a scholar associated with the Critical Refugee Studies Collective, describes the situation in this way: "Refuge provides for little reprieve as the exigencies of the present compound and provoke the haunting of the past" (838). Refugee women are generally responsible for the majority of the work required to continue this daily struggle to survive. Within patriarchal structures in the United States, women are paid less for their work than men and expected to do more of the work in the home. Refugee mothers may also feel that their trauma and sacrifices are overlooked in a society that valorizes the sacrifices of soldiers and the highest wage earners. Families are strained under these conditions, while they feel greater pressure to stay together. In addition, refugees came in waves with later arrivals securing family sponsorship from those already established in the country, which indebted newcomers to their familial sponsors. These realities increase instances of marginalization and violence, primarily for women and children. This social landscape is what writers who were refugees as children draw upon when they write about relationships between mothers and daughters.

The central claim this analysis supports is that ghost mothers in *Short Girls* and *Dragonfish* demonstrate how the absent refugee mother maintains uncanny links to her daughters that ease the full burden of their traumatic history and create new spaces of ancestral connections that disrupt discourses of debt. In their novels Bich Minh Nguyen and Vu Tran, both refugees as small children, respond to familial relationships dominated by unprocessed trauma, debt, and marginalization by portraying mothers who defy the rules governing debt and patriarchy when they leave their daughters behind but maintain ghostly relationships with them. The transformations Nguyen and Tran create in their fiction hint at an opening up of traditional family roles related to gender and generation, especially involving care. Through their explorations of ghost mother-daughter relationships, they challenge assumptions about gendered and generational relationships in refugee families, negotiate generational silences to offer insights into the refugee experience, and highlight the conditions that lead to refugees' initial displacement and continued marginality in their new homes.

In chapter two of *Returns of War,* Long Bui brings together the work of Erin Ninh on filial piety and Mimi Thi Nguyen on the gift of freedom in US colonial discourse to uncover the intertwined affective structures of debt refugees and their children are subject to. According to Bui, the refugee is "aware of her own disciplining as a compliant subject of the family, and the family as duty-bound to the state" (Bui). In reference to refugees being duty-bound to the state, Mimi Thi Nguyen explains that "the gift of freedom and its debt are one and the same" (177). The gift comes with indebtedness, so it is not a gift in the true sense. At the level of the family under liberal capitalism, Erin Ninh defines filial piety as an affective structure that produces a "heightened, habitual sense of inadequacy, of indebtedness" in children, and argues that Asian American families function as productive units of capitalism through filial piety (Ninh 50). Bui suggests that the gift of freedom combined with filial piety create a particularly heavy burden of psychic debt for refugees. Reactions to affective structures of filial piety create emotions "that can yield different, unintended actions and expressions" (Ninh 50). While filial piety can encourage obedience and silence, Ninh points out that the burden it places on children may also produce defiance or depression. Inspired by Ninh and Nguyen's analyses Bui adds that, "the ungrateful daughter who refuses to comport with societal expectations is not simply displaying ingratitude but inhabits 'a state of being resistant to the call of debt'" (Bui). The mothers who leave their daughters defy indebtedness yet remain tied to them as ghost mothers in Tran and Nguyen's novels to deliver their daughters into similar states of resistance to filial and colonial debt.

Women traditionally carry the responsibility for representing the culture of the motherland through the tasks they perform as dutiful daughters and as maternal figures, so collective trauma which entails the loss of home and country is often represented in literature as a separation between mothers and children. As Claire Kahane observes, "the memory-image of a mother being torn from her child, a child from its mother, or the antithesis, a mother's refusal to be separated from her child, even to the point of death" (164) are prevalent in collective trauma narratives. Indeed these themes recur with the drowned woman and Viet Thanh Nguyen's mother. In the case of the mother who abandons her children, Kahane is troubled by a tendency among some authors to ignore trauma as the reason for maternal abandonment and use it to comment on the general humanity of the victimized (Kahane 181). In light of "how profound a level the ideology of gender functions in both the response to and the representation of trauma," Kahane calls on scholars to be especially critical of representations of women as mothers in collective trauma narratives (182).

Rather than see a break in cultural traditions due to mothers abandoning their children, this critical refugee analysis reveals a beneficial relationship between ghost mothers and their daughters that breaks cycles of debt at the family and national level, while it offers a creative relationship to the ancestor even in the midst of collective trauma. Toni Morrison offers insights into the meaning of the ancestor for violently displaced communities beyond the function of the family as an exploitative unit of production. Morrison defines ancestors as "timeless people whose relationships to the characters are benevolent, instructive and protective and they provide a certain kind of wisdom" (342). In her discussion of the ancestor in African American novels, she highlights conflicts over their influence or their traumatic absence before concluding, "If we don't keep in touch with the ancestor . . . we are, in fact, lost" (Morrison 344). Though Morrison's definition makes clear that the ancestor is not necessarily a parent, novels that consider the loss, absence, or displacement of parents address the question of how to be guided by ancestors when one has been cut off from them. For the children of refugees, the ghost mother offers her children the possibility of a deeper connection to the presence of the ancestor than what filial debt in the nuclear family offers.

SHORT GIRLS SHOULD STICK TOGETHER

In *Short Girls* Van and Linny Luong overcome the challenges they face as a result of either conforming to or rebelling against their obligations as the daughters of refugees by drawing on the wisdom their mother, who died nine years before, embedded in her ancestral practices and embrace of liminality. Thus she becomes a ghost mother to her daughters. As the dutiful one who shoulders the burden of financially supporting her father, Van feels alone and ashamed as she faces the dissolution of her childless marriage to Miles Oh, an ambitious and exacting corporate lawyer, and a career crisis as an immigration lawyer (Nguyen 60). Linny, who sees herself as "the bad Asian daughter," feels trapped in her job at "You Did It Dinners" where she helps white upper middle-class suburban Chicago moms provide dinner to their families and her affair with a customer's husband (Nguyen 107). When they return to their childhood home together, the girls find their mother's spirit waiting for them with the lessons they need to navigate their way out of their difficulties.

At first, Mrs. Thuy Luong's marginality in their lives reflects their desire to evade their parents' experience of marginality in the United States, but later they seek their ghost mother's help, which they find in her lingering presence in their childhood home, to find release from their feelings of indebtedness and isolation while connecting to the ancestors and nature.[1] As Van begins to face her crises, she thinks of her mother in relation to her father until she finds she shares her mother's unhappiness and frustration with doing everything right, but never feeling fully accepted (Nguyen 80). Linny could not get out of her parents' house quickly enough after her mother dies. However, as she embraces her mother's cooking and celebration of liminality, she is inspired to leave her lover behind and pursue her dream of becoming a chef.

Van and Linny's memories of their mother create an image of an independent and dutiful woman who leverages her marginality to create her own private place of safety that she ultimately offers her daughters as a ghost mother. Thuy Luong came to America while pregnant with Van on "a ship leaving Saigon in 1975" (Nguyen 24) in deference to her husband Dinh's wishes (Nguyen 205). At not quite five feet tall (Nguyen 61), she often worked overtime as a seamstress at Roger's Department Store, returning home to cook and clean with cramped hands, while Dinh worked part-time laying tile when he wasn't dreaming up unsuccessful inventions (Nguyen 14). She worked hard to care for her family out of duty and love, but her husband's stubborn unwillingness to contribute more to the family's finances frustrated her (Nguyen 207). She smiled at Van's studiousness and disapproved of Linny's make-up and boyfriends (Nguyen 58). Thuy Luong died of a stroke at the age of forty-two in the same year that she and Dinh "decided to live on separate floors of the house they'd had for twenty years" (Nguyen 4–6). This separation that immediately precedes her death suggests she was already transitioning, as if she knew she were dying. Also, this informal separation from her husband highlights her independent spirit and dissatisfaction with being taken for granted. Though she worked hard to pursue the American Dream, she never felt comfortable in the United States. For example, she became a citizen out of fear of being separated from her American-born daughters (Nguyen 107). Linny recalls that she received "photocopies of her [mother's] naturalization certificate in case hers got lost or ruined" (Nguyen 175). Her mother sewed all day with other Vietnamese women "in one large room above the floors of shopping" at Roger's Department Store, but it was "nice to be up here, out of the way" (Nguyen 184). Van "felt both understanding and aversion" when she heard her mother say this because it expressed her own weariness with always standing out as an Asian person in the Midwest (Nguyen 184).

Perhaps because Thuy Luong never felt safe in the United States and worried about her daughters, she made her home into a place where her influence would remain after death. When Van and Linny return to their childhood home together to organize a party to celebrate their father becoming a citizen, they feel her ghostly presence inhabiting her house and the land around it. Her presence lingers in the food she taught Linny to cook. Tom Hanh, a family friend Linny's age, conjures Mrs. Luong when he says, "These are your mom's" after tasting the *cha gio* Linny made for the party (Nguyen 161). "Her ashes in a ceramic urn, her photograph in a gold-tinted frame" sit on the credenza she bought to house a statue of the Buddha and offerings of respect to him (Nguyen 143). The traditional photograph that accompanies her urn comes from a picture Thuy had taken when she took Linny for her senior pictures (Nguyen 155). The credenza is a central feature of the living room, so everyone "paused in the living room to pay their respects to Mrs. Luong" at the party (Nguyen 154). By carrying out these cultural practices, the living ensure that she remains present in her home after her death. Among these practices that make an impression on Van and Linny is their mother's practice of celebrating "*Gloaming; l'heure bleue*," or the blue hour (Nguyen 279). It "is the hour between daylight and night" (*French-Word-A-Day)*. The teak bench her mother placed under a maple tree in the small garden she maintained endures (Nguyen 163). "Mrs. Luong had loved to sit there, counting down the minutes to twilight" (Nguyen 166). She invited her family to join her in this space of contemplation when time seemed to "slow down" and her thoughts turned to her old "neighbors in Saigon" (Nguyen 279–280). She was comfortable in this time and place between night and day as it matched her feeling of being in-between. When her daughters observe the practice again they can almost see their "mother's shadowy outline" (280).

While her actions resonate with them, they also remember her commands and suggestions, which address debt and ancestral links. Mrs. Luong felt that Linny and Van each possessed different strengths that made them a great team. Based on this observation, she commanded them to "Stick together!" (Nguyen 113). She recommended that their partnership follow the example of their celebrated national ancestors "the famous Trung sisters . . . who rebelled against Chinese rule in Vietnam and became queens of the land . . . through skill [and] the support of the people" (Nguyen 144–5). With her encouragement they pretended to be the Trung sisters as girls, and they recover this memory as adults. Her more subtle instructions contain lessons they only begin to understand. When Linny complains that the Oortsemas "didn't sponsor *me*" but rather her parents when they first came to Michigan, Mrs. Luong says "It's the same" (Nguyen 158). In this statement she links Van and Linny to their history as refugees, but it makes Linny feel like she is supposed to owe them something. However, her mother tersely rejects a discourse of debt by stating "They try very hard. Nice people" (Nguyen 129). Though Mrs. Luong appreciates the Oortsemas, she does not acknowledge a debt to their American sponsors. In this discourse she releases her daughters from the kind of indebtedness Mimi Thi Nguyen critiques.

Van and Linny move away from indebtedness and toward ancestral connections as they begin to learn their mother's lessons from beyond the grave: stick together, be skillful and brave like the Trung sisters, be yourself, and connect to your culture and your past. They start sticking together as sisters when Linny comes to stay with Van and they confront Miles, while Van welcomes her and admits she needs help. They confront their fears like modern-day Trung sisters as they develop the required skills for courageous living. Linny becomes a consultant at her job as she starts culinary school and forms a close relationship to Tom Hanh (Nguyen 284). Her actions demonstrate she has overcome the need to rebel against a good girl stereotype (Nguyen 212). Van connects to other Vietnamese women when she finds the jade bracelet she "pried" off in high school, an object her mother gave her in elementary school. She "tried to slide it over her left hand. When it wouldn't go past her wedding set she removed her rings" (Nguyen 146). Removing the rings symbolizes letting go of her failed marriage and choosing to embrace a cultural practice she had previously rejected. After Van files for divorce, decides to sell their house, and takes a lower paying job that does more to help immigrants with legal troubles, she finally jettisons the dutiful daughter image when she tells her dad she can no longer give him monthly checks unless she gets alimony (Nguyen 285).

As Van and Linny begin talking together about their mother, they move away from guilt as they look to the ancestors. Linny says "we should tell her that you're moving" and Van agrees (Nguyen 291). They both embrace Mrs. Luong's celebration of *l'heure bleue* in Van's backyard and in an imagined future, "wishing to save just a little of it, trying to catch the falling hour" (Nguyen 292). This natural connection to their mother and the past becomes part of their future, one that will enable them to go their own ways together.

AN ABSENT PRESENCE IN *DRAGONFISH*

Hong Pham, the central character in *Dragonfish*, is a living ghost mother who encourages her daughter to defy traditional family roles, but also embrace her ancestors. Hong's painful experience of motherhood in the midst of displacement and grief leads her to abandon her daughter Mai to the care of her maternal uncle and his wife in California. When Hong starts writing letters to her years later, Mai is a young adult supporting herself by playing poker in Las Vegas. In the same time frame, Hong leaves her husband Sonny Van Nguyen and takes $100,000 from him. In response, Sonny and his son Jonathan coerce Robert Ruen, Hong's ex-husband and a police officer, to bring Hong and the money back to them, which ultimately places him in the role of surrogate parent to Mai when she appears at a hotel room, as instructed by her mother, to find another letter and a key to a suitcase in the closet that contains the $100,000.

In contrast to Quan-Manh Ha and Chase Greenfield's analysis of Hong/Suzy as a femme fatale with their focus on her relationships with men in *Dragonfish*, this critical refugee analysis of the ghost mother-daughter relationship between Hong and Mai suggests ways of relating to ancestors that stretch beyond or overturn filial relations of debt.[2] In Vu Tran's essay "A Refugee Again," from Viet Thanh Nguyen's edited collection *Displaced: Refugee Writers on Refugee Lives*, he describes Hong when he remarks that the refugee "can be invisible even though her presence is felt . . . a specter both present and distant, both acknowledged and denied" (81). For Robert, Hong is "an absence actually, as though she had gotten lost in whatever world she had escaped into" (Tran, *Dragonfish* 27). In this quote, Robert describes Tran's specter. In other words, Hong is everywhere in the story, but just out of reach to her daughter and husbands.

Tran suggests Hong may not know why she leaves her daughter behind when she disappears from her maternal uncle's home, but in her journal Hong decides she does not feel ready to become a mother and worries she cannot protect Mai.[3] Her pregnancy "was like a sudden and incurable affliction [in which she] . . . was forced into yet another version that seemed not only alien, but unbearably permanent" (Tran 97). This discomfort with her role as a mother, exacerbated by her grief at losing her husband, is expressed when she asks Sonny Van Nguyen, a man who lost his wife at sea and becomes her lover, to take Mai with him and his son Jonathan to give Hong a chance to mourn and figure out who she is as a young widowed mother before she marries him (Tran 210). When Mai falls in the water and Sonny saves her, Hong convinces herself that he is better prepared to protect her (Tran 111–112). His refusal merely postpones Hong's abandonment of Mai as well as her marriage to Sonny (Tran 213). Hong also discusses what the drowned mother ghost reveals of motherhood's perils. At first the woman's actions seem "cowardly," but upon reflection Hong felt "shame" in the knowledge that she "could not have done" what the grieving mother did (Tran 90–91). Though the drowned woman fails as a mother when she leaves an orphan behind, Hong judges her own love for Mai as inadequate in comparison as she realizes even complete devotion is not enough to protect her daughter.

Mai and Hong share uncanny similarities including their physical appearance, ability to see ghosts and a pattern of running away, and Tran uses these connections to create a space for alternative methods of honoring the ancestors. Through their strong resemblance, Hong haunts Robert through her daughter. When he first meets Mai he thinks, "Suzy stood there before me, twenty years younger, both something found and something I had lost" (84). Because she is not physically present, Hong becomes a ghost mother when she reconnects with her daughter through her letters. Reinforcing Hong's ghostliness, Mai regards her as a ghostly presence even after she makes contact. Before Hong writes to her daughter, Mai assumes both parents are dead and refers to them as her "ghosts" (Tran 180). As she explains to Robert about her father's ghostly visitations, "Every time he appears, it's like she does too, and I end up thinking about them both" (Tran 180). After making contact, she enters Mai's consciousness as a palpable presence though she can't see her. Mai explains "It's like she's always just around the corner and at the same time on the other side of the world. Actually that's how it's felt for twenty years" (Tran 132–133). Like her mother, Mai leaves her uncle's home and refuses to feel indebted to him. From these ghostly remnants of her mother and their otherworldly commonalities, Mai moves toward an adulthood that encompasses an understanding of their shared displacement and ancestral ties.

Through the gift of $100,000, Hong gives Mai the means to avoid the requirements of conforming to American capitalist and patriarchal social structures which Hong faced as a young refugee. Hong needed to mourn the loss of her husband and her younger self, but she could not do that while attempting to protect a child from the violence that surrounded them. Without the ability to find well-paid work, Hong had to live with her uncle's family and abide by their traditional values of filial piety that led to her depression and defiance, as Ninh discusses. After leaving Mai, she needs the emotional and financial security marriage offers, but Robert and Sonny Van Nguyen subject her to physical violence when she reacts with rage to not being given the solitude she needs to mourn. By giving Mai the money from Sonny, Hong gives her the opportunity to live without a feeling of filial debt or the need to enter into a marriage that entails violence or oppression. Furthermore, Hong disrupts filial piety by reversing the directionality of debt by trying to pay her daughter a debt for her actions rather than her uncle.

Mai's independence represents a refusal to be debt-bound, but it is not a break from her ancestors because she makes room for maintaining ancestral connections with a possible return to Vietnam and guidance from her mother through Robert as surrogate. As a ghost mother Hong cares for Mai while remaining apart. Besides what the money means for Mai's future, Hong inadvertently puts Robert in the role, albeit awkwardly, of a temporary surrogate mother who helps Mai achieve at least a limited understanding of her mother, which further disrupts the nuclear family's patriarchy that both Mai and Hong reject. It is Robert who nudges Mai toward considering parenthood, with some understanding of her mother's struggles, as well as a return to Vietnam. Mai demonstrates an understanding of her mother's decision to abandon her as a child when she tells Robert why she would like a son: "Raising a daughter would be like mothering yourself" (249). In this statement, she correctly assesses her mother's confusion over who she was as a young mother as a central factor in her decision to leave her behind. This awareness lends credence to the idea that Hong remotely led her daughter to a mature understanding of her. The evidence that Mai includes her ancestors into her adult consciousness is her intention to return to Vietnam, her ancestral home. Through her imagined future as a single mother of a son, Mai refuses to act as the dutiful daughter and avoids creating another economic unity driven by a patriarchal system of filial piety.

In *Dragonfish*, Mai communicates a powerful refusal of the discourse of debt itself, which is the greatest lesson Hong leaves with her. While she acknowledges that Hong's decision to steal money for her is a significant act on the part of her mother, she does not view it in capitalist terms or as a payment for her mother's guilt, which she indicates when she gives Robert half of the money from Hong. Though it might seem Mai shares the money with him out of appreciation for his care, this interpretation is inconsistent with his role as Hong's surrogate. Robert represents her mother, so Mai's decision to leave half of the money communicates a gesture of connection to the ancestors that does not entail taking on the duties of gendered filial piety or indebtedness to a male protector. Furthermore, she eschews a capitalist formula of monetary equivalence of payment for Hong's failure to parent by giving half of it away.

Short Girls and *Dragonfish* both address the powerful, if subtle, ways mothers and daughters refuse to be bound by debt and bear witness to the ongoingness of trauma within the experience of displacement. Though the daughters necessarily come into contact with their mother's traumas as they connect with their mothers, these novels also seem to suggest that the mother's absences and silences protect her children from the full weight of the traumas she experienced. Hirsch identifies the source of the second generation's pain as being consciously removed while physically linked to trauma. The work of the ghost mother, imaginatively rendered by Bich Minh Nguyen and Vu Tran, goes beyond these concerns. The critical refugee analysis in this chapter demonstrates how the second generation might resolve their alienation from the ancestor, while disrupting affective structures of guilt that plague them. With the help of the ghost mother and her surrogates, her daughters draw on the power of deep ancestral connections to refuse to be bound to filial piety or the gift of freedom. Furthermore, Tran uses the surrogate while Nguyen celebrates the bonds between sisters to unsettle patriarchy.

This critical refugee reading of the ghost mother-daughter relationship highlights the importance of paying attention to refugee narratives that reach beyond problematic representations of maternal abandonment. Locating and analyzing the ghost mother trope in other stories of displaced mothers and their children is a promising area for future research. As Khartharya Um explains, "In articulation, we give form and meaning to that which is still unnameable, still incomprehensible, still unacknowledged" (847). In answer to Um, another fruitful avenue for furthering critical refugee studies involves exploring other narratives that make visible and rework affective structures of perpetual indebtedness.

WORKS CITED

Bui, Long. *Returns of War: South Vietnam and the Price of Refugee Memory.* NYU P, 2018.

Espiritu, Yến Lê. *Body Counts: The Vietnam War and Militarized Refugees.* U of California P, 2014.

———. "Toward a Critical Refugee Study: The Vietnamese Refugee Subject in US Scholarship." *Journal of Vietnamese Studies,* vol. 1, no. 1-2, 2006, pp. 410–433.

Ha, Quan-Manh and Chase Greenfield. "'It's oil and water': Race, Gender, Power, and Trauma in Vu Tran's *Dragonfish*." *Asian American Literature: Discourses and Pedagogies*, vol. 8, 2017, pp. 26–42.

Hirsch, Marianne. "The Generation of Postmemory." *Poetics Today*, vol. 29, no. 1, 2008, pp. 103–128.

———. "Past Lives: Postmemories in Exile." *Poetics Today,* vol. 17, no. 4, 1996, pp. 659–686.

Kahane, Claire. "Dark Mirrors: A Feminist Reflection on Holocaust Narrative and the Maternal Metaphor." *Feminist Consequences: Theory for the New Century*, edited by Elisabeth Bronfen, and Misha Kavka, Columbia UP, 2001.

"L'heure bleue." *French-Word-A-Day.com*, 2020.

Morrison, Toni. "Rootedness: The Ancestor as Foundation." *Black Women Writers (1950-1980): A Critical Evaluation*, edited by Mari Evans, Anchor-Doubleday, 1984, pp. 339–345.
Nguyen, Bich Minh. *Short Girls*. Penguin, 2009.
Nguyen, Mimi Thi. *The Gift of Freedom: War, Debt, and Other Refugee Passages*. Duke UP, 2012.
Nguyen, Viet Thanh. "Introduction." *The Displaced: Refugee Writers on Refugee Lives*, edited by Viet Thanh Nguyen, Abrams, 2018, pp. 7–12.
Ninh, Erin Khuê. "Affect/Family/Filiality." *The Routledge Companion to Asian American and Pacific Islander Literature*, edited by Rachel C. Lee, Routledge, 2014, pp. 46–55.
Tran, Vu. *Dragonfish*. Norton, 2015.
———. "A Refugee Again." *The Displaced: Refugee Writers on Refugee Lives*, edited by Viet Thanh Nguyen, Abrams, 2018, pp. 80–83.
Um, Khatharya. "Exiled Memory: History, Identity, and Remembering in Southeast Asia and Southeast Asian Diaspora." *Positions: East Asia Cultures Critique*, vol. 20, no. 3, 2012, pp. 831–850.

NOTES

1. Bich Minh Nguyen was separated from her birth mother when she left Vietnam with her father and paternal grandmother as a toddler as explained in her memoir *Stealing Buddha's Dinner*. *Short Girls* is dedicated to her paternal grandmother who died in 2007, two years before the novel was published.

2. As Suzy, which is Robert's name for her, she is a femme fatale. As Hong, she is the ghost mother.

3. Her journal is translated from Vietnamese, so it is not a reliable source according to Ha and Greenfield. It is an artifact of her existence that Jonathan burns before any of the characters read it (Tran 289).

ns of Identity
PART TWO

Constructions of Identity and Belonging

Chapter Six

Embroidering Intergenerational Threads of a *Roza*

Stitching Together Women's Stories and Solidarity in the Fabric of Diasporic Arab American Fiction

Leila Moayeri Pazargadi

In Arab American women's fiction, the familial bonds between mother and daughter—as they relate to the forging of female homosocial[1] networks—are strands often braided together to form the fabric of diasporic fiction. This is particularly prevalent in Laila Halaby's *West of the Jordan* (2003) and Susan Muaddi Darraj's *The Inheritance of Exile* (2007). In *West of the Jordan*, Halaby adroitly interweaves narrative threads of Palestinian daughters and mothers belonging to the same family. The death of Huda, Hala's mother, serves as a catalyst for progression and self-discovery for Hala, Mawal, Soraya, and Khadija, particularly as the meaning of cultural and familial identities are reevaluated against the backdrop of Huda's decline. Her death can also render her as national allegory;[2] grief for a dying mother replicates grief for the loss of culture and Palestinian homeland. Similarly, in *The Inheritance of Exile*, Darraj expertly weaves a tapestry of diasporic struggles in the lives of four sets of Palestinian American women and their mothers. Nadia, Hanan, Reema, and Aliyah search for a meaningful sense of home while caught in the cultural gap that exists between Palestine and the U.S. These daughters of mothers, Siham, Layla, Huda, and Lamis (Imm Nabeel), respectively, have settled into South Philly, a place wherein each of these woman attempts to reconcile her Arab identity with her American one. Perhaps more pronounced than Halaby's depiction of motherhood, Darraj's inclusion of each mother's story illuminates the oft-troubled relationship between first- and second-generation immigrants struggling to reconcile links to home.

Storytelling is the vehicle driving these thoughtful narratives forward. Invisible invocations of Scheherazade reverberate throughout the novels as each woman takes up the mantle to share her story (and even confront those moments when she trespasses and wrongfully discloses another's). When reading these books side by side, the act of storytelling takes center stage, bookended by Halaby's introductory lines and Darraj's concluding words. Halaby begins her narrative with a personal reflection, "Tell your news the way they tell their stories: slow and tasty . . . no rushing. Make it delicious like the olives, black and bursting with sweetness and sourness" (Halaby 1). Darraj concludes her narrative with Reema's interview of her mother, who advises her daughter, "Just shape the words I said the way you want-fix them and make them sound good. *You* are the writer, habibti, not me" (Darraj 196, emphasis author's). Reema, known throughout as a "collector of stories," not only wants to record her mother's stories for her dissertation, but parallels the fictitious author of *The Inheritance of Exile*, implying the stories we read result from her dutiful collecting. These sets of lines by Halaby and Darraj serve as a pair of chords, heralding the polyphonous voices of Arab American women protagonists that defy the orientalist stereotyping of Arab women as monolithic and silent. These stories sometimes compliment and juxtapose mothers and daughters' experiences in exile, constantly drawing up the mothers' memories of a left-behind homeland with those newly created ones by daughters navigating life in America.

To bring these relationships into more prominence, Laila Halaby invokes the act of embroidering as a motif to represent the way in which each daughter's narrative is linked to her mother's. Through the embroidering of Palestinian *rozas*, a cultural form of stitch work and dress that is prominent in the village of Nawara (the Palestinian epicenter for her characters), embroidering not only serves as an act of cultural production, but also comes to symbolize the stitching together of kinship[3] relationships and ties that extend beyond blood. Adapting this motif and applying it as a lens in Susan Muaddi Darraj's *The Inheritance of Exile* further shows how this network of mothers and daughters create a paradigm of survival and support through the ever-changing landscape of Arab American life. In *The Inheritance of Exile*, mothers like Siham are not only embroidering Palestinian pillows for sale to supplement their livelihood in Philadelphia, but mother-daughter duo, Layla and Hanan, engage in basket weaving learned in Palestinian refugee camps; it is a mode of cultural production that Hanan uses to financially support herself and her son. Ultimately, both narratives show Palestinian American immigrant and refugee women's navigation of the loss of culture and homeland as they resettle in Arizona, California, and Pennsylvania. While the mothers maintain tradition and ties to homeland, the daughters often find comfort and personal strength by temporarily suspending or renegotiating ties to familial and cultural beliefs.

Naturally, the stories are wound around the difficulties concerning relationships, communication, and cultural identity for those in the diaspora. Since each chapter's story is spun around the central female characters, the patchwork narrative structure of both novels becomes incredibly important as an aesthetic parallel to the fabric binding together a female collective. That is, both works' short-story vignettes present a fragmented structure that synechdochically echoes the way in which each woman and story make up the mosaic of the text, and the diasporic Palestinian community. This parallels the forging of cultural and ethnic-based communities that bring together individuals, particularly mothers and daughters, as part of a collective. Drawing on Nima Naghibi's work on homosocial female spaces in *Rethinking Global Sisterhood* (2007), homosociality and the creation of female networks can promote the assertion of women's agency for immigrant and diasporic women. Tracing this concept throughout these two novels shows that 1) reformulation of the family structure that displaces patriarch and 2) female homosocial collectivities within diasporic narratives ultimately allow women to band together and forge relationships beyond blood ties to not only survive, but also thrive in exile. Thus, by evaluating mother and daughter kinship relationships as part of a homosocial network, this chapter explores the ways in which daughters navigate Arab American identity in the U.S., particularly as they draw on the agency and strength of mothers rooted in Palestinian culture. These relationships and networks are manifested vis-à-vis forms of cultural production like embroidering and storytelling, which contribute to the fabric of these narratives, thereby rendering collected stories as allegorical ties to the nation.

SPINNING STORIES: INVOKING SCHEHERAZADE TO VOICE AGENCY

In Arab American women's literature published after the millennium, the image of Scheherazade as courageous storyteller and empowered savior has been repeatedly called forth as inspirational muse to many women writers. In *The Thousand and One Nights*, the Vizier's daughter, Scheherazade[4] takes it upon herself to marry the foolish King Shahriyar, who beheads his recently wed wives before they can cuckold him. After marrying the fickle Shahriyar, Scheherazade begins to spin tale after tale at the behest of her sister, Dunyazad,[5] as a means of not only prolonging her presumed and inevitable death, but to educate the king in the meantime. Weaving story within story (one of the oldest historical examples of the frame-tale structure), Scheherazade manages to capture the king's attentions while teaching him to become a just ruler. At the conclusion of a thousand and one nights, the king has not only learned that she has faithfully borne him children, but how to justly rule his kingdom with even-handed compassion. This collection of stories serves as one of the earliest archetypes for a strong heroine employing her wits and ingenious storytelling to save herself and her kingdom. By the time the stories make their way from the original Persian into Arabic, Scheherazade's image becomes a more pronounced agent who becomes a timeless inspiration to Middle Eastern women storytellers communicating honeyed truths to learning audiences.

Literary scholars of Arab American literature have noted the post-millennium popularity of Scheherazade in literary works, especially due to the 1990s boom of multicultural literature, including a post-Gibran Arab American literary scene, and the catastrophic events of 9/11. Considering literary trends, in the 1990s, Arab Americans were writing themselves into the literary landscape of multicultural literature, while after 9/11, they were faced with the paradoxical duality of visibility and invisibility. As Mejdulene B. Shomali notes in "Scheherazade and the Limits of Inclusive Politics in Arab American Literature": "Any invocation of Scheherazade is at once three pronged: it summons an Arab literary history; it summons the Orientalist and colonial framing of that literary history; and it summons gender and sexuality as key sites for negotiating Arab subjectivity" (Shomali 65). Somaya Sami Sabry also adds that with the revival of attention to Scheherazade and the art of storytelling, Arab American women resist "commodification of otherness" while also articulating "voices and perspectives that cannot be silenced" (Sabry 200). In part, Arab American writers are reclaiming a pre-European reimaging of Scheherazade prior to colonialism that not only saw an influx of French and British mandates ruling over the fallen territories of the Ottomans following World War I, but also witnessed increased European orientalist appropriation of Arab cultural production, art, music, literature, etc. As a response, many writers are reclaiming the image of Scheherazade to repair European misrepresentations of her as hypersexualized and frivolous.

In fact, the image of Scheherazade as alluring seductress did not come into being until colonialism brought images of Scheherazade to Europe. Suzanne Gauch points out in *Liberating Shahrazad: Feminism, Postcolonialism, and Islam* that European rivalry with Ottoman power, in particular, prompted an objectification of Scheherazade that reduced her to nothing more than an odalisque-type seductress (Gauch xi). Moreover, as Susan Muaddi Darraj points out in her non-fictional study of Scheherazade, she "became nothing more than a harem sex kitten when Antoine Galland, and later Richard Burton, introduced the *Nights* to the European canon in the eighteenth and nineteenth centuries. An intelligent woman, schooled in literature, philosophy, and history, reduced to an erotic, shallow, sex-crazed body behind a veil—it happened many times, with many Arab and/or Eastern women, including Cleopatra, Khadija, and Aisha" (Darraj, *Scheherazade's Legacy* 2). Likewise, Fatima Mernissi similarly notes in *Scheherazade Goes West*, it was because of Western orientalist and colonialist encounters with Scheherazade that she loses her agency. She concludes: "Strangely enough, the intellectual Scheherazade was lost in all these translations, apparently because the Westerners were interested in only two things: adventure and sex. And the latter was expressed only in a bizarrely restricted form confined to the language of the female body" (62). To Arab women, Mernissi notes, Scheherazade symbolizes a "political crusader" combating King Shahriyar's authoritarian rule through the power of her stories (64). Along with Mernissi, Eva Sallis in *Scheherazade: Through the Looking Glass*, asserts that European orientalists often penalized Scheherazade for her power and described in Victorian terms that flattened her complexity, pronounced by Antoine Galland that she be a lady of "courage, wit, and penetration infinitely above her sex" (Galland quoted in Sallis 100). For writers from the margins, this consistent exoticization of Scheherazade (and Arab women by proxy) creates an impetus for "un-learning and untangling" with the goal of resuming the "grandmother's interrupted storytelling" (Trinh 148). In Sabry's view, the grandmother that Arab American women writers are reviving is Scheherazade (200).

The consistent Western reduction of Scheherazade, beginning with Galland in 1704 through to the millennium, builds to an explosion after 9/11, when Arab American writers reclaim her while rejecting increasing hostility and racism lodged against Arabs while subverting neo-orientalist attitudes objectifying Arab women. For many writers like Laila Halaby and Susan Muaddi Darraj, reclamation is paramount in carving out a space for Arab American women writers into the bedrock of ethnic American literature.[6] In this study, I am interested in how numerous women use acts of storytelling expressed through writing, embroidery, and weaving to bring a community into focus. Rather than focus on Scheherazade or a singular character, both Halaby and Darraj break through monoliths with emphasis on the community and a collection of intertwining stories that assert agency.

For the mother and daughters in Halaby and Darraj's texts, their narratives recalling Palestine, the loss of homeland, and conciliation with American culture offer reflections of the past in the present as all the characters contend with displacement either in the U.S. or what remains of Palestine. This synchronistic cultural memory at times fragments Palestinian and American identities, speaking to the way in which displacement becomes a central theme woven throughout the mothers and daughters' narratives. Strung together, the daughters' stories become a mirror for their mother's experiences, sometimes echoing similar themes of un-belonging in both America and an ever-shrinking Palestine. Together, however, the mothers and daughters of *West of the Jordan* and *The Inheritance of Exile* create all-female networks that help those in Palestine and in the diaspora to manifest agency. What is helpful here to consider are feminist theories by Chandra Mohanty, Mahnaz Afkhami, and Nima Naghibi concerning second wave projects promoting and expanding on notions of "global sisterhood," particularly in response to colonial and imperial hegemonic structures. Each investigates the notion of "universal sisterhood" in relation to "Third World women's" agency, advocating for a solidarity that is not only locally rooted, but one that can also transcend national and cultural boundaries (Mohanty 116, Afkhami 17, and Naghibi 102). For Mohanty in *Feminism Without Borders: Decolonizing Theory, Practicing Solidarity*, "universal sisterhood," in its Utopian definition of transcending a "male world," erases the political location of women of color who do not have access to the same power as white, Western feminists (Mohanty 116). Mohanty asserts "solidarity" instead of "sisterhood" as a mode in which "mutually accountable and equitable relationships among different communities of women" (193). In her earlier work in *Third World Women and the Politics of Feminism,* she first draws attention to the way in which Western feminism ignore their privilege in evaluating "third world" women. This becomes particularly apparent in the context of Middle Eastern and Muslim women when Western feminists perceive them along the following narrow paradigms:

> So, while on the one hand women attain value or status within the family, the assumption of a singular patriarchal kinship system (common to all Arab and Muslim societies) is what apparently structures women as an oppressed group in these societies! . . . Not only are all Arab and Muslim women seen to constitute a homogeneous oppressed group, but there is no discussion of the specific practices within the family which constitute women as mothers, wives, sisters, etc. ("Under Western Eyes," 61)

Mohanty specifically draws attention to the way in which lingering colonial attitudes gaze at Muslim women as monolithically oppressed, silent, and without recognizable power, which could not be further from the truth. Considering this notion of solidarity, Iranian feminist, Mahnaz Afkhami notes that in the Iranian case, to avoid these types of assumptions, Iranian women must not only resist responding to white Feminist gazes that limit their mobility, but at the same time, draw on indigenous identity and expand outwards to global practices that defy patriarchal discourses embedded within Iranian culture (Afkhami 17). Nima Naghibi, Iranian feminist and literary scholar, provides an interesting framework that expands on her feminist predecessors so as to provide future modalities for feminist praxis. In *Rethinking Global Sisterhood: Western Feminism and Iran,* she builds on Mohanty, Afkhami, and Eve Kosofsky Sedgwick's arguments[7] concerning solidarity and sisterhood to draw attention to the value of a female homosocial collectivity. To counter cultural patriarchal norms, in addition to Western feminism that renders Muslim women as "backward" or "victimized," Naghibi articulates a vision of empowerment facilitated by all-female support networks. Reclaiming the all-female space of the *andaruni,*[8] Naghibi investigates the way in which Iranian women, particularly after the 1979 Iranian Revolution, use segregated spaces to build support and strength to counter patriarchal norms and newly Islamic state-mandated gender roles. Her study of post-revolutionary Iranian films discloses the way in which a return to women's homosocial spaces "enable women to draw on the possibilities of female bonding as a way of negotiating a disciplinary masculine culture" (Naghibi 111). Ultimately, what Naghibi finds is that each Iranian woman of her film study defies patriarchal mandates and authority through platonic and possibly sexual navigations of female relationships that are either intrinsic or manifested. On a "microlevel," mothers, daughters, and friends are able to carve out spaces for themselves via a "transient network" that attempts to mitigate the absence of women on the "macrolevel" (122).

When applying this argument to the context of Palestinian American literature, the women's homosocial network in *West of the Jordan* and *The Inheritance of Exile* show the ways in a transnational, Palestinian feminist framework reinforces the empowerment and survival of women in Palestine, Jordan, and the U.S. This is further highlighted in the novels since men are mostly absent, killed, ridiculed, or cast off. When more prominent male figures do appear, most are depicted as dutiful, kind, loving, and caring, thereby, dispelling stereotypes that they are violent Arab men (save for Khadija's father in *West of the Jordan*). When the male characters are minimized, they are replaced by central female storytellers who 1) must rely on one another to navigate daily life on a microlevel and 2) ensure group survival and preserve memory of homeland on a macrolevel (especially where it concerns racism lodged against them by Israelis and Americans). Taken together, the mother and daughter groups in both novels create networks of solidarity that show their wit, intelligence, determination, and forbearance (all attributes set forth in early examples of Scheherazade). By assessing the homosocial formations within these texts, it becomes clear that these female collectivities help create a means of asserting power and replacing patriarchal control among immigrant and refugee Palestinian women in the diaspora.[9]

EMBROIDERING AS STORYTELLING: CULTIVATING HOMOSOCIAL NETWORKS THROUGH CULTURAL PRAXIS

West of the Jordan

In Leila Halaby's novel, *West of the Jordan* (2003), the author creates a narrative told from the first-person perspective of four Palestinian women of the same family spread between the Palestinian village of Nawara, Jordan, and the U.S. As is the case with many Middle Eastern-American narratives examining themes of migration, the text moves back and forth between the U.S. and the Middle East to explore perpetual movement, fragmentation, and displacement, even in the homeland (due to the creation of illegal Israeli settlements). Though it is written through Hala, Mawal, Khadija, and Soraya's perspectives, the text begins and ends with Hala, who becomes the focal point of the novel. She is half-Palestinian and half-Jordanian (a reminder of her mother's displacement), and she explores the way in which she connects with "home" while in her newly adopted country of the U.S. She originally grew up in Jordan, but moves to Arizona with her uncle and his American wife to pursue her education (and fulfilling the dying wish of her mother, Huda). Unlike many ethnic American narratives that focus on cultural differences by localizing the plot in the U.S., the author allows Hala to confront her "Arabness" and increasing Americanness in Jordan when she returns for her mother's funeral. There is a double displacement here since Hala returns to an enclave of Palestinian refugees (many from her mother's village, Nawara) in Jordan. The rest of the novel's short stories proceed to show the progression and self-discovery of Hala and her cousins during the period of mourning for Huda, a mother lost to illness and restrictive borders preventing salvation without incurring great financial expense.

What immediately emerges throughout Hala and the other girls' narratives is the emphasis on speaking and storytelling as a means of forging a transnational community among Palestinian women engaged in preserving familial memory and cultural heritage. It is not surprising that questions about family, culture, and identity come up over and over again at the trauma of a dying mother, who can be seen as allegorically paralleling the dying nation. The narrative disclosure employed throughout the novel immediately challenges leftover colonialist and Western attitudes stereotyping Middle Eastern or "third world" women as silent or unable to build solidarity (Mohanty, *Third World Women* 61). Embroidering, in particular, is posed as both cultural product and literary device metaphorizing life storytelling and community building. To begin, Hala first introduces the way in which her mother's village, Nawara, "is known for lovely, cleverly embroidered dresses (*rozas*) in an area of villages where almost no one embroiders, for lack of time and money" (Halaby 10, author's emphasis). The dresses come to symbolize the dressmaker's stories, her connection to others in her community, which also serves as an act of preservation of a disappearing culture. Moreover, as means of cultural production and compensated labor, they allow women in the village to survive and thrive. As Brinda Mehta points out in *Rituals of Memory in Contemporary Arab Women's Writing,* ritualized acts such as "cooking, bread making, weaving, purification rites, and beauty treatments demonstrate the sensory, embodied aspects of memory that connect women to their past as they reclaim their subjectivity denied by the intersecting forces of orientalist discourse, colonialism, imperialism, masculinist wars" (Mehta 4) and what Fatema Mernissi terms "petro-dollar engineered Islam" (Mernissi 1986, ix quoted in Mehta). This connection to roza making serves a cultural praxis that channels the "mother-spirit" into the aesthetics of weaving and stitching, as women often share stories and disclose feelings throughout its production. In Palestine, there are present day projects focused on this art of embroidery and how it can preserve precious history.[10] For those in the diaspora, mothers use this art to culturally transmit and share this form of cultural production to create "safe spaces" for Arab exiles, refugees, and migrants abroad (Mehta 18).

While Hala's stories serve as bookends for the short story collection novel, her cousin, Mawal's perspective and stories offer a helpful focus for life in Palestine, the cultural epicenter for the novel. Since she is the only character to live in Nawara (not having ever left), she serves as a cultural anchor, representing life in the original village to which Hala, Soraya, and Khadija have ties from abroad. Mawal spotlights the way in which one can still be displaced in Palestine, feeling loss of homeland as she is confined to her town and the West Bank, never able to travel to Gaza or other territories lost or restricted after the 1967 Six-Days War and ensuing Israeli occupation.[11] Furthermore, because of the disadvantaged economic conditions of remaining Palestinian villages, many have to leave for Jordan or the U.S. to provide for their families. About the politics of embroidering rozas, Mawal adds:

> The complicated embroidery on our *rozas*—with both Palestinian and western stitches and patterns-captures the spirit of Nawara, which sits at the top of the West Bank, just west of the Jordan River, east of Jenin and far enough away from both of these places to be a peaceful village that only every so often releases an avalanche of stones and fire. This is something that happens more often as the Israelis take parts of our village to build their settlements. (15)

As Amal Talaat Abdelrazek notes in *Contemporary Arab American Women Writers: Hyphenated Identities and Border Crossings,* although Mawal's character and storyline are not fully developed within the text, she highlights the other cousins' displacement vis-à-vis her discussion of "the politics of location in Nawara with its political upheavals, gender struggles, and social conflicts" (Abdelrazek 127). The political placement of Nawara as in-between changing Middle Eastern cartographies is echoed throughout the hybridization of the stitch pattern that blends Palestinian and Western styles.

Already, this cultural form of expression is shifting, though it still stands in for Palestinian modes of indigeniety when so many immigrate to America to send money back home. Skeptical of America, Mawal accuses the country of being a "greedy neighbor who takes the best of you and leaves you feeling empty" (96). Her stories, and her attention to the rozas and its stitching serve as what she calls "little histories," which preserve group identity in the face of those immigrating abroad:

> I tuck this story into my pocket, wishing I could stitch it into my skin, like one of the Bedouin tattoos my grandmother wears. Are there stories like this in lovely, tempting America? Do my cousins there even know these little histories? I doubt it.
> Stitch in red for life.
> Stitch in green to remember.
> Stitch, stitch to never forget. (Halaby 103)

What is noteworthy here is Mawal's alliteration linking "story," "stitch," and "skin" together to highlight the importance of remembrance concerning one's origins and the preservation of it. Bedouin heritage is reclaimed through matriarchal lineage as a way of recalling bonds to a disappearing culture and nomadic way of life, not unlike Palestinian culture today. The threads of the rozas, with their bright colors, often represent the cycles and conditions of life. In this chapter's epigraph, the colors first referenced for stitching intuitively use red for blood, white for purity, and black for death. In Mawal's aforementioned example, red now stands in for life (as it is fueled by blood), and green represents remembrance so that those who are stitching and embroidering to "never forget." The stitching takes on its own language and semiotics, as colors generate "multiplicity of meaning within the text" and the fabric of the roza (Sabry 257). On a semiotic level, embroidering offers social camaraderie and meaning as a lasting signifier of cultural identity and its preservation. Using its own language, Palestinian embroidery offers codes for gauging sociocultural makers of identity and group kinship relationships, especially those facilitated through female homosocial networks and mother/daughter bonds. In this way, gendered perspectives are layered in the semiotics of roza making. The language and colors of the roza render it as such so that the fabric of the roza stands in for life and the stitching for the storytelling of it. Quite literally, life storytelling is grafted onto the creation of these uniquely Palestinian dresses, which are not only infused with self, but also with cultural significance.

Life story, therefore, becomes *preserved* in the roza and it is shared between embroiderer and wearer. This is not unlike discussions of ethnographic autobiography that seeks to transform the autobiographical "I" of remembrance into sites of collective memory expressed through the embodiment of "we." In *Reading Autobiography: A Guide for Interpreting Life Narratives*, life writing scholars Sidonie Smith and Julia Watson assert that cultural modes of expression, including visual art and textiles, can become a terrain in which the producer "revalues a past moment and links the personal, communal, and ethnic" (Smith and Watson 176). Surveying contemporary ethnographic artists in their work, Smith and Watson focus on the autobiographical body, whether present or alluded to through biological markers and artifacts. In Mawal's case, the materiality of both her roza and her skin serve as fabrics to preserve life story. Not unlike her grandmother's Bedouin tattoo, the stitching of the roza signals grafting onto the autobiographical body, seen here as the roza itself. Smith and Watson note that in postcolonial national contexts (seen her as Palestine), these types of cultural acts and artifacts can signify a reconfiguration of official memory that seeks to silence or suppress personal and communal memories perceived as threatening national authority (177). The roza, therefore, becomes a site of cultural life storytelling that seeks to not only preserve self through an autobiographical process, but also preserve communal and cultural history in the face of colonial erasure.

Mawal's stories offer a complexity to life storytelling and personal disclosure (albeit fiction), as they are not only embedded in speaking, but also in witnessing. As she notes, "Sometimes stories in our house come from watching, watching just the right way and seeing the underside of things, the thinking things and the forgetting things" (122). Stories, therefore are not always freely shared, but discreetly learned, particularly by mothers, daughters, wives, and sisters navigating their way through the complexities of women living in Nawara. These enduring women not only have to navigate the patriarchal norms within the internal space of some Palestinian households, but also Israeli dominance that controls external, sociopolitical spaces. In a world where agency is under attack, "watching" and "seeing" serve as two actions that women can take when they feel limited in speaking. For survival, storytelling must become multivalent in how it is produced, shared, and recorded. Ultimately, stitching and storytelling become acts of survival since "So many women spill their secrets and their joys and their agonies because they know my mother—and I—will keep them safe do no more than stitch them into the fabric of our *rozas*" (17). Mawal and her mother must preserve the "secrets," "joys," and "agonies," of the women in her community, demonstrating the homosociality becomes a keeper of tales and stitcher of stories, particularly throughout the political changes governing Nawara and its economic dependence on Israel's economy. Furthermore, it suggests access to women's agency, since they are producers and wearers of cultural garments of their own making, threading together wearers in a homosocial network of agents willing to help one another in the village.

It is for this reason that Hala, on her return journey from Jordan to the U.S. dons her mother's roza despite her father's protestations. After journeying back to her family in Jordan, Hala confronts many moments of identity fragmentation and in-between-ness that she cannot quite reconcile. Halaby's choice to highlight these disconnections during the return to homeland, as opposed to the initial departure, suggests a finality of un-belonging and change for Hala. Back "home" in Jordan, Hala concedes, "I am unconnected. There *is* comfort to be in my own house, to wake up in my own language, but all those faces I've carried with me for so long wear suspicion in their eyes as they greet me. I have walked so far away from them" (77). The tension of un-belonging occurs throughout Hala's journey, first in Arizona, then in Jordan, ultimately forcing her to choose where she feels there is the most opportunity for her: the U.S. Before her flight back to her uncle's home in Arizona, Hala declares: "I am wearing a *roza* that my grandmother made for my mother as part of her trousseau ... I remember her wearing it and being happy. It is not a fancy one, but the pattern is clever and it suits me. I even imagine it still carries her scent" (203). The roza not only stands in for her connection to Palestine, but to her kinship relationships with her mother and grandmother. Even though she is leaving Jordan and her displaced Palestinian family behind, the roza is her connection to her family lineage, heritage, and network, which empowers her to move forward.

In a touching final scene at the novel's conclusion, Halaby repeatedly invokes the trope of remembering as a means of ensuring cultural preservation and the survival of Nawara. After returning from "home," having laid her mother to rest in Jordan, Hala evaluates her bare, Arizona bedroom with new eyes, recognizing its starkness devoid of any cultural signifiers. After papering over the wall with travel posters of Egypt and Morocco (as stand-ins for Jordan and Palestine) Hala repeatedly echoes her mother's command to "remember." She recalls, "remember for yourself and for your tomorrow, my mother used to say.... Remember the stories of Nawara: everything, including the tragedies.... Remember the ones who left, who fled, whose memories are vague and lives are changed ..." (218–219). Memory here is Huda's lasting commandment to her daughter so that she does not forget where she came from and to preserve her community's stories as an act of solidarity. Brinda Mehta observes that the use of memory as a trope in Arab American literature allows the writer to explore generational issues witnessed and reexamined through writing (Mehta 3). Women writers and storytellers are also able to add a layer of complexity to "transformative textualities, when her particular gender concerns are articulated in a commemorative script of (self-) discovery and social critique" (3). In *West of the Jordan*, the recitation of memory serves as a political act reclaiming space for Arab women in the fabric of national and cultural discourses. As a recent immigrant who has been denied her Palestinian homeland all her life, Hala begins to reconcile the identity crisis and fragmentation she has been experiencing between Arab and American identities.

The Inheritance of Exile

This crisis of reconciling Palestinian and American identities is a bit more fleshed out between mothers and daughters in Susan Muaddi Darraj's *The Inheritance of Exile* (2007). Similar to the collection of stories in Leila Halaby's *West of the Jordan*, Darraj organizes her novel according to a short story cycle alternating between four female protagonists, Nadia, Hanan, Aliyah, and Reema, and their respective mothers, Siham, Layla, Huda, and Lamis. The daughters, who are all friends in Philadelphia, are second generation Arab women attempting to create space for themselves as both Arab and American. In the U.S., they are negotiating their status as "hyphenated[12]" Americans, and upon return to Jerusalem (as evidenced by Aliyah), these women feel as though they must also prove their "Arabness" within their community. This is the most pronounced when one of the daughters, Aliyah notes, "I'd flinched, and reminded him that I was an *Arab*-American. There was a hyphen there, connecting the two things that created me: the one that drew me to him and the other that kept me at a distance" (Darraj 69). The hyphen undoubtedly signals identity politics at the core of Arab American women's writing: the process of reconciling what is on both sides of the hyphen. What results is a narrative that shows the conflict of identity formation, since the girls are undoubtedly in-between Palestinian culture and American way of life. The push and pull of identity politics threatens fragmentation, but ultimately, moments of cultural crisis are resolved through hybrid identity and the memory of home preserved in the present locale of South Philadelphia vis-à-vis stories and cultural modes of expression.

Just as in *West of the Jordan*, storytelling in *The Inheritance of Exile* serves as an extension of cultural praxis that becomes enmeshed in identity. Stories are regarded as personal possessions in the novel; someone else's story should never be shared, particularly when it threatens group embarrassment. This becomes evident when one of the protagonists, Aliyah, fuses her uncle's drunkenness at his daughter's wedding into a quasi-fictional short story published in a magazine for all of her family to read. After this embarrassing disclosure, her father justly reprimands her, shouting, "It is not your story!" It is his. Make up your own, for Christ's sakes!" (55). This cautionary advice is echoed when Reema's mother, Lamis (also referred to as Imm Nabeel for her eldest son) begins telling her daughter about her time living in the UNRWA refugee camps following the 1967 Six-Day War. About to disclose her friend, Dina's story, she hesitates, admitting "I shouldn't talk about Dina anymore. I don't want to. No, I will not. It's not my right to tell her story. I can only tell you mine. You? You can tell mine because I am giving it to you to keep safe, or to tell all the people, or to tell your sociology professor. Do as you like. It is yours now" (Darraj 192, author's emphasis). This is a touching moment at the novel's end when a mother passes on her heritage to her daughter, entrusting her to keep her story safe, while also protecting the story of her friend. Her daughter serves as ethnographic preserver, both as cultural insider, and as a sociology student collecting stories for her dissertation. Stories, therefore, become the torch passed from mothers on to their daughters to light the way of remembrance. To remember is to engage in a political act that offers testimony about the squalid conditions for Palestinian refugees following the onslaught of the Six-Day War and the loss of Palestinian sovereignty. Through the retelling of these life stories, they have the capacity to slowly form into postmemory,[13] which becomes remembered and *almost* experienced by future generations, thereby, reinforcing group bonds and preserving revisionist histories in the diaspora.

Further exploring the image of the storyteller, Aliyah and Reema are two central characters of note that engage in storytelling projects to expand their cultural network and create solidarity among network actors. Reema, who academically studies sociology as part of her PhD formalized her relationship to storytelling as she collects the story of her community for ethnographic work in her dissertation. Fueled by her interest in her parents and refugees experiencing war, her dissertation began as a "collection and study of eyewitness accounts of war" (170). The omniscient narrator muses how Reema, a cultural insider, has been listening, witnessing, and collecting her community's stories, observing "Reema was becoming a collector of stories, something she'd always imagined Aliyah would do instead. But as her childhood friend reminded, "I invent stories, for the most part. You record them" (180). For Aliyah, stories fuel her passion, particularly those that she records and creates: "One day, she finally boarded the subway and returned home to tell her father that all the stories in the world had to be hers, or else she would never find her own voice, never write from the heart" (55). The dynamism of storytelling is two-fold here as they are produced and preserved through oral tradition and testimonial writing. In fact, it would seem as the collected stories bound in *The Inheritance of Exile* could be a product of their collective efforts: to write and gather stories that make up the fabric of the community.

The image of Scheherazade shines through the examples of Reema and Aliyah, who invoke storytelling as a political act of cultural preservation, not to entertain, as the early European translators of *A Thousand and One Nights* would have us believe. This rejection of a frivolous Scheherazade becomes most evident when an over-the-top, almost comical orientalist caricature, Alex, projects the specter of an exoticized Scheherazade onto Reema. When Alex begins to date Reema, he poses her like an odalisque painted by Matisse and refers to her as his "houri" from *The Sheik* (1921). Reema reflects on this orientalist fetishization, acknowledging,

> When he asked her to tell him stories of her childhood, about her parents and their idiosyncrasies, about her brother and how he'd met his wife during a two-week vacation to Palestine, and then said that he felt like Sultan Shahrayar of the *Thousand and One Nights*—which Reema supposed made her like Scheherazade.... Since she had been old enough to understand it, she'd been bothered by the fact that people told her that she looked "exotic" (which, until the age of fourteen, she'd confused with "erotic"). (174–175)

This image of Scheherazade as entertaining is precisely what Reema and the other girls reject. She is asked to provide stereotype after stereotype about her family throughout their courtship, as evident in Alex's misperceptions that her brother entered an arranged marriage upon returning to Palestine or how her family could potentially engage in an honor killing if they find out Reema is dating Alex. She recoils at being told she's "exotic," which as she notes, is reminiscent of "erotic." Instead, as a doctoral student intent on continuing this storytelling legacy in academia, Reema dons the more serious face of Scheherazade. Reema's stories, taken alongside her mother's refugee experiences, show the way in which life storytelling is recorded to provide testimony and cultural revisionist history. Her mother, Imm Nabeel, reminds Reema the importance of life narratives, stories, and truths that are exchanged in a community, advising her, "When you tell the truth, you allow people the chance to heal" (185). Storytelling, therefore, is shown as having the capacity to alleviate trauma through the acts of disclosure and catharsis.

Just as in *West of the Jordan*, storytelling serves as cultural praxis like embroidering and basket weaving; they are all means for women to forge alliances and create spaces for themselves. For Siham, Nadia's mother, who had been taught by her grandmothers, she uses it to create pillows and sell them in the Donato's flower shop downstairs. From this work, she is not only stitching in her heritage into these pillows, but she is also able to financially profit from them and supplement her husband's income, particularly after he is killed in a car accident. Siham describes embroidering as having a lasting trace, since "Thread would imprint itself forever" (28). Echoing the motif of embroidery reverberating throughout *West of the Jordan*, this Palestinian mode of cultural production allows Siham to tap into generations of artistry and collectivity as women come together to practice embroidery and roza making. Through her embroidery, Siham continues on the stories and traditions of her mother and grandmother, stories that were interrupted with the Six-Day War in Palestine, which necessitate group memory and continuation in the diaspora.

In addition to Siham's Palestinian embroidering, Hanan's basket weaving and story arc with her mother serve as compelling examples of cultural production, negotiation of motherhood, and confrontation with Arab American identity. Hanan and her mother, Layla, provide for enthralling character foils that bring complexity to kinship relationships in the diaspora. Layla, who grew up in a UNRWA refugee camp in Jordan, attempts to make a new life for herself in America with her new Arab American husband, Michel. She endeavors to understand her daughter, Hanan, who constantly struggles between Arab identity and American nationality. What compounds this situation further is that Layla suffers from the paradox of Arab hyper-visibility and invisibility in a post-9/11 world that simultaneously sees her before erasing her.[14] This makes it that much more difficult for her daughter to *see* Layla through her own fragmented gaze. An estrangement between mother and daughter ensues after Hanan marries and separates from John since Layla had cautioned Hanan against marrying an "Amerikani" in the first place. As a result, Hanan temporarily suspends her mother/daughter bond at just the time that she gives birth to her son, Michael, thereby, isolating her from a support system that could aid in her navigation of motherhood. To support herself, she engages in basket weaving, eventually creating and selling her Palestinian baskets at a local Philly arts and crafts shop. As Hanan first discusses her basket weaving, she identifies the matrilineal tradition passed between mothers and daughters, affirming that she learned from her mother, and that her mother "learned all that stuff from her mother—embroidery, weaving, all that stuff" (36).

When she discusses the basket weaving process, culture and politics become intertwined since the Six-Day War and ensuing displacement necessitated the learning of this handcraft for economic survival. About the baskets, Hanan reflects,

> My parents' house was also filled with these baskets, which my mother used to make by weaving strips of olive branch wood, soaked in paint, into round or flat shapes. First she built a foundation, then the sides, and finally she weaved in other strops as a decorative pattern. "In the camp, A UNRWA program come and tell us, do this and we give you money," she said, "so we do it." Her mother and

aunts had done it for years, and though my mother didn't particularly enjoy it, she had discovered that she could make money by weaving these designs. (118)

In times of need, both Hanan and her mother use basket weaving to support themselves. For Hanan, through the labor and profit from her baskets, she is able to support herself, only by way of participating in industry. For Layla, her basket weaving program was a byproduct of The Vocational Center at the Jordanian Red Crescent, which was established in 1953. Its purpose was to create a community of empowered women who could draw on new skills for sources of income that would allow them to achieve economic security (Jordan Red Crescent). Yet, as Hanan concedes, while her mother did not particularly enjoy it, she was incentivized by the economic viability of basket weaving. In *Transnationalism,* Steven Vertovec notes that in transnational networks, survival is tied to globalization in that the free flow of not just capital, but also of products, images, ideas, cultural output can become "creolized or hybridized," particularly in the diaspora (Vertovec 7). For Hanan, this "hybridized" practice of basket weaving is learned from her mother and adapted to styles and materials found in Philadelphia. Hanan's basket weaving, therefore, takes on extra significance, as its hybridized form facilitates the continuity of cultural modes of artistry, localizing its production in the diaspora. Ultimately, for both mother and daughter, the creation and the selling of baskets for economic survival allow for independence and the matrilineal preservation of culture through the memories and stories woven into each basket.

Basket weaving is a significant example in the discussion of group affiliation because it represents a history of Bedouin and Palestinian homosocial networks that produce cultural artifacts in all-female systems for the aim of economic security and prosperity. Stories, memories, and patterns are interwoven in the creation of these baskets to signify personal and collective histories. As Brinda Mehta notes, there is a ritualized aspect to Palestinian basket weaving that communicates its own language of negotiation as storyteller or weaver sets a story and pattern into the creation of the basket (Mehta 97). Furthermore, Mehta notes the way in which "Woven fabric as woman-text represents an empowering act of articulating the female body in prescriptural form and broadens the parameters of our appreciation of the technique of 'writing the body' . . ." (97–98). For Hanan, when John attempts to manage her life and push her into a degree and career, claiming, "There's a lot of *potential,*" she instead recedes into familiar cultural terrains of belonging (130). In response to the confrontation, she admits, "Instead, I stayed up late in the basement, weaving gold strips through the bottom and sides of a dark brown basket" (131). In this way, basket weaving serves as a familiar and comforting custom that eventually helps her to reconcile with her mother, while at the same time, bolstering alliances with friends and community members. Ultimately, each basket becomes a site for memory and for the preservation of culture passed onto her in the diaspora, which is critical since Palestinian territories and culture are vulnerable to illegal Israeli settlement building and suppression.

For Hanan, basket weaving not only facilitates reconciliation with her mother (as they share in cultural acts of memory), but also her independence from her husband, who attempts to control her life. Finally open to taking her place in this network of female actors, Hanan becomes interested in storytelling and recording stories about her family so that she can pass them on to her newborn son. Keen to continue family oral traditions, Hanan excitedly exclaims to her father, "I can't believe I never heard that story before," I said to Baba. "I'm glad you told me." "There are many stories," he replied. "And I want Michael to hear them all" (164). The power of storytelling here also allows for Hanan's father, Michel, to become a facilitator for cultural and familial remembrance, not to patriarchally control her, but to engage in communal memory work in the diaspora. As a single, Arab American mother in the diaspora, Hanan fights against the invisibility of immigrant mothers and the fetishized visibility of Arab Americans by forging her own hybridized navigation of identity. With the help of her community, she not only has a place of belonging, but she has the strength, means, and agency to advocate for herself and her son.

CONCLUDING THOUGHTS: EMBROIDERING THROUGHOUT MIDDLE EASTERN WOMEN'S LITERATURE

In the literary landscape of Middle Eastern literature, both *West of the Jordan* and *The Inheritance of Exile* use the structure of the short story cycle in the pursuit of presenting female homosocial spaces conducive to building solidarity. Their focus on Palestinian embroidering and basket weaving present cultural forms of production that not only sustain women economically, but also preserve culture, especially when it is threatened in Palestine or in the diaspora. As a motif, embroidering not only serves as a form of matrilineal expression, but it also exists as a form of storytelling that echoes throughout other Middle Eastern literary works. One of these echoes appears in Iranian author, Marjane Satrapi's *Embroideries* (2008), a graphic memoir exploring intergenerational, female relationships before and after the 1979 Iranian Revolution. The stories within the graphic novella, which breaks through the traditional frames and gutters of *les bandes dessinées* comics,[15] uses the open space of the page to explore themes of love, family, motherhood, and daughterhood. Set against the backdrop of a post-revolutionary Iran, the women in the text look back on their lives and compare how they fit in, particularly as it relates to the relationship between mothers and daughters. Yet, its namesake, *Embroideries*, does not derive from a type of stitching belonging to Iranian dress (as it does in the Palestinian context), but rather the procedure to "restore" the hymen to make a non-virgin appear a virgin again. It is a clever reference to invoke because it does not just show the survival of homosocial female networks, but their active undermining of religious and state-imposed values. Embroidery here, therefore, comes to stand in for more than genital surgery, but the stitching together of resistance narratives, particularly against patriarchal values. Strung together, texts like *Embroideries*, *West of the Jordan*, and *The Inheritance of Exile* create all-female spaces in which Middle Eastern women gather in solidarity to discuss the delicious morsels of their lives, and in defiance of those who would restrict their agency.

On a final note, as I sit in the comforts and confines of my home in the U.S. amid the global COVID-19 pandemic, kinship relationships, particularly intergenerational ones between women, seem that much more significant and urgent to research. I am sure that by the pandemic's end, social scientists will have studied the ways in which our interpersonal dynamics will have changed, and how the marginalized will have become that much more marginalized. But, in the meantime, what previous studies have already told us is that women, especially, are intergenerational caretakers of the young and the old, and that their labor is mostly invisible. These caretakers are not only a link between generations, but they can also serve as cultural transmitters between homeland and the *new* world within the context of immigration. Immigrant mothers, and more specifically, Arab American mothers within these fictional works bridge gaps between their parents, who also represent Middle Eastern homelands left behind, and their children, who come to symbolize new cultural modes of belonging (or conversely, *un-belonging*) in the U.S. Their navigation of life in the diaspora is fraught with simultaneous waves of visibility and invisibility, while their daughters navigate confusing and murky waters of belonging. What emerges, as a potential resolution, is the way in which women must band together in solidarity to help one another survive adversity and patriarchal oppression in societies that seek to minimize their labor, especially in the U.S. With one another, Arab American women, including storytellers and artisans, can weave culture and agency into the fabric of their diasporic communities, ensuring that their cultures and voices survive in a world rapidly changing with each exhalation.

WORKS CITED

Afkhami, Mahnaz. "Women in Post-revolutionary Iran: A Feminist Perspective." *In the Eye of the Storm: Women in Post-Revolutionary Iran,* edited by Mahnaz Afkhami and Erika Friedl, Syracuse University Press, 1994, pp. 5–18.

Ahmad, Aijaz. "Jameson's Rhetoric of Otherness and the 'National Allegory.'" *In Theory: Classes, Nations, Literatures,* Verso, 1992, pp. 95–112.

Alfarra, Jehan. "Weaving the History of Palestine." *Middle East Monitor.* 26 January 2017. https://www.middleeastmonitor.com/20170126-weaving-the-history-of-palestine/ Accessed 10 April 2020.

Al-Haj, Majid. "The Changing Arab Kinship Structure: The Effect of Modernization in an Urban Community." *Economic Development and Cultural Change,* vol. 36, no. 2, 1988, pp. 237–258.

Alshaibi, Sama. "Memory Work in the Palestinian Diaspora (Personal Essay and Art). *A Journal of Women Studies,* vol. 27, no. 2, 2006, pp. 30–53.

Darraj, Susan Muaddi. *Inheritance of Exile: Stories from South Philly.* University of Notre Dame Press, 2007.

———. *Scheherazade's Legacy: Arab and Arab-American Women on Writing.* Praeger, 2004.

Doraï, Mohamed Kamel. "The Meaning of Homeland for the Palestinian Diaspora: Revival and Transformation." *New Approaches to Migration: Transnational Communities and the Transformation of Home,* edited by Nadje Sadig Al-Ali and Khalid Koser, Routledge, 2002, pp. 87–95.

Gauch, Suzanne. *Liberating Shahrazad: Feminism, Postcolonialism, and Islam.* University of Minnesota Press, 2007.

Halaby, Laila. *West of the Jordan.* Beacon, 2004.

Hirsch, Marianne, "Surviving Images: Holocaust Photographs and the Work of Postmemory." *Yale Journal of Criticism,* vol. 14, no. 1, 2001, pp. 5–37.

Jameson, Frederic. "Third-World Literature in the Era of Multinational Capitalism." *Social Text* 15 (Autumn): 1986, pp. 65–88.

Jordan Red Crescent. "The Jordanian Red Crescent's Vocational Center concludes Training Courses for Syrian-Refugee and Local Community Women." 24 Aug 2015. https://reliefweb.int/report/jordan/jordanian-red-crescent-s-vocational-center-concludes-training-courses-syrian-refugee. Accessed 10 April 2020.

Marshall, Susan E., and Jen'nan Ghazal Read. "Identity Politics Among Arab-American Women." *Social Science Quarterly,* vol. 84, no. 4, 2003, pp. 875–891.

Mehta, Brinda. *Rituals of Memory in Contemporary Arab Women's Writing.* Syracuse University Press, 2007.

Mernissi, Fatima. *Women's Rebellion and Islamic Memory.* Zed Books, 1986.

———. *Scheherazade Goes West: Different Cultures, Different Harems.* Washington Square Press, 2010.

Mohanty, Chandra Talpade. *Feminism Without Borders: Decolonizing Theory, Practicing Solidarity.* Duke University Press, 2003.

Naghibi, Nima. *Rethinking Global Sisterhood: Western Feminism and Iran.* University of Minnesota Press, 2007.

Sabry, Hafez. "Food as a Semiotic Code in Arabic Literature." *Taste of Thyme*, edited by Zubaida and Tapper, 2000, pp. 257–280.

Sabry, Somaya Sami. "Performing Scheherazade: Arab-American Women's Contestations of Identity. *Alif: Journal of Comparative Poetics*, vol. 31, 2011, pp. 196–219.

Salaita, Steven. "Ethnic Identity and Imperative Patriotism: Arab Americans before and after 9/11." *College Literature*, vol. 32, no. 2, 2005, pp. 146–168.

Sallis, Eva. *Scheherazade: Through the Looking Glass: The Metamorphosis of the Thousand and One Nights*. Routledge, 1999.

Satrapi, Marjane. *Embroideries*. Jonathan Cape, 2008.

Sedgewick, Eve Kosofsky. *Between Men: English Literature and Male Homosocial Desire*. Columbia University Press, 1985.

Shakir, Evelyn. "Mother's Milk: Women in Arab-American Autobiography." *MELUS*, vol. 15, no. 4, 1988, pp. 39–50.

Shomali, Mejdulene B. "Scheherazade and the Limits of Inclusive Politics in Arab American Literature." *MELUS*, 2018, pp. 65–90.

Smith, Sidonie, and Julia Watson. *Reading Autobiography: A Guide for Interpreting Life Narratives, Second Edition*. University of Minnesota Press, 2010.

Trinh, T. Minh-Ha. *Woman, Native, Other: Writing Postcoloniality and Feminism*. Bloomington: Indiana University Press, 1989.

Vertovec, Steven. *Transnationalism*. Taylor & Francis Group, 2009.

NOTES

1. I am using homosocial and homosociality to refer to a network forged from all-female relationships that can also have kinship ties. In particular, I will draw on Nima Naghibi's work on Iranian homosocial networks in Iran, as explored in *Rethinking Global Sisterhood: Western Feminism and Iran*, and adapt similar notions of women's collectivities between Arab women in the diaspora.

2. Unlike Frederic Jameson in his controversial essay "Third-World Literature in the Era of Multinational Capitalism," I do not believe that "third world" literature is *necessarily* allegorical. I agree with Aijaz Ahmad in "Jameson's Rhetoric of Otherness and the 'National Allegory'" wherein he objected to Jameson's arguments noting that *all* "Third-World texts" should neither be homogenized nor essentialized as performing culture. In this case, however, Huda's long-ravaging cancer and subsequent death parallel the ever-shrinking landscape of Palestine, particularly after the Israeli occupation of Palestine in 1967 when Hala's mother "lost her freedom to visit her family" and Hala's father had lost much of his land (Halaby 11).

3. Here, I am employing kinship to not only refer to traditional notions of blood ties, but of networks socially constructed, also referred to as "fictive kinship." As Majid Al-Haj notes in "The Changing Arab Kinship Structure: The Effect of Modernization in an Urban Community," in his study of Arab kinship relationships in Israel, the definition of kinship relations has had to expand due to the dwindling of

blood ties (249). In the diaspora, this has certainly been the case since families have had to forge communities beyond blood ties.

4. Or *Shahrzād*, meaning "city freer" in the Persian etymology.

5. Or "world freer" in the Persian etymology. Both the Persian etymologies of Shahrzad and Dunyazad are significant testaments to their power, specifically that which is facilitated via the act of storytelling.

6. In so doing, however, Shomali rightly points out that the way in which Arab American writers like Darraj and Mohja Kahf (in her celebrated *E-mails from Scheherazade* poetry collection) reclaim Sheherazade can sometimes be a bit narrow, following traditional feminine and hetero-normative lines (Shomali 68).

7. Naghibi builds on Kosofsky Sedgewick's notion of homosocial desire, albeit between men, as "the affective or social force, the glue, even when its manifestation is hostility or hatred or something less emotively charged, that shapes an important relationship" (Sedgewick 2, quoted in Naghibi 109).

8. Persian word denoting the architectural and social space designed for the women's quarters.

9. Because of the narrowed scope of this study, there is not sufficient space to analyze the stories that show friendship and camaraderie between all the mothers and daughters. Rather, surveying all the stories with an eye towards the collective makes clear that these stories create a mosaic of the community that firstly, counters individual fragmentation, and secondly, creates solidarity between transnational Palestinian women.

10. The Palestinian History Tapestry project aims to capture the stories and histories of Palestinians and their lives through the art and tradition of embroidery in tapestries that will be on display in Ramallah and in the U.K. (Alfarra).

11. With the 1948 Arab-Israeli war and the post-Six-Days War 1967 occupation of Palestinian territories, the West Bank essentially became a colony of Israel, becoming economically dependent on Israel. As a result, many Palestinians, especially men, fled to Jordan, Europe, and abroad for economic opportunity. As Amal Talaat Abdelrazek points out, Palestinian women became heads of their household, running the home, while also having to find ways to economically provide for their families (128). This further resulted in the feeling of loss of homeland and being uprooted in one's nation, a crisis point which resulted in the forging of transnational networks for survival (Doraï 88).

12. The hyphen in ethnic American identities offers insight into how those writing about identity grapple with themes of home, identity, and belonging. I do not choose to hyphenate Arab American as the hyphen would too neatly resolve questions of cultural in-between-ness. Rather, I am invested in investigating both sides of the hyphen and the liminal spaces in which Arab American women writers inhabit.

13. As Marianne Hirsch defines this in the body of her prolific work on postmemory, it is "the response of the second generation to the trauma of the first" (Hirsch 8).

14. There are many moments in the text wherein Layla feels self-conscious about her accent and her insistence of traditional Palestinian customs while living in the U.S. This comes to a head when Hanan asks her to not attend Parent's Day at school (Darraj 100). As Steven Salaita notes, after 9/11, Arab Americans "suddenly were

visible, and because of the pernicious intentions of various law and intelligence agencies, that visibility was not necessarily embraced" (Salaita 149). As a result, a process of *seeing* and *unseeing*, or ignoring, Arab Americans ensued.

15. In reference to the Franco-Belgian style of comics popularized by *Tintin* and *Asterix*, which have been emulated in graphic novels by David B., Marjane Satrapi, and Zeina Abirached.

Chapter Seven

Mothering on Enemy Land

An Analysis of Japanese Picture Brides' Motherhood in Julie Otsuka's The Buddha in the Attic

Kaori Mori Want

INTRODUCTION

Japanese picture brides were migrant women who moved to the United States of America (hereafter referred as the US) as the wives of Japanese male laborers in the early twentieth century. They married their husbands only by exchanging pictures without meeting them in person. When the Japanese picture brides moved to the US, Japan was a poor agricultural country. The Japanese saw the US as a country of gold, where the Japanese picture brides could have a luxurious life. Their future husbands also promised them a better life in the US. With the hope of having a bright future, many young Japanese women ventured into this picture marriage.

When they arrived in the US, however, most picture brides found that their husbands were poor indentured laborers working on plantations. They needed to live in a shack, and they needed to work in the plantation fields with their husbands. Some picture brides fled their husbands while others remained and became mothers. They made up the foundation of the Japanese American community. Yet, their stories are usually unknown.

A historian Yuji Ichioka writes about the invisibility of Japanese picture brides in American history. He writes that "Despite playing a crucial role in the growth of Japanese immigrant society, Japanese immigrant women are absent from most historical accounts of Japanese immigration" ("Amerika Nadesiko" 339). As if responding to this historical void, a Japanese American writer, Julie Otsuka's *The Buddha in the Attic* delineates the life stories of the picture brides. The story is based on Otsuka's interviews with them. Otsuka writes about the experiences of Japanese picture brides in a collective voice of "we." Roth Maxey discusses the effect of the collective voice in *The Buddha in the Attic*. She contends, "It is a fluent voice, allowing women with sometimes little English, who are silenced by mainstream society, the literary space to speak, their words gaining incremental impact through the power of shared narration" (10). In fact, Otsuka explains her attempt to unbury the silenced Japanese picture brides' voices in the book in an interview.

> While researching these women's lives, I was struck by how much loss they suffered. It was almost unimaginable. And yet, they kept on going. They simply endured (a very Japanese attitude—you stick it out and you don't complain, because complaining would be unseemly). And, really, what choice did they have? I was also struck by how little we hear about the lives of women in the official historical accounts. Most of history is written by men, and about men. So I wanted to give a voice to these invisible unsung women—the ones who didn't make it into the pages of the history books—because their lives are just as heroic and dramatic (if not more so) as the lives of the men who "officially" make history. (Yuhas)

The Buddha in the Attic is a story of Japanese picture brides whose voices are rarely heard in "his"tory documents. Their experiences as women were treated as trivial in history. Yet, as the wives of Japanese immigrants, and the mothers of second-generation Japanese Americans called the Nisei, their experiences are worth listening to. The book tells of their life struggles including mothering in the US where they could not speak English, and did not know the social rules. Mothering Japanese children in the US in the early twentieth century was especially challenging for many picture brides because this was the time when anti-Japanese sentiment among some white Americans was very intense.

Through carefully reading Julie Otsuka's *The Buddha in the Attic* and referring to historical and theoretical accounts on Japanese picture brides, this article will examine how the migrant status affected the mothering of Japanese picture brides, and discuss what kind of principles enabled Japanese picture brides' mothering, which gave their children strength and wisdom to survive on enemy land.

HISTORY OF JAPANESE PICTURE BRIDES

In the late nineteenth century, Japan was an agricultural nation. Due to their primogeniture system, which allowed the inheritance of land only to the first-born son, many Japanese men could not inherit land for farming, and had no way to make a living. Japan started government-sponsored immigration to the US in 1868. Some men went to Hawaii to work on the sugarcane plantations as cheap laborers. Some of them moved to the mainland to look for better job opportunities (Takaki 42).

These men originally planned to leave plantation work and to go back to Japan after saving some money. However, some men could not make enough money to go back home. In addition, the Gentlemen's Agreement prohibited the migration of Japanese laborers from Hawaii to the US in 1908. Japanese mobility was limited to Hawaii or the US mainland (Lee 23).

In order to settle down in the US, these Japanese men tried to make their own families. However, since the anti-miscegenation acts of the time prohibited Japanese men from marrying white American women, they had to find wives from the same racial group. For this purpose, Japanese men asked intermediaries such as their families, relatives, or matchmakers back in Japan to find wives for them. Intermediaries selected possible brides for the Japanese men in the US. After a series of photo exchanges and final agreements between the families, Japanese brides underwent the traditional marriage ceremony, registered their names under the spouse's family register, and applied for a US passport. When the passport was issued, they finally crossed the Pacific Ocean by ship to meet their husbands (Yanagisawa 46). Between 1912 and 1920, approximately 13,000 Japanese women moved to the US (Yanagisawa 52).

Picture brides came to the US for various reasons. The Meiji era (1868–1912) saw a rapid Westernization of Japan, and through that process, some Japanese women grew a strong interest in Western countries. They used picture marriage as a way to go to the West (Tanaka 123). Others knew their future husbands in their early childhood, and agreed to marry them through intermediaries (Yanagisawa 57). When picture marriage was practiced, the average marriage age for the women was about twenty years old. Some unmarried women over twenty felt social pressure to marry. They found a picture marriage as a way to evade social pressure (Yanagisawa 61). For many reasons, Japanese women decided to go to the US as the wives of strangers.

The picture brides only knew their future husbands through pictures and some were shocked to see their husbands in the US because the husbands were sometimes older than they were in their pictures, and they were poor laborers unlike the wives' expectation that their future husbands were rich in the US. Some picture brides left their husbands but most stayed with their spouse mainly because they had no other way of survival in the new land other than staying with their husbands. They gradually took root in the US, and made families with their husbands and children (Glenn 46–49).

The growing visibility of Japanese families along the West Coast spurred anti-Japanese sentiments among some white Americans. They set up the Asiatic Exclusion League in San Francisco in 1905. The league's members consisted of a wide range of individuals and organizations. In 1908, the league had approximately 100,000 members. The main body of the league was made up of labor unions (Takaki 201).

The purpose of the league was to prevent the immigration of Japanese to the US. "Keeping California White" was their slogan. The members of the league felt that Japanese immigrants threatened their labor opportunities. They claimed that the Japanese were unassimilable to American culture. They believed that for the preservation of the Caucasian race upon American soil and for the protection of job opportunities for white laborers, they insisted that it be necessary to take all possible measures to prevent or minimize the immigration of Japanese to the US (Takaki 198–200).

The Asiatic Exclusion League took several extreme actions to oppress Japanese immigrants. For example, they penalized hiring Japanese workers. They demanded that the school board segregate Japanese students from white students. They boycotted Japanese businesses. The league lobbied political leaders to legally ban Japanese from having various rights such as naturalization, land possession, etc. (Takaki 201–203).

As a result of intense anti-Japanese activism, the 1920s saw anti-Japanese legal enactments. They first pressured the Japanese government to abolish picture marriage insisting that the system was uncivilized. The Japanese government had long worried about the intensifying anti-Japanese sentiments in California. With a purpose of sedating the anger of some white Americans and of protecting Japanese nationals from xenophobia, the Japanese government decided to stop issuing passports to picture brides in 1920 (*The Issei*, Ichioka 173).

On November 13, 1922, the US Supreme Court ruled against a Japanese immigrant Takao Ozawa, declaring that he was ineligible for citizenship because he belonged to the Mongolian race. Ozawa came to the US in 1894 to study. He graduated from University of California, and worked in Hawaii. He settled down in the US, and decided to apply for American citizenship in Hawaii. Yet, the US District Court for the Territory of Hawaii rejected his application in 1916. He brought his case to the Supreme Court but was denied citizenship eligibility (Takaki 208). This ban clearly showed the State's will that the Japanese were unassimilable aliens, and they could never be Americans no matter what.

Anti-Japanese Americans were not satisfied with the legal decisions mentioned above. They lobbied to the Congress to ban the entire immigration of Japanese to the US. One of these exclusionists, a journalist Valentine Stuart MacClatcy claimed to the Congress as follows:

> Of all races ineligible to citizenship, the Japanese are the least assimilable and the most dangerous to this country. With great pride of race, they have no idea of assimilating in the sense of amalgamation. They do not come to this country with any desire or any intent to lose their racial or national identity. They come here specifically and professedly for the purpose of colonizing and establishing here permanently Yamato race. They never cease to be Japanese. (Takaki 209)

As a result, the Congress passed the Immigration Act of 1924, which ended the immigration of all Asians mainly targeting Japanese to the US. Thus, The US made its attitude quite clearly known that the country was an enemy land for Japanese picture brides. How did they raise their children while surrounded by hostility?

MOTHERING ON ENEMY LAND

Japanese picture brides started their life in the US when anti-Japanese sentiments were very intense. Otsuka writes of the harassment Japanese immigrants went through as follows:

> Sometimes they drove by our farm shacks and sprayed our windows with buckshot, or set our chicken coops on fire. Sometimes they dynamited our packing sheds. Sometimes they burned down our fields just as they were beginning to ripen and we lost our entire earnings for that year. (36)

We can see that Japanese lives were exposed to danger. They asked for help to the police but white police officers did not dare to persecute peer white racists (36). As a result, in order to protect themselves from whites, Japanese immigrants "slept with [their] shoes on, and hatchets beside [their] beds, while [our] husbands sat by windows until dawn" (37).

Child Birth

Japanese picture brides quietly fought against xenophobia alongside their husbands. They worked hard, saved money, and bought land. Against the expectation of some whites that Japanese immigrants would run away from the US, they stayed, built houses, and gave birth to a new generation. Planting roots in the US would be the picture brides' quiet resistance to racism. Yet, the birth of the children in the US was not easy for them.

During the Meiji period of Japan, midwives usually assisted with childbirth, and new mothers went back to their maiden houses with their babies to recover (Ayukawa 111–112). They could physically and mentally relax under the care of their mothers, yet, in the US, childbirth was a totally different experience for them. Some picture brides were lucky enough to have Japanese midwives help with their childbirth in the US if they were available, but most delivered babies by themselves or with the help of their husbands. Otsuka describes the Japanese picture brides' delivery of babies.

> We gave birth under oak trees, in summer, in 113-degree heat. [. . .] We gave birth on remote farms in the Imperial Valley with the help of only our husbands, who had learned from The Housewife's Companion what to do. [. . .] We gave birth alone, in an apple orchard in Sebastipol, after searching for firewood one unusually warm autumn morning high up in the hills. I cut her navel string with my knife and carried her in my arms. (55)

From the moment the picture brides became mothers, they could not expect any help, and became isolated mothers.

Child Rearing

With the birth of babies, the picture brides were busier than before and busier than men. Evelyn Nakano Glenn explains why the picture brides' life was busier than the men.

> The men worked long hours, often at physically exhausting jobs, but the women's days were longer. Their work began before other members of the household arose with the preparation of the morning meal, and ended after others were relaxing with the clean-up following the evening meal. (209)

Most Japanese picture brides had to work both inside and outside of the house. They worked paid jobs such as farming or as housemaid. They were responsible for their house chores. Otsuka writes of how Japanese picture brides raised their children while working.

> We laid them down gently, in ditches and furrows and wicker baskets beneath the trees. We left them lying naked, atop blankets, on woven straw mats at the edges of the fields. We placed them in wooden apple boxes and nursed them every time we finished hoeing a row of beans. (61)

If they were in Japan, children were usually taken care of by their grandmothers so mothers could concentrate on working (Ayukawa 112). Yet in the US where Japanese picture brides were displaced from their motherland, and had no one to ask for help, they had to take care of children by themselves while working. The birth of children thus increased Japanese picture brides' labor. Did their husbands help them? Otsuka writes,

> Usually, our husbands had nothing to do with them. They never changed a single diaper. They never washed a dirty dish. They never touched a broom. In the evening, no matter how tired we were when we came in from the fields, they sat down and read the paper while we cooked dinner for the children and stayed up washing and mending piles of clothes until late. They never let us go sleep before them. They never let us rise after the sun. You'll set a bad example for the children. They never gave us even five minutes of rest. (63)

Husbands were not only reluctant to taking care of their own children and house chores but also had no consideration for the well-being of their wives. How could Japanese picture brides bear that life? It is because Japan used to have a patriarchal system called the *ie*, which means house. This system, which put the patriarch in the center of the family and gave all rights to the patriarch, had long existed in Japan, and the Meiji government legalized the system in 1898. Gentaro Oido explains the women's role under the *ie* system in the Meiji period. He contends, "Married women have no place to live and perform their duties other than their husbands' house. Women marry, work, and deliver children only for the *ie*. Women's duties are all for the preservation of the *ie*" (206–207). In short, Japanese women were forced to exist not for themselves but for others in the past. Japanese women were socialized to sacrifice themselves.

Hideko Maruoka analyzed the labor of farming women, and claims that "farming women worked as hard as men, but they had no status" (68–69). Many Japanese women in the Meiji era including the picture brides incorporated the *ie* ideology, and accepted their non-status existence in the family. Japanese men also incorporated the *ie* ideology, and demanded the total obedience of wives as a patriarch of the household. This system justified the obedience of women under the name of *ryosai kenbo*, which literally means good wife and wise mother (Koyama 482). Even if Japanese women felt it unfair that they alone had to accept the non-status in the *ie* system, they were convinced that the obedience made them a good wife and wise mother.

Japanese picture brides brought the *ie* and *ryosai kenbo* ideology to the US with them. For the preservation of the *ie*, the picture brides were demanded to sacrifice themselves for their husbands and children and they accepted that lot believing that self-sacrifice made them a good wife and wise mother.

Japanese picture brides worked selflessly for the family. Dennis Ogawa explains the *ryosai kenbo* mentality of the picture brides who devoted themselves to the children as follows:

> [They were] sustained by the belief that for the sake of children, kodomo no tameni. [. . .] If one worked hard, saved, sacrificed, and gathered strength from one's cultural roots, then material, social, and spiritual well-being would be possible for the coming generation. (xxii)

Japanese picture brides could bear the hardships of life in the US with the hope for their children. *Buddha in the Attic* describes the selflessness of picture brides and given an impression that they did not have free will. Yet, some scholars give us different views on Japanese picture brides. For example, Ikumi Yanagisako researched the oral history of picture brides, and concluded that they were not enslaved to their family. While admitting the harshness of labor, Yanagisako claims that picture brides acquired new farming skills such as using machines in the US, and worked as a partner to their husbands not a subservient worker to them (78). Yanagisako points out that some picture brides even saved their own money from their labor (78). They would enjoy some independence and control of their labor.

Their selfless child rearing is also given another interpretation. Glenn writes that "sacrifice and hard work for the sake of children enhanced issei women's self-esteem and also their reputation in the community" (217). If the Nisei children excelled at school, picture brides were praised for their successful mothering in the community. In fact, the presence of their children legally improved the lives of Japanese immigrants.

As stated, the Asiatic Exclusion League's lobbying resulted in the passing of the Alien Land Act of 1913. They pressured California state legislature to pass the Act, which did not allow Japanese to possess land, and to settle down in the US. The implementation of the Act invited protests from the Japanese government. The government sent a letter to the US Secretary of State. The letter said that the Act was jeopardizing the friendly relationship between Japan and the US, and depriving Japanese immigrants of their livelihood. Despite the protest, the Act was practiced in California. An article of the Act stated that it prohibited aliens ineligible for citizenship from owning land, and from leasing land for more than three years. It did not explicitly refer to Japanese, but since Japanese immigrants were not eligible for naturalization, it was obvious that the Act targeted Japanese immigrants. Many Japanese immigrants were engaged in agriculture in the US, so the Act was a big blow to them because the Act took away their means of living (Want 144).

Yet, the Act actually had a loophole. The Act banned the Japanese from purchasing and leasing land, but it was possible for the US-born children of Japanese picture brides, to purchase and lease land as a proxy for their parents, and the parents could use the land as the caretakers of their children. This loophole was possible because of the US Nationality Law which allows US-born children to be American citizens by birth. Since the Nisei were Americans, the Act could not prohibit the Nisei from leasing and purchasing land (Ferguson 70).

The children were thus the source of hope for Japanese picture brides in the US. They had the legal rights Japanese picture brides were not entitled to. With children, the picture brides could improve their life on enemy land. Otsuka writes of the picture brides' jubilation on having the Nisei children. They say, "We gave birth to babies that were American citizens and in whose names we could finally lease land" (58). The picture brides worked harder for the sake of children. Yet, when children grew, another problem came up.

The Emergence of Cultural Conflicts

The Nisei children were taught English and American ways of thinking at school, and they were more comfortable communicating in English language and living an American life style. As a result, language and culture became the barrier between the picture brides and their children as the children grew. Otsuka writes that the picture brides felt cold attitudes from their children. She writes, "[The children] were ashamed of us. Our floppy straw hats and threadbare clothes. Our heavy accents. Every sing oh righ [sic]? Our cracked, callused palms. . . . They wanted different and better mothers who did not look so worn out" (75). Japanese picture brides sacrificed for their children. They raised their children very hard when they did not have any support from anyone. Yet, their efforts seem to end in the alienation from their own children.

Another issue that made Japanese picture brides worry about their children was the never-ceasing racial discrimination against the Japanese and poverty. As noted, legal measures were practiced one after another to restrict the rights of the Japanese. These legal recourses justified racial hatred and discrimination against the Japanese. Just being Japanese made even Nisei children a target of racial intolerance in the US. The legal measures put many Japanese into financial difficulties. One Nisei child told her mother that "She wished she's never been born" (Otsuka 65) because of poverty and social exclusion. Upon hearing the child confession, the mother says, "We wondered if we had done the right thing, bringing them into this world. Not once did we ever have the money to buy them a single toy" (65). Japanese picture brides might feel that they failed to give their children any material and social happiness. Because of their Japanese roots, their Nisei children's future might be hampered by many obstacles due to the spreading anti-Japanese sentiments. As a result, the Nisei children were quiet students at school.

> At school they sat in the back of the classroom in their homemade clothes with the Mexicans and spoke in timid, flattering voices. They never raised their hands. They never smiled. At recess they huddled together in a corner of the school yard and whispered among themselves in their secret, shameful language. (Otsuka 74)

Yet, being quiet students at school does not mean that they were academically inferior. Some picture brides did not stop encouraging their children to study. Otsuka writes that Japanese picture brides told their children, "study hard. Be patient. Whatever you do, don't end up like me" (72). They knew that education could give their children a better life, which picture brides could never achieve. Their strong belief in education may derive from a Meiji era's work ethics called *risshin shusse*, which means success in career and life. Atsushi Kadowaki explains that *risshin shusse* work ethics encouraged the Japanese to achieve upward social and economic mobility through education. By studying and working hard, people could gain social position, wealth, and prestige, and to acquire admiration (222–223).

Japanese picture brides may have believed that if their children studied hard and spoke perfect English, white Americans, who were of a higher social status, would accept their children, and the US would finish being an enemy land for their children. Some Nisei children incorporated the *risshin shusse* work ethics their mothers instilled in their minds. Takaki introduces a comment by a Nisei woman. "We Nisei were told over and over about the importance of school and education—how knowledge in one's mind could never be taken away and that learning could be the ladder toward success and security and equality" (217). Responding to the mother's encouragement, some Nisei did well at school. Otsuka writes, "some of them developed unusually good vocabularies and became the best students in their class" (76). Although some children felt linguistic and cultural conflicts between themselves and parents, others incorporated Japanese ideologies from their mothers, and strove to have a better life.

Incarceration

Despite their efforts to achieve a better life for the sake of children, the picture brides faced a harsher reality when the Japanese military attacked Pearl Harbor on December 7, 1941. It was the time when many Nisei started college. *The Buddha in the Attic* ends with a chapter titled "A Disappearance." It is a chapter on the scene of the Japanese American incarceration. Approximately 120,000 Japanese Americans disappeared from the West Coast of America.

Upon the attack, Lieutenant General John DeWitt wrote to Secretary of War Henry Stimson about the military necessity to remove Japanese Americans from California. He wrote, "The Japanese race is an enemy race and while many second and third generation Japanese born on United States soil, possessed of United States citizenship, have Americanized, the racial stains are undiluted" (Kitano 391). Against DeWitt, Curtis Munson, who was commissioned as a special representative of the State Department reported to President Franklin Roosevelt that Japanese Americans were loyal to the US, and there was no need to incarcerate them (Kitano 386). Yet, the President listened to DeWitt, and issued Executive Order 9066, and incarcerated Japanese Americans as the government supported De Witt's view to regard Japanese Americans as enemy aliens (386).

The incarceration deprived of all the property and investment the Japanese picture brides had accumulated for years. They were again thrown into the pit of American society. They were incarcerated till the end of World War II in 1945. Yet, it was their Nisei children who restored the mother's property and dignity by serving in the military and sacrificing their lives for the country.

The Nisei were originally denied serving the military due to their enemy alien status, yet as the war progressed, the US government needed more soldiers. They admitted the Nisei to military service on the condition that the Nisei were limited to their own battle unit. The 442nd Regimental Combat Team (the 442nd RCT) was created. They were sent to some of the most intense battle grounds in Europe. Their most difficult mission was to rescue the 1st Battalion of the 141st Regiment in France. The battalion consisted of 211 soldiers from Texas who were surrounded by German soldiers. The 442nd RC was ordered to rescue the battalion, and succeeded with the loss of more than 200 lives and more than 600 wounded. Many members of the 442nd RCT were awarded the Purple Hearts and became the most decorated unit in the history of the US military (Grubb 392–394).

The bravery of the 442nd RCT impressed many Americans. President Harry Truman complimented the 442nd RCT when they returned to the US in his message on July 15, 1946. "I think it was my predecessor who said that Americanism is not a matter of race or creed, it is a matter of the heart. . . You fought not only the enemy, but you fought prejudice—and you have won" (Nisei Veterans Legacy). Truman's message officially eradicated the disgrace of Japanese Americans as enemy aliens, and they were wholeheartedly accepted by Americans as their peers for the first time. William Petersen, a sociologist, even wrote an article "Success Story, Japanese American Style" in 1966. He lauded the success of Japanese Americans despite their hardships such as the incarceration during World War II, and attributed their success to the Japanese cultural mores of hard work and strong family ties, and their belief in education (38). His article spread the Asian American stereotype as a model minority. The Nisei climbed the social ladder from enemy aliens to the model minority. The picture brides' efforts to educate their children to be successful in American society may appear rewarded. Yet, the stereotype is criticized by contemporary Asian Americans. For example, Kim Park Nelson criticized the model minority stereotype as follows.

> [Model minority stereotypes] often described as positive stereotypes, are ultimately harmful to Asian Americans; the stereotype of Asian Americans as naturally high achieving prevents high achieving Asian Americans from getting credit for their work; instead, they are viewed as average performers within a population that is expected to excel. (128)

Were the picture brides' efforts to educate their children detrimental to the present Asian American community? It is true that there are some Asian Americans who feel uncomfortable with the model minority stereotype, yet it is this mentality that helped Japanese Americans from the devastation of wartime incarceration. Being the model minority was a way of survival, which the picture brides bestowed on their Nisei children.

CONCLUSION

This article intends to shed light on Japanese picture brides as an example of forgotten migrant mothers in American history. They were discriminated against in the US as unassimilable enemy aliens. They were not allowed to have access to any American resources. Their mothering strategies were as a result to stick to Japanese ideologies of the Meiji era such as *ie*, *ryosai kenbo*, and *risshin shusse*. To be a good mother, they worked hard for the well-being of the household, and encouraged their children to study hard so they could succeed in the US. Their obedience to the Japanese ideologies sometimes caused conflicts between themselves and their children. Yet, these age-old Meiji Japanese ideologies would support the picture brides while they bore their painful life in the US, and enable the Nisei children to succeed in American society.

Migrant mothers exist all over the world, and they contrive their own unique mothering strategies in new land so they could ensure the well-being of their children. Research on the mothering of migrant women is still scarce but knowing more about the strength and wisdom of migrant mothers will open up a new perspective to the migration scholarship.

WORKS CITED

Ayukawa, Midge. "Good Wives and Wise Mothers: Japanese Picture Brides in Early Twentieth-Century British Columbia." *BC Studies*, Spring/Summer, 1995, pp. 103–118.

Ferguson, Edwin. "The California Alien Land Law and the Fourteenth Amendment." *California Law Review*, Vol. 35, No. 1, 1947, pp. 61–90.

Glenn, Evelyn Nakano. *Issei, Nisei, War Bride: Three Generations of Japanese American Women in Domestic Service*. Temple UP, 1986.

Grubb, Abbie. "442nd Regimental Combat Team." *Asian American Society: An Encyclopedia*, edited by Mary Yu Danico, Sage, 2014, pp. 392–394.

Ichioka, Yuji. "Amerika Nadeshiko: Japanese Immigrant Women in the United States, 1900-1924." *Pacific Historical Review*, Vol. 49, No. 2, May 1980, pp. 339–357.

———. *The Issei: The World of the First Generation Japanese Immigrants 1885–1924*. New York: Free Press, 1988.

Kadowaki, Atushi. "Nihonteki Risshin Shusse no Imi Hensen" [Process of Changes in the Conception Risehin-Shusse in Meiji Japan]. *Kyoiku Shakaigaku Kenkyuu*, No. 24, 1969, pp. 222–223.

Koyama, Shizuko. "Ryosai Kenbo [Good Wife Wise Mother]." *Joseigaku Jiten [An Encyclopedia of Gender Studies]*, edited by Teruko Inoue. Tokyo: Iwanami, 2002, pp. 481–482.

Lee, Catherine. "Prostitutes and Picture Brides: Chinese and Japanese Immigration, Settlement, and American Nation-Building, 1870-1920." *Center for Comparative Immigration Studies*, 2003, pp. 1–47.

Maruoka, Hideko. *Nihon Noson Fujin Mondai [Problems of Japanese Farming Women]*. Domes, 1980.

Maxey, Ruth. "The Rise of the "We" Narrator in Modern American Fiction." *European Journal of American Studies*, Summer 2015, pp. 1–15.

Nelson, Kim Park. *Invisible Asians: Korean American Adoptees, Asian American Experiences, and Racial Exceptionalism*. Routledge, 2016.

Nisei Veterans Legacy. "442nd Awards, Return to Hawaii." https://www.nvlchawaii.org/442nd-awards-return-hawaii. Accessed February 6, 2020.

Ogawa, Dennis. *Kodomo No Tame Ni For the Sake of Children: The Japanese American Experience in Hawaii*. University of Hawaii, 1978.

Oida, Gentaro. *Nihon Josei Hattatsushi [The History of Women Development in Japan]*. Seikyo, 1934.

Otsuka, Julie. *The Buddha in the Attic*. Penguin, 2011.

Petersen, William. "Success Story, Japanese American Style." *The New York Times*, January 9, 1966, pp. 19–21, pp. 36–43.

Takaki, Ronald. *A History of Asian Americans: Strangers from a Different Shore*. Backbay, 1998.

Tanaka, Kei. "Japanese Picture Marriage and the Image of Immigrant Women in Early Twentieth-Century California." *The Japanese Journal of American Studies*, No. 15, 2004, pp. 115–138.

Yuhas, Alan. "Six Questions for Julie Otsuka." *Harper's Magazine*, 13 June 2012, http://harpers.org/blog/2012/06/six-questions-for-julie-otsuka/. Accessed December 10, 2019.

Yanagisawa, Ikumi. "Shasin Hanayome wa Otto no Dorei Datttanoka?: Shashin Hanayometachi no Katari wo Chushinni [Were Picture Brides the Slaves of their Husbands?: An Analysis of the Picture Brides' Narratives]." Shashin Hanayome Senso Hanayome no Tadotta Michi [*Crossing the Ocean: A New Look at the History of Japanese Picture Brides and War Brides*], edited by Noriko Shimada, Akashi Shoten, 2009, pp. 46–85.

Want, Kaori Mori. "The Webb-Haney Act Passed by California State Legislature," *25 Events That Shaped Asian American History: An Encyclopedia of the American Mosaic*, edited by Lan Dong, Greenwood, 2019, pp. 140–155.

Chapter Eight

Guiding, Shaping, and Resisting

Refugee Mothers' Educational Strategies as They Navigate "Unsettlement"

Lucy Hunt

SETTING THE SCENE

Three women sit around a low children's school desk in a community center, beneath an old whiteboard held up with string: a mother and her teenage daughter, who fled Syria together and claimed asylum here in Greece; and myself, a British teacher and doctoral student volunteering for and studying the educational response for refugees.[1] Hala,[2] 15, pours cardamom coffee into our plastic cups while her mother, Safaa, rubs her eyes, frustrated. Safaa has been trying to get help with applying for scholarships for Hala, but is struggling to find support in her school. "Why don't they push the good refugee?" she complains, taking a sip of coffee. "I tell them she is smart, but the teachers do not listen. Nobody listen."

Safaa sighs. The last time I met her, her youngest son had burst into the room with his school backpack askew and cheeks pink from playing football outside. He had proudly shown his mother a letter from school, detailing his grades for the term. She had clapped her hands and squeezed his cheeks, congratulating him, before gesturing for him to show me, too: they were all As. He had asked his mother if he could go back outside, and she had agreed. "Yeia sas," he had said to me in Greek, using the polite form to say goodbye, as he had sped off around the corner.

INTRODUCTION

This chapter describes mothering strategies in a context of precarity—namely, the uncertain conditions associated with forced displacement in Greece—and specifically how mothers navigate these conditions in and through learning spaces. In doing so, it presents the (young) refugee mother as a figure of strength and resistance, in an attempt to disrupt (particularly current European) conceptions of what it means to be "young," "displaced" and/or a "mother." When combined, these facets of a woman's identity compound the perception of her as vulnerable. However, drawing from Vigh's concept of "social navigation," this chapter highlights the often-neglected stories of how, rather than being passive victims, mothers instead strategically navigate the challenges of displacement; and in particular, how educational outcomes and spaces become involved in this process. The aim is not to "give voice" to these women—as they have their own voices—but to share their perspectives, from my position as a teacher, doctoral student and outsider. While there is a growing body of research exploring refugee parents' involvement in education (e.g., Bergset; Sarikoudi and Apostolidou) and what it means to be a mother during (forced) migration and resettlement (e.g., Lenette; Levi), this work aims to contribute to a particular understanding of refugee mothers' relationships with education.

The chapter begins by presenting the precarious conditions in which forced migrants find themselves in Greece and the educational opportunities provided for this group by both the state and civil society. It then outlines the theoretical framework and methodology of the larger DPhil study, and the data from which this chapter draws, before presenting the mothering strategies observed during fieldwork in relation to education: such as legitimizing spaces for family members, shaping educational offers and resisting education due to issues of trust and understandings of displacement. It concludes by summarizing the commonalities among these strategies and the implications for those providing refugee education.

Refugees in Greece: A Country of "Unsettlement"

Since 2015, more than one million migrants have entered Greece (UNHCR, "Greece" 1). While in the early days of the refugee "crisis" many passed through on their way to northern and western Europe—a strategy facilitated by the Greek government—after the implementation of "migration management" strategies (such as border closures to the north, and the implementation of the so-called "EU-Turkey deal") tens of thousands became trapped in the country (Stathopoulou). Due to the high number of asylum applications to be processed, the refugee status determination process now takes years; meaning that for many young refugees, they will become "adult" before receiving their travel documents (AIDA). Of the 121,000 refugees currently in Greece, over a third are under the age of 18, and the vast majority are accompanied (UNHCR, "Fact Sheet," 1; UNICEF 1). Almost two thirds of the asylum seekers arriving in 2019 were women and children (Fernandes). While some girls arrive unaccompanied, most often it is teenage boys aged 14–17 who travel alone (EKKA 1). As it may be just one stop on their route to their intended country of "resettlement," Greece is often described as a "transit" country (e.g., Tsitselikis and Agelopoulos); however, here I will term it a country of "unsettlement." This is because for many, their asylum case remains unsettled, and their life is characterized by uncertainty and, often, relocation within the country—making it difficult to "settle." It is through this uncertainty, and competing social forces, that mothers are forced to navigate, with attention to both their family's everyday survival and long-term goals. As they do so, education becomes implicated in various ways.

Refugee Education in Greece

For refugee children, Greek schools are—theoretically—open for enrollment. They may join elementary or junior high school from the ages of 6–15 (both of which are compulsory for both refugee and Greek children) or senior high school from age 15 and beyond (Ministry of Education). Reception classes taught by substitute teachers are in place in schools in many Zones of Educational Priority (ZEPs), to prepare learners for a full program with host community peers in their second year. For adult refugees (i.e., over 18), formal options are limited: technical high schools may allow enrollments well beyond 18 in their evening "shifts," or there are Second Chance Schools—for those who have a elementary school completion certificate—which lead to an equivalent of the junior high school (*gymnasio*) certificate. Alternatively, they may engage in non-formal[3] (NFE) learning opportunities which are widely available across the country for all ages—mostly run by international or local non-governmental organisations (NGOs)—which predominantly constitute Greek and English language classes (OECD). These may be what I will call here "peri-formal" opportunities, designed to support and encourage participation in formal schooling, or more distinctly non-formal activities designed to build specific skills or address psychosocial issues, such as jewelry-making courses or drama workshops. Some of these offers specifically target women or (young) mothers, combining accommodation, childcare support and other services alongside learning activities for themselves and their children (Eurochild and SOSCVI 67; Sirigos).

While official statistics suggest that half of all youth have enrolled in Greek schools, drop-out rates are high and attendance in both formal and non-formal education is inconsistent (Theirworld). Common reasons include the difficulty of studying secondary-level subjects in Greek; legal uncertainty; the costs and time spent reaching schools from camps; the belief that the stay in Greece is only temporary (meaning that there is no need to invest time, energy and much-needed money to attend courses where they may understand very little); and perceptions of the importance of (girls') education. As Sarikoudi and Apostolidou have found, parents can play an important role in guiding their children in this regard; often acting as educational agents and encouraging attendance, while also making learning decisions for themselves. This chapter builds on this work by contributing observations on the navigational and relational dynamics involved in this educational decision-making process.

Navigating Precarity: Strategies and Relationships

To counter popular media representations of refugees as passive victims of circumstance, an increasing body of research depicts the ways in which forced migrants navigate their way through and out of adversity; simultaneously negotiating everyday challenges and long-term planning towards what they perceive to be beneficial outcomes. This process of "motion within motion"—or the constant re-adaptation of praxis to "get by" in contexts of insecurity, where social formations are in flux—is encapsulated in Vigh's concept of "social navigation" ("Motion Squared"; "Youth Mobilisation"). As an analytical optic, it brings to light how migrants' "tactics" and movements are decided upon, realized and renegotiated in line with emerging opportunities, barriers and evaluations of the sociopolitical environment; requiring a flexible navigation of social relations and possible manipulation of rules. Other researchers have also applied this lens in research with refugees (e.g., Daniel et al.; Denov and Bryan), noting how its focus on deliberate and calculated decisions can contradict the image of the "powerless, passive, and/or pathological" migrant (Denov and Bryan 16).

Here, the optic of "social navigation" is used to analyze mothering practices; and as such, it necessarily positions women in relation to their children. However, relations beyond the family also come into play, making a relational approach to analyzing praxis more fitting. Daniel and colleagues (4) take a similar line. They cite recent research (Comstock et al.; Huijsmans et al.) which emphasizes the connections between actors, dimensions and forces, and the ways in which power and friction manifest and shape connections in the everyday life of networks; with attention to the influence of institutions and time. This chapter follows suit.

METHODOLOGY AND DATA

This chapter is based on data collected during ethnographic fieldwork undertaken in Thessaloniki, Northern Greece, between October 2019 and June 2020. During this time, I conducted individual and pair semi-structured interviews and participant observation as a volunteer teacher, teaching one to three times per week for three organizations (one of which had a women-only space) and observing one further program. This qualitative design was chosen to provide "thick description" (Geertz) of the everyday realities of a small sample of forced migrants in this context, as they decided to engage with or resist state or non-state educational opportunities. Due to the nature of the sample size and design, the findings are not generalizable or representative, but offer themes for further exploration. In this chapter, I focus on participants' references to "mothering," or the role of motherhood in their educational decision-making. Additional data comes from my field notes and experiences of everyday life as a volunteer teacher; particularly in the women-only space of a community center. All data was entered into NVivo and coded according to the three-step "constant comparison" process (Strauss and Corbin).

Participants in the wider DPhil project were recruited via convenience and snowball sampling. They were 12 refugee and asylum-seeking youth (aged 15–25, and arriving in Greece during or since the peak of the "refugee crisis" in 2015) and 38 educational stakeholders with first-hand knowledge of their experiences: such as parents, teachers, educational assistants, coordinators, social workers, "caretakers"[4] and cultural mediators. Young participants (under 18) were interviewed in pairs while in-country, while interviews with stakeholders and youth aged 18+ were mostly conducted individually—apart from where they requested a joint interview. As COVID-19 caused all in-person educational activities to be suspended from March 2020, all interviews and teaching activities between March and June 2020 took place online via Zoom, Skype, WhatsApp or Viber. To protect the identity of participants, all names presented here are pseudonyms and I avoid giving many details on their background or the names of organizations or centers. Ethical approval for the study was granted by the Social Sciences and Humanities Interdivisional Research Ethics Committee at the University of Oxford.

MOTHERS' EDUCATIONAL STRATEGIES

Negotiating Access to "Legitimate" Learning Spaces

For Safaa, the lady with whom we began this chapter, the continuation of her children's education was one of her first concerns after the family's arrival in Greece. She had persuaded the family's social worker to accompany her to the school and translate, and in the end was successful in registering all three of her children. She proudly described being the mother of the "first" refugees in Greek schools, despite the fact that no organizations were yet prepared or well placed to assist families in the enrollment process—and indeed, principals had also been unaware of how to respond to her request. After I had known her for some months, she also enlisted my help with university scholarship applications: Did I know anything about the process? Did I know someone who she could talk to about it?

For other mothers of older youth, their children's access to education raised concerns relating to trust and protection. With a government which hosts new arrivals on the Aegean islands in inhumane conditions (RRE), it is natural that families would be hesitant to send their children alone to be "educated" in a state institution—especially if they have no concept of what "schooling" means in the European context. To counter this and enable their daughters to participate in some form of learning, some mothers "legitimised" non-formal learning spaces for the family before allowing them to attend alone. Alex, an NFE coordinator, recalled how when girls wanted to join their workshops, "the first week her mother was coming with her . . . to see who we are and what we are doing." This is one way in which mothers act as agents for their children's education: ensuring that they and their reputation will be safe in this space, rather than resisting their participation outright.

Once women begin engaging in alternative learning spaces themselves—particularly when women-only—they can become sites of ownership and privacy away from the family. As Melissa, the coordinator of the women-only space suggested, they are a "legitimate" space to spend time—especially as studying languages can be seen as productive and adding value to the family, as well as being known to husbands and fathers and therefore "trusted." Many members encouraged family members to come: daughters brought mothers, and mothers brought daughters. In this way, they gave the learning space "validation" for one another and the rest of the family, as Melissa termed it. "When there's another family member that comes along, it's almost like a bit more awareness—you know what's going on there, and it's not so secretive. It's more widely accepted."

Engaging in and Shaping Accessible Opportunities

Especially if alone, young mothers I met—who were also occasionally teenagers—sought out educational opportunities as a means of survival; with Greek and English language skills being the priority, to find employment and communicate with doctors and teachers. However, with a limited support network to care for their child, support with childcare was a necessity. As the public system does not cater for such students, many young refugee women joined our non-formal activities in the women-only space of the community center, as these practical obstacles were removed. Alexandra, a teacher in a non-formal setting, explained: "If they don't have anybody to leave their child, for even a couple of hours to attend the lesson, or to attend school—it's really difficult. I think it's the most difficult target group to welcome them to a lesson. Just for practical reasons, not for any other reason." When children are cared for and/or welcomed in NFE spaces, this can provide an option to overcome such obstacles. Alexandra shared her surprise that in her non-formal program, "I had one mother that she was breastfeeding in my class!" This would not be possible in the formal context in Greece, as it currently stands. This was recognized by coordinators of NFE programs I spoke to, who noted that it was essential to provide such support if the space was going to be equitably accessible to all young women.

As such an accessible option, the entrance and reception to our women-only space were commonly crowded with pushchairs and small children in the mornings, and babies would bounce on laps and wait to be cared for by volunteer staff as young mothers took their lessons. Before a volunteer could be found for the "baby room," women would sit around the long table in the classroom with children on their laps, gurgling, or at a smaller table to the side with coloring pens and paper. They would for the most part chat quietly, or mimic my emphatic pronunciation—or sometimes chase one another or play until their mothers shushed them or took them outside. The other ladies were for the most part supportive, showing solidarity and understanding, with unfaltering attentiveness to the lesson and dedication to learn. On various occasions, young mothers requested homework material when they could not come due to their children's medical appointments or school enrollment. This demonstrates how mothers not only directly negotiate their child's access to school, but also seek out learning opportunities for *themselves* as a means of vicariously benefiting their children's education and other spheres of their lives; as also found by Sarikoudi and Apostolidou.

Beyond legitimizing and engaging in these spaces, the mothers I met also took steps to adapt the educational offer to better fit their needs—which, most often, were to communicate with educational and health care staff to benefit their children. It was common, when I first started, to have ladies telling me: "Teacher, we do not want grammar. No worksheets. We need how to go to the doctor, how to ask for things. To talk to my children's teacher. For every day." This strategy—practiced as a collective act—was confirmed by Alexandra, whose organization had originally established two educational offers: a language course for youth, aged 16–24, and one for older adults. She remembered how mothers shaped these groupings to enable them to share childcare responsibilities with their partners:

> A lot of girls they were young mothers. We had a session that it was for youth, and another slot for adults. So what happened after one or two months . . . they made it in a way that it was gender "slots" and not age slots, and so it became a separate zone—because also a lot of these couples, they have younger children, so one of them should stay at home, to attend them.

Resisting Schooling: Norms and Needs

Some mothers—whether in Greece, at home or in the "destination" country—resisted their children's participation in education due to gendered expectations of youth and understandings of the family's needs during "unsettlement." As Lydia, a coordinator, noted, mothers can resist their son's education as she "thinks that her 18-year-old son is a grown man, that should get married and find a job and support the rest of the family"—especially due to the necessity of an income in a context of financial precarity. In some cases, mothers encouraged their sons to undertake non-formal language classes to find employment, rather than studying secondary-level academic subjects in Greek public schools. Others needed to delegate family responsibilities to their daughters, such as caring for their infant siblings, meaning that they could not attend educational activities either. Elena, a teacher in a camp setting, described how 10-year-old girls would come to her "with babies in hand," saying that they could not come because their mother had gone to the market. She understood their mothers's "very valid arguments," as they told her "'I cannot leave the baby alone. Where can I leave the baby?' And that's it."

In a similar vein to Lenette's findings ("Mistrust"), I was told that mothers' resistance to their daughters' participation in education could also be related to concerns about community expectations and stigma. Katerina, a teacher, explained the dynamics of living in camps with many people from the same community:

> Community expectations sometimes are important, especially when we consider gender as well. Because if, for example, you are a mum, and you have a girl,

and you might be ready to invest on her education—if the community sees that you send your child to the school, then they're gonna think that this kid is not appropriate for their boys, or for her to make a family.

Therefore, in this case, their resistance to education is grounded in concerns about a successful future; with "success" defined according to the family and/or community's cultural norms. In some cases, this successful future is expected to be elsewhere in Europe, due to the deep-rooted belief and hope that they will receive travel documents or family reunification approvals before long (despite that fact that these processes are now taking years to complete, and may not be successful). As such, some mothers (both in Greece and abroad) instructed their children not to waste their time and energy on education at all—particularly in Greek—when they will shortly leave. This is also based on a concern for their well-being, in their desire to avoid their children expending the psychological effort of studying in a new language before starting all over again elsewhere.

Being a "Mother-Teacher": Managing Cultural Distance

Even when mothers supported their children in their new forms of learning, on occasions at the community center I could see intergenerational distances and disagreements growing as a result of their participation in the learning process and new peer groups. Siblings argued among themselves in fluent Greek, to avoid being understood by their mothers, with the latter complaining that she could not keep up; and mothers were concerned when their teenage daughters asked to spend time with school friends in the afternoons or changed their appearance. Children, for their part—according to Nadia, a cultural mediator—may feel more comfortable telling teachers about their problems, as they feel "less distance between the teacher and them."

This topic of distance arose during a conversation with Irina, a teacher, who believed that being abroad makes it more difficult for mothers to "control" their children. She reflected:

> The children—even teenagers, the girls—many of them integrate fast. I mean that they are adapting this different style, this European style. It's something they like, I feel. And you notice also changes at their appearance. A lot. Especially for girls—you see for example in five, six months, teenagers are changing their appearance, because they are living in a different environment . . . Their parents are a little bit stressful about that . . . because they feel that their children are changing.

Safaa echoed how "everything is changing" when we were chatting about fashions one day. In reference to piercings, she said she sees "all this kind of stuff here"—but was not averse to it. As well as the parental efforts to "make community gatherings" in camps and "be all together" which Irina mentioned, Safaa too would manage this distance by organizing Arabic and culture classes for Syrian youth in the city—while women in the community centers and families with children in public schools shared recipes and arts from their countries during workshops and community events. This aligns with other research on the tensions (dis)continuity can cause within refugee families (e.g., Rousseau et al.), and how mothers may take on an instructional role to manage it (e.g., Sarikoudi and Apostolidou).

DISCUSSION: LEARNING TO NAVIGATE CONTINUITY AND RUPTURE

Navigating Displacement Time

For mothers who studied or guided their children into education, learning was seen as having instrumental benefits: both immediately, in the short-term, and for the child or young person's imagined future. The immediate benefits included the opportunity for contact with (Greek or international) support staff in non-formal spaces who could provide assistance with practical tasks; the chance to develop a wider support network for themselves, to replace that which was lost as a result of flight; and having somewhere which was considered a "legitimate" space to spend time. When mothers took courses themselves, this allowed them to develop their own skills (and to vicariously benefit their children), as well as carving out a space in the city where they felt welcome and had ownership. All of these factors promoted their own ability to practice care as a mother and guide youth on a more stable path. In terms of longer-term benefits, these were perceived to be a stronger asylum application (as it demonstrated a willingness to integrate); the chance to continue along the educational path their children had started in their home country; and the opportunity to develop skills and knowledge to find work to support the family in Greece, at "home" or in the eventual country of resettlement. For mothers who resisted their children's education—whether they were with them in Greece or not—education also played into their navigation of displacement "time." In their efforts to keep their children safe for the time that they were in a country they perhaps did not trust, and to preserve their reputation within their community, some mothers refused to allow their children to partake in (particularly formal) education.

Navigating Culture and Identity

As well as mothering through issues of temporality (i.e., not knowing if or when the family or child will leave Greece), the strategies described above show how mothers were also dealing with issues of cultural continuity and ruptures within the family. As Levi also found, one of the biggest challenges for displaced mothers—or in the Greek context, also for transnational mothers of displaced youth—is the growing symbolic distance between her and her child. This is not to say that mothers' own identities and attitudes remain static; but rather, that they are negotiating their own changing ideas and practice of motherhood alongside a desire to maintain stability for their children. (Indeed, some children influenced their mothers too: by bringing them to lessons, encouraging them to try new things and guiding them into and through the new society.) These changes in mothers' identities became apparent as they mentioned enjoying going to school for the first time (even if only a weekly language lesson at a community center) after not being able to do so in their home countries, while simultaneously organizing Arabic lessons or community meetings for their increasingly (symbolically) distant children. While these intergenerational divides inevitably exist around the world and across all populations, it is possible to see how the distance grows further and faster when children are socialized into a new, potentially culturally distant society through the medium of the school. The longer they remain outside of their home country, this distance may grow; requiring a constant renegotiation of the practice of mothering.

Navigating (via) Relationships

New social networks were prominent in the strategies of mothers I met, as both a source of support and of possible conflict. Overall, the ladies demonstrated how mothering can be a collective act, as they drew from the support of social workers, educators and other staff, volunteers and mothers to assist them with various tasks for their children's education; while struggling to re-establish a wider, more stable and more trusted support network in an unfamiliar setting. Here, accessible non-formal learning spaces provided an essential service. Young mothers could find childcare or other social support—from trained staff and fellow members from a variety of backgrounds—and in women-only spaces, they could socialize and share their culture and skills in cooking, tailoring or crafts. They could, and would, come to staff with a variety of requests: regarding everything from their physical and mental health needs to filling out forms and calling their children's schools to translate messages. As such, these spaces became much more than learning sites: as the posters around one center attested, it had become a "family" and a place of "solidarity," and thus an important "space of encounter" (Valentine) for "meaningful contacts" (Mayblin et al.) between women who had discovered unexpected commonalities.

However, this is not to say that new relationships were inherently supportive—indeed, some mothers would share their disagreements with peers or staff with me—but rather that they *can* be employed as a means of support. Lenette reminds us that while there is an assumption in migration studies that "stronger networks equate to less vulnerability" (also of refugee mothers, in her case), they too involve power relations which can have negative impacts; such as ostracizing single mothers or creating "a minority inside a minority" ("Mistrust" 5). Similarly, Willmann Robleda described how social networks had both positive and negative effects on the refugee women she interviewed. This highlights both the heterogeneity of refugee and migrant populations and confirms how cities can become sites of "overlapping displacements," in which the "hosts" may be other migrants (Fiddian-Qasmiyeh); as well as what Vigh ("Youth Mobilisation" 155) described as the "diffuse and unclear" dynamics of power. Both Lenette and Willmann Robleda note how relationships outside of the refugee or national community—i.e., "bridging" social capital, rather than "bonding," to use Putnam's terms—can be more trusting and valued. Throughout my time in different learning spaces, I witnessed how both forms were valuable, and often for different reasons: whether for socializing, childcare, providing translations at school, teaching a particular skill or simply having a friend with whom they could discuss the challenges of "displacement mothering" in their mother tongue.

CONCLUSION

Drawing from Vigh's concept of "social navigation," this chapter has attempted to describe how education is implicated in refugee mothers' navigation of "unsettlement" in Greece. Their strategies involved engaging in or resisting various forms of education and learning space as a way of managing temporal, cultural and social (dis)continuity and rupture. Overall, the findings above align with other accounts of refugee women's educational agency, which have documented how women have individually and collectively "created and actioned opportunities for resistance or change" to overcome "social, political, gendered and familial constraints"; in line with the Foucauldian notion that while the parameters of the "game" are set, various moves are still possible (McPherson 128). However, further research is needed to better understand what it means to "mother" in contexts of forced displacement specifically; as well as how a mother's identity shifts over time, and how mothering practices shape young people's experiences of life in the new society and their future plans. A key question for future studies, as originally posed by Levi (493), remains that of "determining how the host society can manage this difference in parenting ideology in a way that does not undermine or punish the parents." Beyond this, there is a need to help create "new stories of motherhood" (Kelly, Nel and Nolte 264) and promote good-quality family relationships which can support mothers as they navigate the experiences of forced migration.

For those who wish to learn themselves, these findings highlight the importance of accessible, welcoming and "valid" spaces for women and their daughters to learn; both for mothers to build their own knowledge and skills, and to indirectly benefit their children. Having social and practical support in this space—which can be as simple as a private area to conduct Skype calls, a social space to spend time with other women (such as a kitchen) and staff who can provide information—encourages and supports women to attend. Beyond this, the findings remind us that young refugees—who are expected and encouraged to attend public school by the international education community, in line with European and intergovernmental organizations' conceptions of adulthood trajectories—may be mothers themselves. It cannot be forgotten that for teenage mothers, the conditions can be especially difficult in Greece (Kotsiou et al. 4); and the amount of support provided must correspond with the extraordinary agency they demonstrate in their strategies to overcome these challenges and continue learning, for themselves and their children.

CLOSING

For Safaa, the mother with whom we began this chapter, having such support—alongside her own efforts—had been crucial. Thanks to help from willing social workers and understanding directors, all three of her children were in school and progressing well despite the difficulties of "unsettlement." However, as far as Safaa was concerned, her job was far from done. She was looking well into the future: researching prestigious university scholarships and pushing her children's teachers to recognize and nurture their talents. "If the refugee is the best in the school," she told me, "they need more care!" It became apparent that she would not rest until her children received it.

WORKS CITED

Asylum Information Database (AIDA) (2020). "Regular Procedure: Greece." www.asylumineurope.org/reports/country/greece/asylum-procedure/procedures/regular-procedure.

Bergset, Kari. "School Involvement: Refugee Parents' Narrated Contribution to Their Children's Education While Resettled in Norway." *Outlines - Critical Practice Studies*, vol. 18, no. 1, 2017, pp. 61–80.

Council of Europe (2019). "Key Terms: Formal, Non-Formal and Informal Learning. *COE*, www.coe.int/en/web/lang-migrants/formal-non-formal-and-informal-learning.

Daniel, Marguerite, et al. "Intergenerational Perspectives on Refugee Children and Youth's Adaptation to Life in Norway." *Population, Space and Place*, e2321, 2020.

Denov, Myriam, and Bryan, Catherine. "Tactical Maneuvering and Calculated Risks: Independent Child Migrants and the Complex Terrain of Flight." *New Directions for Child and Adolescent Development*, vol. 136, 2012, pp. 13–27.

EKKA (2020). "Situation Update: Unaccompanied Children (UAC) in Greece. 15 June 2020." www.unicef.org/eca/media/12776/file.

Eurochild and SOS Children's Villages International. "Let Children Be Children: Lessons from the Field on the Protection and Integration of Refugee and Migrant Children in Europe." 2017, www.sos-childrensvillages.org/getmedia/32eeb951-d731-48ae-86fb-96b9aff63f3e/Let-Children-be-Children_Case-studies-refugee-programmes.pdf.

Fernandes, Deepa. (July 22, 2019). "Mothers and Babies Lack Basic Needs in Greek Refugee Camps." *The World*, 22 July 2019, www.pri.org/stories/2019-07-22/mothers-and-babies-lack-basic-needs-greek-refugee-camps.

Fiddian-Qasmiyeh, Elena. "Refugee-Refugee Relations in Contexts of Overlapping Displacement." *International Journal of Urban and Regional Research*, 2015, www.ijurr.org/spotlight-on/the-urban-refugee-crisis-reflections-on-cities-citizenship-and-the-displaced/refugee-refugee-relations-in-contexts-of-overlapping-displacement/.

Geertz, Clifford. "Thick Description: Toward an Interpretive Theory of Culture." *The Interpretation of Cultures: Selected Essays*, edited by Clifford Geertz, Basic Books, 1973, pp. 3–30.

Kelly, Aisling, Nel, Pieter W., and Nolte, Lizette. "Negotiating Motherhood as a Refugee: Experiences of Loss, Love, Survival and Pain in the Context of Forced Migration." *European Journal of Psychotherapy & Counselling*, vol. 18, no. 3, 2016, pp. 252–270.

Kotsiou, Ourania S. et al. "Impact of the Refugee Crisis on the Greek Healthcare System: A Long Road to Ithaca." *International Journal of Environmental Research and Public Health*, vol. 15, no. 8, 2018, pp. 1–18.

Lenette, Caroline. "Mistrust and Refugee Women Who Are Lone Parents in Resettlement Contexts." *Qualitative Social Work: Research and Practice*, vol. 14, no. 1, 2013, pp. 119–134.

Lenette, Caroline. "I Am a Widow, Mother and Refugee": Narratives of Two Refugee Widows Resettled to Australia." *Journal of Refugee Studies*, vol. 27, no. 3, 2013, pp. 403–421.

Levi, Meredith. "Mothering in Transition: The Experiences of Sudanese Refugee Women Raising Teenagers in Australia." *Transcultural Psychiatry*, vol. 51, no. 4, 2014, pp. 479–498.

Mayblin, Lucy, et al. "Experimenting with Spaces of Encounter: Creative Interventions to Develop Meaningful Contact." *Geoforum*, no. 63, 2015, pp. 67–80.
McPherson, Melinda. *Refugee Women, Representation and Education: Creating a Discourse of Self-Authorship and Potential*. Abingdon, Routledge, 2015. Ministry of Education, Research and Religious Affairs. "Integration of Secondary Education Schools in the Educational Priority Areas (ZEP), Where Reception Classes Operate." 22 October 2018, www.minedu.gov.gr/news/37829-22-10-18-entaksi-sxolikon-monadon-defterovathmias-ekpaidefsis-stis-zones-ekpaideftikis-proter-aiotitas-zep-opou-dynantai-na-leitourgisoun-takseis-ypodoxis-t-y-i-zep.
Organisation for Economic Co-operation and Development (OECD) (2018). "Education For a Bright Future in Greece: Reviews of National Policies for Education." *OECD*, 2018, www.oecd-ilibrary.org/education/education-for-a-bright-future-in-greece_9789264298750-en;jsessionid=-znxYmtnw3SAmWco-mAijlTOK.ip-10-240-5-167.
Putnam, Robert. D. *Bowling Alone: The Collapse and Revival of American Community*. New York: Simon and Schuster, 2000.
Refugee Rights Europe. "No End in Sight: The Mistreatment of Asylum Seekers in Greece." 2019, refugee-rights.eu/wp-content/uploads/2019/08/RRE_NoEndInSight.pdf.
Rousseau, Cécile, et al. "Remaking Family Life: Strategies for Re-Establishing Continuity Among Congolese Refugees During the Family Reunification Process." *Social Science & Medicine*, vol. 59, no. 5, 2004, pp. 1095–1108.
Sarikoudi, Georgia, and Apostolidou, Anna. "Parenting and Education: The Example of Refugee Parents in Greece." *Refuge: Canada's Journal on Refugees*, vol. 36, no. 1, 2020, pp. 40–49.
Sirigos, Constantine S. "Looking Out for Children and Young Mothers in Greece in the Time of Coronavirus." *The National Herald*, 22 April 2020, www.thenationalherald.com/archive_coronavirus/arthro/looking_out_for_children_and_young_mothers_in_greece_in_the_time_of_coronavirus-266377/.
Stathopoulou, Theoni. "Surveying the Hard-to-Survey: Refugees and Unaccompanied Minors in Greece." *Humanitarianism and Mass Migration: Confronting the World Crisis*, edited by Marcelo M. Suárez-Orozco, University of California Press, 2019, pp. 165–185.
Strauss, Anselm, and Corbin, Juliet. *Basics of Qualitative Research: Techniques and Procedures for Developing Grounded Theory*. Thousand Oaks, SAGE, 1998.
Theirworld. "Finding Solutions to Greece's Refugee Education Crisis." 2020, reliefweb.int/sites/reliefweb.int/files/resources/RefugeeEducation-Report-240420-2.pdf.
Tsitselikis, Konstantinos, and Agelopoulos, Georgios. "Temporary Migrants and Refugees in Greece: Transformative Challenges." *Temporary Migration, Transformation and Development: Evidence from Europe and Asia*, edited by Pirkko Pitkänen et al., Routledge, 2019, pp. 121–142.
UNHCR. "Greece: Sea Arrivals Dashboard. September 2019." 2019, reliefweb.int/sites/reliefweb.int/files/resources/71691.pdf.

UNHCR. "Fact Sheet: Greece. 1-30 April 2020." 2020, reliefweb.int/sites/reliefweb.int/files/resources/77120.pdf.
UNICEF. "Refugee and Migrant Children in Greece: As of 31 May 2020." 2020, www.unicef.org/eca/media/12771/file.
Valentine, Gill. "Living with Difference: Reflections on Geographies of Encounter." *Progress in Human Geography*, vol. 32, no. 3, 2008, pp. 323–337.
Vigh, Henrik. "Motion Squared: A Second Look at the Concept of Social Navigation." *Anthropological Theory*, vol. 9, no. 4, 2009, pp. 419–438.
Vigh, Henrik. "Youth Mobilisation as Social Navigation: Reflections on the Concept of *Dubriagem*." *Cadernos de Estudos Africanos*, vol. 18/19, 2010, pp. 140–164.
Willmann Robleda, Zubia. "Re-Inventing Everyday Life in the Asylum Centre: Everyday Tactics Among Women Seeking Asylum in Norway." *Nordic Journal of Migration Research*, vol. 10, no. 2, 2020, pp. 82–95.

NOTES

1. In this chapter, the term "refugees" refers to both those who have gained refugee status and those who have applied for it (i.e., asylum seekers) for brevity and to align with the international literature, while recognizing that these legal categories do not define experience.

2. All names in this chapter are pseudonyms, to protect the identity of study participants.

3. The Council of Europe "Key terms" defines *formal* education as that which takes place in educational systems, follows a syllabus and involves assessments; while *non-formal* education (NFE) —despite also being organized and intentional—mostly takes place outside of the formal system and does not result in accreditation. It may be more focused on particular activities, skills or areas of knowledge and take place in community settings such as NGOs.

4. In Greece, "caretaker" is the name for a member of staff who provides pastoral care in a shelter for unaccompanied minors.

Chapter Nine

Iraqi Mothers, Diasporic Sons
Narrative Patterns of Identity and Belonging in Baghdad Twist

Lamees Al Ethari

In those moments as we locked the doors to our home in Baghdad for the last time, my mind was busy generating possible scenarios with border officers, things I may have forgotten to pack and my 3-year-old son sleeping on my shoulder. I never thought about the losses that this moment of migration would lead to, nor did I think about the sense of displacement that would come with it. In the pit of my stomach, I had that feeling of irrepressible loss. The 2003 American invasion had left us, like millions of other Iraqis, in a state of violent aftermath and instability that affected the lives of each and every one of us. So, at that moment of departure, if there was anything I actually focused on, it was that small fluttering light of hope that we would finally find a safe place for our young family.

    As a mother, my first instinct was to help my son learn English, adjust to daycare and find friends. It wasn't until a few months later, after we settled into life's routines, that I began to notice the little losses we did not anticipate. When Ameen refused to speak in Arabic for the first time, I laughed. He stood in the middle of the living room of our small apartment in his blue onesie pajamas, his arms crossed, his eyebrows tightly knitted, and stubbornly refused to talk to me in our native tongue. But as the weeks passed, he began to forget words in Arabic and then, as if suddenly, he altogether stopped speaking in our language. For me, losing his language meant losing his identity and his ability to connect to people back home; it meant losing his connection to Islam, as Arabic is the language of the Quran. For some, the fact that Ameen began to speak English after a few months of our arrival meant that he was smart and quick to learn. For me, it was the first loss that came with displacement. The connection between loss of language and loss of identity, although not clear at first, became vividly undeniable as he grew up in this new environment. Reflecting on Gloria Anzaldúa's statement, "Until I can take pride in my language, I cannot take pride in myself" (*Borderlands/ La Frontera: The New Mestiza* 59), I knew that the only way to ensure he maintained his Iraqi identity was to persist that he re-learn Arabic and teach him (constantly) about his culture, his religion and his history. Our bedtime stories, post-prayer chats and car rides became his only connection to home and to his Iraqiness.

Years later while working on my PhD at the University of Waterloo, an Iraqi friend sent me a link to the National Film Board documentary *Baghdad Twist* (2007) directed by Canadian filmmaker Joe Balass. The film was about a thirty-minute glimpse into the Iraqi Jewish experience through an interview between Balass and his mother Valentine. While the documentary uncovers this rarely explored part of Iraqi history, it is ultimately the conversations between mother and son in *Baghdad Twist* that frame the work. Through the production of the documentary and Joe's role as coaxer, he creates a space for his mother's narrative in which Valentine reclaims her identity as an Iraqi, an identity that was challenged and fragmented by subjugation, displacement and multiple migrations. However, Joe's connection to Iraq and his understanding of his Iraqi identity (his Iraqiness) is only established through his mother's stories, personal clips of home videos and photographs of life in Iraq.

I saw myself in Valentine's place, trying to share all my experiences of a past life with my son. However, the Jewish Iraqi experience was not something I studied at school back home, nor was it a topic that my family discussed. They would mention that Jewish tradesmen, shop owners and even popular government ministers had lived in Baghdad in the early twentieth century, but these fleeting references were so insignificant that they were never discussed in depth. I first learned that Jewish Iraqis were still living in our communities in grade eight. After the 1991 Gulf War, schools reopened to allow students to complete their second term and take their final exams. In the midst of the post-war chaos, my father was abruptly reassigned to a new position at work which meant that we had to move back to Baghdad from Samarra, where we had been living for over almost two years. For the next six months, we lived with my maternal aunt and her family in a two-bedroom house without electricity or running water,[1] waiting for an opening in government housing. My siblings and I were temporarily placed in nearby schools with my cousins as we began to adjust to the post-war conditions.

One of the most vivid memories I have of Khawla Bint Alazwar Girls Middle School was during chemistry class. After finishing up the lesson, the teacher moved closer to our desks and unexpectedly whispered, "We have two Jewish girls in the school!" I remember that moment after all these years because the excitement in her voice as she disclosed this "secret" made us all lean forward in our wooden desks, eager to hear more. I remember that moment because I had never met a Jewish Iraqi. I wondered briefly if they too were momentarily displaced because of the war but before I could ask, my classmate shouted eagerly, "Who are they? Can you point them out?" Over the hum of our excited chatter rising in the classroom, the teacher whispered, "I can't share that information. We are not allowed," she raised her eyebrows and motioned to us to stop talking. I wondered if her resistance to share their names was built on fear for their well-being. The Palestinian-Israeli conflict was one of the most talked about subjects in our classrooms, apart from Iraqi history and the Ba'ath regime.

The second time the topic of Iraqi Jews came up was after the 2003 American invasion. I sat playing on the floor with my son in our home in Baghdad, watching a reporter on television interview a small, elderly man dressed in a traditional Iraqi dishdasha. He was frail and quiet as the reporter gave a brief history of Jewish presence in Iraq and related that the number of Jews left in the country was a total of eighty people. I listened intently as she interviewed him about why he had remained after all his family members had left the country. He simply replied, "This is my home."

That statement echoed in my mind when I viewed *Baghdad Twist*. Valentine's narrative, while different in some ways, reiterated similar stories I had heard over the years about Iraqi women's experiences of trauma and displacement. There was a familiarity in her narrative that described an Iraqi mother's forced exile from her beloved home and her persistence to hold on to her Iraqiness. She followed the oral traditions of mothers passing that thread of identity found in the language, the culture, the experiences and the memories to her son in the diaspora. I was astounded by how the history of a group of people can be, almost completely, removed from the consciousness of a nation. To me being Iraqi was not limited to a specific faith, a race or a social class. I shed the preconceptions I grew up with; I became persistent in learning about this part of my country's history and culture that I knew almost nothing about.

The documentary led me to search for more North American narratives that dealt with Iraqi Jewish experiences.[2] At the time, I found few scholarly works (see Abbas Shiblak, Nissim Rejwan and Letal Levy) and almost no documentaries or narratives that discussed these experiences. I did, however, find the documentary *Forget Baghdad: Jews and Arabs-The Iraqi Connection* (Samir 2002), which deals with the Jewish diaspora from Iraq but focuses on Jewish migrations to Israel and the impacts of that movement on their sense of nationality and Iraqi identity as Arabs in Israel. *Forget Baghdad* also focuses mostly on Jewish Iraqi male writers and their perspectives on their deportation from Baghdad, without any substantial attention to the experiences of women during this era in Iraqi history (out of four or five authors, Ellah Shohat is the only female writer/scholar portrayed). *Baghdad Twist*, on the other hand, moves from the political to the personal as Valentine Balass reflects on her family's social life, her education and her marriage in addition to the incidents that led to their forced exile from Iraq. When I saw the work for the first time, I was reminded of all the photographs that my mother had of her own family growing up in Baghdad. The people in the documentary were familiar and their stories were relatable.

I also noticed a pattern in the way we both told our stories; the act of narrating identity is not haphazard or spontaneous. It is well thought of and follows an organized strategy, even when it is done subconsciously. As a migrant mother, I noticed that in the process of narrating my past life and experiences of and in the homeland to my son, two main concerns seemed to reoccur: the first is the fact that our children will never experience our culture and our sense of belonging in the same way because they have been, of course, displaced from it; the second is the need to present adequate reasoning behind our departure from that state of belonging to a place of *ghurba*[3] and disbelonging. In order to reflect on the depth of loss that immigrants experience, they have to first present a narrative of the past life, in the homeland, that is somewhat perfect and, especially for their children, relatable. This was an approach that I had used myself in my own memoir,[4] but also as a newly landed immigrant. The nostalgic images of home flooded my conversations with my son as I tried desperately to keep the faces of relatives and places alive in his young mind. I focused on positive memories that included family gatherings, feasts during Ramadan and exciting vacations to the north of Iraq. On our car rides around Kitchener, I would talk about my days spent at my grandfather's house, taking time to recall the smallest details like the scent of Ambar rice[5] in the early mornings or visits from fortune tellers who read our futures in the images created by the coffee grounds in our *fanajeen*.[6] Looking back, I feel that the image I created was somewhat fantastical and unrealistic in its exaggerated descriptions. Strategically, in the beginning, I left out all the images of fear and desolation that filled my memories during and after the war. Those stories would come later, after he reconnected to and related to those parts of home and my culture that I could not leave behind.

Going back to other life-writing texts by Iraqi women in the diaspora, I found that we seem to create patterns in the way we relate our narratives of home and migration. While some minor inconsistencies exist between narratives due to form and style, the basic construction of the narrative seems to be similar:

1. the pattern generally begins with the narrator reflecting on the loss of home and family by recreating nostalgic images of the homeland, idyllic pre-traumatic experiences, and a state of belonging;
2. then the narrator moves to establishing agency through invalidating stereotypical images and connecting to Western cultural norms (through dress, education, social status, etc.);
3. this is followed by relating the traumatic events that led to displacement (sometimes within the native country) and ultimately leaving the homeland;
4. which ends in some form of establishing/re-establishing identity, which can be a confirmation of the native self or a hybrid self that contains elements of the native and the diasporic self.

Valentine's narrative followed this pattern of storytelling, which allows her to reaffirm her Iraqiness and reconstruct her son's Iraqi identity and his connection to his native home.

However, in order to understand the context of *Baghdad Twist*, I needed to understand the history that led to her forced migration from Iraq and the importance that this documentary has in building on the narratives of Iraqi women in the diaspora.

DENATURALIZING THE JEWISH COMMUNITY IN IRAQ

In his work *Iraqi Jews: A History of the Mass Exodus* (2005), Abbas Shiblak states that Iraqi Jews were "indigenous to the country. . . . They were thoroughly Arabized in the sense that their tradition, superstitions, and language were Arabic" (34). Lital Levy, in his article "Self and the City: Literary Representations of Jewish Baghdad" (2006) adds that the Jewish population in Iraq "prided themselves on their deep roots in the region, on the enduring legacy of the Babylonian geonim, and on their economic and cultural contributions to the building of modern Iraq" (167). However, with the emergence of Zionism in the late nineteenth century and, later the establishment of the State of Israel, the Jewish communities were slowly rejected and evacuated from Iraq and other Arab countries. Although the migration of Jewish families from different Arab countries to the Holy Land began at least a century before the actual establishment of Israel (Rejwan *The Last Jews in Baghdad* 201), these migrations were, according to scholars like Rejwan and Shiblak, based on religious motives, rather than Zionist beliefs. The affiliation of the Jewish communities with their Arab identities led many to reject Zionist theory and even refuse, in countries like Iraq and Syria, the concept of a Jewish state. Nevertheless, the establishment of Israel and the strict Arab nationalist views led to the collapse of ties between Jewish Iraqis and other Iraqi citizens of different faiths.

The threat against Jewish Iraqis escalated as they became the target of angry mobs and rioters in what was named "Farhud" or the "Violent Dispossession" in June of 1941. Even after their open and persistent announcements of loyalty to Iraq, Jewish neighborhoods and businesses were attacked and an estimated 170–180 "Jews were killed and many more wounded, and even larger numbers of non-Jews, including rioters, security men and Muslims who came to the defense of their Jewish neighbors, were among the dead and injured" (Rejwan 222). The solidarity between the diverse Iraqi religious groups was not strong enough to keep Iraqi Jews in the country and their numbers began to dwindle during the mid-twentieth century. In addition, the passing of Law 1/1950, the denaturalization law, allowed for the cancellation of Iraqi citizenship of whoever wished to leave the country willingly and never return (Shiblak 104). Letal Levy explains:

> Between 1950 and 1951, some 120,000 Jews—approximately 90 percent of the Iraqi Jewish community—left for Israel and the West in the whole-scale emigration the emigrants referred to as the *tasqit*. The few thousand who remained would gradually trickle out of the country, most fleeing after the Ba'th-sponsored repression of 1969–71, leaving only some twenty or thirty Jews in the capital to witness the fall of Saddam Hussein's regime. (168)

The law was severe for people who had, for generations, been a part of the history of Iraq, however the choice to stay was no longer a safe option. Within the frame of this traumatic history, Valentine's testimony addresses experiences of denaturalization on a very personal level as she embodies the position of witness to the unraveling of her community.

PATTERNS OF NARRATING IDENTITY

Step 1—Reflecting on the Loss of Home and Family

Valentine's narrative begins with that initial reflection on being displaced from Iraq and re-rooted in Canada. With the opening of the documentary we see the images of airports, baggage belts and a Canadian city's somewhat empty streets covered in heavy layers of snow far from the crowded streets of her hometown, Baghdad. Arriving in winter, Valentine's first memories of Canada are connected to its drastically different weather in comparison to Iraq. The snow and all it symbolizes for her—exile, loneliness, and otherness—contrasts her first narrated memories of Baghdad, which are passionate and whimsical. Nadje Al-Ali explains that:

> Aside from the physical and material realities and hardships related to living in a strange place away from home, exile also refers to a state of mind and being. Received notions and ideas as well as set practices and traditions are unsettled when people are forced to leave the known and familiar behind. While many of those exiled face a "crisis of meaning," others fervently and desperately hold on to the past and everything they knew and did before. (*Iraqi Women* 17)

The clips from home videos and photographs show a young, elegant and carefree Valentine at her engagement party and wedding, surrounded by multiple generations of family members and close friends. She builds up the positive images of home to create an image that is intriguing for her son and the viewer. She goes on to speak about her own privileged childhood; the special treatment she received because she was the only girl in the family; and focuses on her own mother's attention to dressing her in expensive clothing made by the best dressmakers in Baghdad. These reflections on the positive images of home, of being loved and cared for allow the viewer to understand the depth of loss she feels when she is forced to leave her country.

Her connection to Iraq is not merely a connection to a place, but to a history and an identity. Therefore, we see Valentine repeatedly identify herself as if she is still trying to defend and renegotiate her Iraqi status with those who denied her this status almost half a century ago. The viewer hears Valentine assert her identity when Joe asks her, "Did you ever question the fact that you were Iraqi?" and she persistently replies, "No, I did not. I was Iraqi and that was it. I was Iraqi, I was a Jewish Iraqi. [in Arabic] The two always went together. I am Iraqi, I am Jewish. That is how it was" (Balass). According to Valentine, her identity is non-negotiable; she eliminates any doubt of her Iraqiness by repeatedly asserting her Iraqi identity to her son and the viewers.

Nevertheless, Valentine's sense of exclusion and loneliness are evident as memories and images of family gatherings is replaced with her reflections on the shrinking Jewish community at the time. According to the conversation between mother and son, she relates that after the 1950s Jews began to keep a low profile and, eventually, "the majority gave up their nationality and went to Israel" (Balass). The population diminished from around 180,000 at the time to "about 10, 12 thousand" (Balass).

Gradually, Valentine and her immediate family are one of the only families left in Baghdad to face the oppression and persecution by the Iraqi government. When the conditions turn more dangerous her parents also leave the country, I listened as she stated, "My father was leaving with my mother . . . and they did leave in 1957" (Balass). I connected with that moment because

I had lived through a similar one. Watching my immediate family members leave one by one, while I stayed with my young family thinking that I could face the aftermath of the invasion alone. After all, I had my husband and my son to keep me busy. However, similar to my experience, the separation from loved ones began to fragment her daily life and her ability to maintain that sense of belonging to a country that was forcing her out.

Step 2—Establishing Agency

When putting together research on Iraqi women's life narratives for my PhD dissertation, I faced an issue that I had not thought about. As members of a minority, these women's authority and agency are the first to be questioned, especially when authority is part of how these women defragment and reconstruct their identities through writing or relating their experiences. The act of life-writing or life narration, in general, is a form of establishing agency through constructing an image of the self and of the history of that self from the perspective of the life narrator, it is an urgency to define the self and comprehend its place as an active subject first. Suzette A. Henke asserts that "[t]he act of life-writing [or in this case, life narration] serves as its own testimony and, in so doing, carries through the work of reinventing the shattered self as a coherent subject capable of meaningful resistance to received ideologies and of effective agency in the world" (*Shattered Subjects* xix). For Valentine, in addition to confirming her Iraqi identity, narration enables her to establish an identity that rejects the stereotypical Western perceptions of Arab women and their abilities to be independent agents capable of presenting their own narratives. Dwight F. Reynolds in *Interpreting the Self: Autobiography in the Arabic Literary Tradition* states that,

> structural and rhetorical characteristics of the western chronological, narrative-based autobiography have become the gauge by which the scholars seek to measure the level of "self-consciousness" and "individual identity" present in other historical periods and other cultures, bypassing the changing literary conventions that mediate these expressions of the self. (19)

Unlike Western autobiographers, non-Western life narrators are considered unlikely to present a developed testimony of their experiences. Wail Hassan adds, that "it is not enough for the marginalized autobiographer to undermine socially constructed identity; he/she must be able to engage the dominant discourse dialogically in order for his/her intervention to negotiate a viable identity effectively" (9). As the subaltern, these writers come from a history of colonization, from occupation, and have become part of the minority in the diaspora. Furthermore, the image of Arab women in the West always seems to pre-determine the identity of individual Arab women, without acknowledgment of their diversity or uniqueness of character, history, experience and education. As Nawar Al-Hassan Golley claims, the "Western stereotype of the Arab woman remains that of an invisible and silent woman shrouded in mystery" (xxvi). Thus, the need to prove that we have the agency to tell our stories becomes part of that narrative pattern through which we reaffirm our identities.

Additionally, there needs to be more for the Western viewer and for Joe Balass, who has lived most of his life in Canada, to connect with. No matter how inviting Valentine's memories are, they are still very much removed from the Western perceptions of Arab women and Eastern cultures. The only way to combat the stereotypes is to present images of a very modern, very Westernized culture, especially in the exhibition of women's lives and interests. For instance, *Baghdad Twist* integrates video clips in which girls in Western clothes play sports at schools, work in fashion, in labs, and in hospitals. Even Valentine shows her pride in the fact that her mother had dresses made for her just like the ones that Shirley Temple wore.

Joe takes this process of Westernization a step further by including clips from mid-twentieth century British documentaries which display a side of the massive changes that took place in the lives of urban Iraqi women and girls around that time. We hear the British narrator state:

> When you see these young girls in their Western clothes, so assured and confident, you're inclined to forget how surprised their mother would have been at the idea of training for jobs their daughters take in their stride. Jobs they thought that only men could and should do. And it's natural with all these modern developments, the women in Iraq are breaking away from their traditional style dress, unaltered for centuries, to wear the practical, comfortable clothes that are right for this life. (Balass)

The pictures of "civilized" Iraqis, who dance the Twist and dress in Western clothes, relate a strong sense of the images planted in the Iraqi conscious that views the positivity of replicating the West rather than the cultural Iraqi dress and traditions which are always presented as backward or negative. Although Valentine speaks of the restrictions that she faced as a girl, these restrictions are limited to insignificant experiences, like her inability to swim in the river like her brothers. Nevertheless, Valentine was well educated and taught not to let the men in her life take advantage of her. Growing up with five brothers, her mother wanted her to defend herself and find her equal place among them. The image Valentine presents is far from the oppressed or abused Middle Eastern women presented in Western media. The documentary tries to present a counter-image of Iraqi women in general, not only Jewish Iraqi women.

Laura Nader states that "the grid through which we rank the humanity of the [Middle East], is based on how we perceive their treatment of womenfolk. The way in which we construct the place of Arab women is one of the keys to the control of others. . . . The West is more civilized by the status and rights of its women" (quoted in Elie 140). This focus on the strength of Valentine's character, her education and, somewhat, Westernized lifestyle is supported by the fact that she is narrating her own story. The act of life narration is, therefore, a declaration not only of existence, but also of authority over the presentation of her unique self. As she reexamines her past from a different place and time, the act of narration enables the realization of identity through the "process and the product of assigning meaning to a series of experiences, after they have taken place, by means of emphasis, juxtaposition, commentary, omission" (Smith 45). Through her narrative, she presents herself and her stories in the image that she desires.

Step 3—Relating Testimonies of Trauma

As I expanded my research, I found that traumatic experiences are main topic of Iraqi women's life narratives in the diaspora,[7] as was mine. The 2003 American invasion took up most of my memoir. For me, and many other Iraqis, it disrupted and redirected our paths in life. We were uprooted from a considerably settled life surrounded by our families and our communities and thrust into the unknown, into a state in which we were spread across the continents.

Valentine's traumatic experiences are also the dividing factor between that idyllic life and the displacement that follows. Up to this point in her narration, Valentine dismisses the need to leave Baghdad, which confounds her son. He is confused about his family's persistence to remain in spite of these difficult times in Baghdad, stating that he is unable to comprehend how people were able to live normal lives with the violence that was shown towards the Jews in Iraq. His mother explains, in both Arabic and English that, "every year or two, when it's calm people forget and live their own lives. If someone has a fear of something, there's a revolution, a month, two months, three months passes, everything is back to normal and everybody lives their own life" (Balass). However, Valentine's strong connection to her country does not last for long. She relates, "after 1967 everything collapsed, everything. People we used to laugh with, sit with, they did not want to show themselves as though they know a Jewish person" (Balass). The government begins broadcasts on the radio to encourage citizens to watch their Jewish neighbors and inform officials if they suspect them of being spies. "So, you can imagine in what state we were," she continues, "scared to death, not moving. A week later they cut all our phone lines" (Balass).

The sense of being imprisoned in her own home affects the way she perceives her own identity as an Iraqi. She, like other Jews, was made to feel unwelcome by the government, and in turn by her own neighbors and friends of different faiths. The violence against her community escalates further as she discloses that one day her older sons surprisingly returned from school at 9:30 in the morning, "I said what happened? They said the school closed and there were Jews who were hanged. One [of the Jews] had two kids, two little kids, I knew them very well" (Balass).

The situation in Baghdad becomes very intense for the Jewish community who are trapped in their city and in their homes. The only way to cross the Iraqi border was by surrendering their Iraqi citizenship, something that she and her husband refused to do. The tremor in Valentine's voice reveals the extent of the traumatic event, even after all these years; the alteration in the volume and the pitch of her voice is clear to the viewer, as she seems to relive the incidents once again. "On Thursday," Valentine continues, "they came ringing the house, two police cars. We were all asleep. It was quarter to 6:00 in the morning. I knew they were coming to get your father, I knew that" (Balass). The officials tell her that they will bring him back soon, but she begins to scream. With accusations of sending money to Israel, she knows that proving his innocence will be impossible.

The viewer does not see Valentine's expressions but clearly hears her sense of anguish through her voice. The family pictures that were shown earlier are substituted with a photo of Valentine enclosing her son in her arms, her face serious and despondent. We see the shift from the cheerful family photos and videos, which represent "the cohesion of the family and [are] an instrument of its togetherness" (Hirsch 7), to fragmented images of immobility and foreboding. Thus, both her voice and the images presented help recreate the anguish of the situation felt, not only by Valentine, but by the community as well.

Not only is Valentine's life fragmented by the trauma of her husband's incarceration, but her role as a woman, as a mother, and as a housewife are also fragmented, as she is forced to leave the safety of her home and go to the police station to negotiate her husband's release. She narrates, "Every single day, I tried, I stood in the burning sun for hours. I had to go find a way to get your father out of prison" (Balass). Her narration of waiting for hours under the hot sun in order to meet with the police and arrange her husband's release is accompanied with the images in the film of shadows of people lined up and the sound of police sirens in the background; they help construct a scene for the viewer to better understand the situation. Furthermore, by going to the police herself, Valentine is seen as defiant because she takes on a man's role and breaks the image of Iraqi women's social conduct. She relates this difficult time to her son, showing her persistence in trying to free her husband. As a woman, she is told to go home and send a man in her place. But Valentine knows that as a woman she has a stronger chance of appealing for her husband and avoiding prison, unlike their male friends and relatives. She reflects on the terror she felt; her voice becomes more anxious and her fear is perceptible as she states, "I don't know what is going to happen to me, I don't know what's going to happen to your dad and I don't know what is going to happen to my children. I don't know how to protect my children" (Balass). She has no choice, but to take on the position as the family's protector, which adds to her sense of displacement from her society and alienates her from familiar social constructs. Her belief system in the safety and protection of her community is shattered by the traumatic events that take place.[8]

Accordingly, Valentine's sense of powerlessness resurfaces as she seems to relive the trauma and even her speech changes from the past tense to the present tense. She not only relives the fear of her husband's imprisonment, but she also relives the fear of her inability, as a mother, to protect her children. Anne Whitehead makes an interesting point concerning repetition in trauma fiction, which may be applied to Valentine's dialogue. Whitehead states that repetition "mimics the effects of trauma, for it suggests an insistent return of the event" (86). Whitehead also adds that "in its negative aspect, repetition replays the past as if it was fully present and remains caught within trauma's paralysing influence" (86). Thus, we sense that the impression of the traumatic incident is still threatening to her and her sense of safety for herself and her family.

Valentine's husband was imprisoned three times and released on bail, which made him an easy target for persecution. The sense of being displaced from home, community, and country leave Valentine desperate for change that will bring security. Her persistence to remain Iraqi, within the borders of Iraq is finally shattered by her fear for the lives of her loved ones. Therefore, she decides that they have to leave the country. Throughout the documentary, Valentine narrates the continuous loss of family, a lifestyle, safety, and freedom. Thus, her sense of fragmented identity and displacement is established while she is still in her native country, but this displacement becomes tangible when she leaves her home and city. She narrates the hasty and highly secretive escape by saying, "We left the house. You should see it. It's like someone is still living there; the beds, the furniture, the table, the food in the fridge, everything" (Balass). The focus of the pictures and scenes during Valentine's narration of her family's escape are on stagnant, lifeless objects, contradicting the former lively images of joyous gatherings, dancing, and celebration. The physical appearance of the home remains, like the pictures that Joe presents, intact in her mind. According to Mohanty and Martin, the relationship between the self and home and community is crucial because the "the giving up of home will necessarily mean the giving up of self and vice versa" (quoted. in Wiley and Barnes xvii). The loss of home is also a loss of self, the self that is safe and connected to the memories that her home presents.

Step 4—Establishing/Re-establishing Identity

One of the main contradictions that kept resurfacing as I watched *Baghdad Twist* was the role that Joe played in constructing the documentary, after all he was the director of the film. His organization of the shots, decisions on what was kept and what was cut from the dialogue must have impacted the final product, and thus Valentine's voice. Undeniably, the documentary is a collaboration between mother and son. At one point, Joe asks her if she has a good memory. Through these questions, Joe attempts to prove to the viewer and to himself that his mother is capable of reconstructing a credible history of her past life. She confidently answers, "Yes I think I do I have a good memory." But Joe is not satisfied with this answer alone, as he proceeds to ask, "You understand why I ask you all these questions?" (referring to the interview in general) to which Valentine answers laughing, "Maybe you want a memory for yourself of Iraq, no?" Valentine's statement reinforcing her role in helping him establish his Iraqi self through his mother's narrative.

In other sections of the documentary, Valentine's ability to remember is challenged as she tries to remember a Mary Hopkins song from the late sixties, "Those Were the Days," but her memory fails her, so she instead hums the tune. Balass, persists in pushing her to talk about the memories that our minds select to retain. He completes the words for her and reminds her that she would sing the song to him often. The conversation tackles the concept of remembering as it reveals what Valentine chooses to remember from her past. Joe in this instance is not only the interviewer, but the coaxer of her memories. He helps her fill gaps in her narrative by asking questions and directing the conversation. In addition, Joe confesses that his own recollection of the song is actually built on his mother repeatedly singing the song to him. Thus, the conversation sets the dynamic between mother and son: the mother is the authoritative figure, who holds the key to the family history and the son, who needs and encourages the narration of this history to reaffirm his own identity and understand his own position within it.

The more I thought about it, the more I felt that this documentary would not be possible without her narrative. For Joe, his connection to Iraq and his understanding of his Iraqi identity is established through his mother's recollections. His mother's narrative functions a as relational connection to his Iraqi self as his departure from Iraq, before the young age of four, leaves him with only blurred memories of his homeland. He is dependent on the memories presented through his mother's narrations and on the videos and fragments of documentaries that she carries with her when she leaves Iraq.

Although Joe pieces together these memories through assembling the documentary and conducting the interview, at the same time the fact that these memories are his mother's establishes her influential role in the work and on her agency as a storyteller. Furthermore, her narrative becomes a historical document of some of the experiences that the Iraqi people endured and presents "the wider sociopolitical implications of that historical moment to the community" (Grace 71). On one hand, she presents a personal narrative, while on the other a communal narrative in which the history of a nation and a people are brought to light.

The interaction between mother and son kept me thinking about the stories that I shared with my son (now sons). These days, I notice their effort in trying to speak words in Arabic, I notice and appreciate their persistence to fast during Ramadan, I notice their interest in understanding their cultural history. I know that there is a thread of that story that I carried with me from Iraq, tied to their own sense of Iraqiness, even if my youngest has never seen our native home.

WORKS CITED

Al-Ali, Nadje Sadig. *Iraqi Women: Untold Stories from 1948 to the Present*. London: Zed Books, 2007.

Al-Radi, Nuha. *Baghdad Diaries*. New York: Vintage, 2003.

Anzaldúa, Gloria. *Borderlands: The New Mestiza-La Frontera*. 3rd ed. Aunt Lute Books, 2007.

Balass, Joe. *Baghdad Twist*. 2007. <http://www.nfb.ca/film/baghdad_twist/>.

Elie, Serge D. "The Harem Syndrome: Moving Beyond Anthropology's Discursive Colonization of Gender in the Middle East." *Alternatives: Global, Local, Political* 29.2 (Mar.–May 2004): 139–68.

Golley, Nawar Al-Hassan. *Arab Women's Lives Retold: Exploring Identity through Writing*. Syracuse: Syracuse UP, 2007.

Grace, Daphne. *Relocating Consciousness: Diasporic Writers and the Dynamics of Literary Experience*. Amsterdam: Rodopi, 2007.

Hassan, Wail S. "Arab-American Autobiography and the Reinvention of Identity: Two Egyptian Negotiations." *Alif: Journal of Comparative Poetics* 22 (2002): 7–35.

Henke, Suzette A. *Shattered Subjects: Trauma and Testimony in Women's Life-Writing*. New York: St. Martin's, 2000.

Jenoff-Bulman, Ronnie. *Shattered Assumptions: Towards a New Psychology of Trauma*. Free Press, 1992.

Kerby, Anthony Paul. *Narrative and the Self*. Bloomington: Indiana UP, 1991.

Levy, Lital. "Self and the City: Literary Representations of Jewish Baghdad." *Prooftexts*. Spec. Issue *Literacy Mappings of the Jewish City* 26. 1–2 (Winter/Spring 2006): 163–211.
Martin B., Mohanty C.T. "Feminist Politics: What's Home Got to Do with It?" Ed. Teresa de Lauretis. *Feminist Studies/Critical Studies. Language, Discourse, Society*. Palgrave Macmillan: London, 1986. <https://doi.org/10.1007/978-1-349-18997-7_12>.
Nader, Laura. "Orientalism, Occidentalism, and the Control of Women." *Cultural Dynamics* 2 (July 1989): 323–55.
Rejwan, Nissim. *The Jews of Iraq: 3000 Years of History and Culture*. London: Weidenfeld and Nicolson, 1985.
Reynolds, Dwight F., ed. *Interpreting the Self: Autobiography in the Arabic Literary Tradition*. Berkeley: U of California P, 2001.
Samir, *Forget Baghdad: Jews and Arabs-The Iraqi Connection*. Directed by Samir. Arab Film Distribution, 2002.
Shiblak, Abbas. *Iraqi Jews: A History of the Mass Exodus*. London: Saqi, 2005.
Smith, Sidone. *A Poetics of Women's Autobiography: Marginality and the Fictions of Self-Representation*. Bloomington: Indiana UP, 1987.
Whitehead, Anne. *Trauma Fiction*. Edinburgh University Press, 2004.
Whitlock, Gillian. *Soft Weapons: Autobiography in Transit*. Chicago: U of Chicago P, 2007.

NOTES

1. With the coalition attacks on the main infrastructure, most of the population was left with very limited access to water and electricity.

2. A more recent documentary is the British film *Remember Baghdad: Iraq's last Jews Tell the Story of Their Country* (2017) directed by Fiona Murphy.

3. Estrangement or alienation.

4. *Waiting for the Rain: An Iraqi Memoir*. Toronto: Mawenzi House, 2019.

5. Fragrant rice grown in the south of Iraq.

6. Small coffee cups.

7. See authors like Zainab Salbi, Dunya Mikhail, Leilah Nadir, Alise Alousi, and Nuha Al-Radi among others.

8. See Ronnie Janoff-Bulman's *Shattered Assumptions: Towards a New Psychology of Trauma*.

Chapter Ten

(Un)inhabitable "homes" for mothers and daughters

The transmission of memories of "home" in Sri Lankan Tamil diasporic women's writing

Sabreena Niles

The Incomplete Thombu by T. Shanaathanan is a compelling rendering of homes, which through its architectural designs, ground plans, dry pastel drawings, and written narratives, captures the fluidity of "home" for those displaced during the war in Sri Lanka.

> I have resettled in our own house after nearly twenty years. I was displaced to Puttalam. Everything has changed here. My street does not look like it did before. Most of those who were displaced have yet to return . . . our house does not have a roof. With the help of a well-wisher we managed to fix a roof for one room. It is difficult to manage in a single room especially during the rainy season. Home is about community, family and friendship. Even in the refugee camps in Puttalam we lived with our relatives and friends. Now I am living with strangers. I am a stranger on my own street. (Shanaathanan 80)

This quote extracted from a narrative in Shanaathanan's work gestures at the elusive nature of "home" that characterizes the lives of internally displaced persons among the Tamil community in Sri Lanka. It suggests that notions of home, and the stability and security associated with "home," are radically transformed against the backdrop of a volatile climate of war. Shanaathanan's project thus depicts the transient nature of "home," especially in a climate of unprecedented transformations, for the Tamil community living in Jaffna. It suggests that in a context where the material space of the home is underlined by impermanence, especially for the Sri Lankan Tamil diaspora[1] whose sense of "home" drastically changes due to dispersion from their homes in Sri Lanka, what often remains is the intangible structures of "home," particularly that of family and community. Hence, the stability provided through family and community and the collective forms of identification derived from these structures, become crucial to resettling in new homes outside Sri Lanka.

As its point of departure, this chapter attempts to address questions that emerge in a discussion that centralizes the transmission of memories from mothers to their daughters in the Sri Lankan Tamil diaspora: how does one inherit her mother's "home," or family and community? Is it possible for a daughter to re/inhabit the "home" of her mother's past? How does the trauma experienced by Sri Lankan Tamil mothers shape the relationships they share with their diasporic daughters who are spatially and temporally distanced from those sites of trauma? This chapter seeks to grapple with these questions through focusing on the work of Sri Lankan Tamil diasporic women writers: *Love Marriage* by V.V. Ganeshananthan and selected narratives from *Song of the Sun God* by Shankari Chandran and *Bodies in Motion* by Mary Anne Mohanraj.

Inevitably, the questions that frame this chapter also probe my own positionality as a Sinhala-Tamil woman residing in Sri Lanka. Born in Scarborough, Toronto, to mixed-race parents, who left Sri Lanka in the wake of the 1983 riots (a day marked by the massacre of the Tamil community living in Colombo),[2] the trajectory of my own life would have been vastly different had not my mother returned to Sri Lanka, a journey that has tremendously influenced my ontological location. In many ways, the questions that are posed in this chapter are not merely those I ask myself today, but those that dwell on the different space and location I may have potentially inhabited in relation to this research, which studies the bonds shared by mothers and daughters among the Sri Lankan Tamil diaspora.

Thiranagama's study on the Tamil and Muslim communities living in northern Sri Lanka, frames the contours of "Tamil-speaking Jaffna," as both a material and an intangible "home," the loss of which is conflated with the demise of her mother, Rajani Thiranagama,[3] a leading activist who was murdered by the LTTE[4] at the age of thirty-five: "her body returned like us to 'our home,' my *ur*,[5] our grandparents' house and village where she and we had been born and had lived most of our lives" (*In My Mother's House* 1). It locates the narrative in a deeply personal tragedy, mirroring the collective mourning of families and communities consumed in a war, marked by the subsequent loss of homes. Titling the study *In My Mother's House*, Thirangama writes, "this book is about returning to my mother's house" (2). It thus dwells on the possibility of revisiting a spatial and temporal location that was once inhabited by her mother, an abode marked by the searing memory of loss. The renewed hope of restoring that which was lost, of family and community, hinges on the relationships espoused between mothers and their daughters. "Home" is thus articulated and made tangible in the form of such bonds that women share, which are integral to denoting a sense of identity, continuity and belonging for both mothers and their daughters.

An analysis of literary representations of home, "home" and "homeland," in relation to Sri Lankan Tamil diasporic writing, is potentially politically contentious because of the inherently spatial nature of these terms that are vividly mapped into the Sri Lankan national imaginary, with divisive claims for a Sinhala-dominated south and a Tamil homeland with the right to self-determination in the northeastern provinces (Jazeel; Orjuela). The war[6] that raged for nearly three decades was battled in the northern and eastern provinces in Sri Lanka, within the geographical contours of the imagined Tamil homeland or Tamil Eelam. Thiranagama posits that the "impossibility of Tamil Eelam enables the possibility of life in Toronto," the "ultimate desired location" ("Making Tigers from Tamils" 275) in the mythical "homeland."[7] Sivamohan concurs that "the birth of the Tamil nation, 'Tamil Eelam' in the diasporic imagination" is made possible as "in the context of marginalisation within the metropolis, transnational 'hybridity' acts as a space to reimagine the safe space, the national space, with a crucial difference from the one left behind: it is a space drained of contradictions" ("The Middle Passage" 18). This is vastly different in Jaffna, the primary site of the war, which conjures diverse meanings for the various groups and communities that inhabit this space. As Thiranagama elucidates, "one is a caste notion, it is also a Vellala notion, in some ways. For who lives inside the *ur*? The *ur* is not the same for everybody. Even in one village it is not necessarily the same for everybody" (interview). While acknowledging the complexities in prying these overlapping notions of "home" apart, for purposes of clarity, in this chapter "home" refers to the families and communities of the Sri Lankan Tamil diaspora in Jaffna or Sri Lanka, and "homeland" is the imagined Tamil homeland or Tamil Eelam.

(UN)AVAILABLE SPACES: CONSTRUCTING MOTHERHOOD

The intrinsic association of motherhood with the rhetoric of "home" plays out in the spatial negotiations, as Walker observes, of the "everyday life of a mother in eastern Sri Lanka" (54), in a war-torn context in which "physical barriers mapped out the town, militarization and the anticipation of violence circumscribed behaviour and kept people tightly anchored to strategies of silence and protection" (29). Nationalist discourse is often saturated with the enduring presence of the woman as a mother or a maternal figure, who in her capacity to reproduce, is shaped by the transitions of the sociopolitical landscape of Sri Lanka (Silva *The Gendered Nation*). The issue of space in such conversations pertaining to women as procreators, is integrally, not merely about spaces that women inhabit, but also about conceptual and physical spaces and structures that women are prohibiting from accessing. Commenting on the circumscribed role of women within the deeply gendered Tamil nationalist discourse in Sri Lanka, Coomaraswamy and Perera-Rajasingham posit that "powerful in the home, she ironically reproduced and represented a worldview that re-inscribed the subordination of women" (117). Sivamohan draws attention to the "unavailability of the nation" or the "curious lack of available positions" for "transnational women, transnational Sri Lankan women, who have lost all claims to the space of the national and yet are compelled to reimagine it" ("The Middle Passage" 15).

While Sri Lankan Tamil diasporic women play a critical role in reproducing the "home" that was left behind, often their seeming passivity and immobility can be ascribed to that very role in which they have been involuntarily cast, as the strategic positioning of women's bodies as the "being" or the static, untarnished, reproductive sphere, upon which external aspects of "becoming" occur, is framed within discourses on "reproduction-as-stasis" that limit the significance of the reproductive activities of women to a "logic of sameness" (Gedalof 92). As Gedalof highlights, the embodied practices in which women engage, from material to emotional and culturally-specific work, are aimed at maintaining appearances of stability and replicating the "home" of the past, despite the backdrop of transition against which these practices of home-making take place (101–102). In Chandran's *Song of the Sun God*, Nala, upon migrating with her husband Rajan, following the brutal treatment to which she was subject during the 1983 riots, attempts to transfer the experience of "home" in Sri Lanka to their new residence in Australia. Chandran describes the process of purchasing crabs and preparing a curry for dinner, one that is unfamiliar to Nala but more so in a foreign land. Her determined efforts to recreate the warmth of home in her newfound surroundings in Sydney are evident as "Nala wanted everything to be perfect. She wanted everyone to know that she and Rajan were fine in their new home" (ibid., 221–222). Therefore, despite her longing for cherished moments with her grandchildren, in Sri Lanka, she is convinced that "she would have more days like that in Sydney," as she surveys "the inner perimeter of where she was expected to live," decides that "it was fine," considers lighting the spitting lamp in her shrine, applies holy ashes on her forehead, tastes the crab curry and feels that "it needed a little more lime, but aside from that, it was perfect" (ibid.).

Similarly, Lakshmi in Mohanraj's *Bodies in Motion* is determined to thrive in her capacities as a wife and a mother, primarily, to compensate for her sense of inadequacy as a daughter in comparison to her accomplished siblings: "I will have many children, and a beautiful home, and I will cook perfect meals for my Raksha - at least I can cook" (106). The ideal of a "perfect mother," for Lakshmi (ibid., 105), stems from the assurance that she will excel within the sphere of the home, a construct which, as she perceives, endorses her value as a woman within her Sri Lankan Tamil diasporic family and community. However, she ruefully records in her diary that she could be deemed a failure in her duties as a woman, and therein the roles in which she set out to prove herself: "I wanted to be a good daughter, a good wife, a good mother. I am not sure that I succeeded in any of those, even the last" (ibid., p. 120). Walker observes of one of her participants, "Meena followed the central thread of life, which she framed mainly within a domestic setting and structured by the societal conventions, which cast her as daughter, wife and mother" (98). The trajectories of women are thus often shaped by the roles they perform in relation to their families, which are critical to forming their sense of belonging and identity. In her analysis of *If the Moon Smiled* by Chandani Lokugé and *Homesick* by Roshi Fernando, Silva posits that the childhood home becomes a central space, especially in a Sri Lankan diasporic context within which the "construction of the self" and "notions of "ideal" daughter/wife/mother are internalized through religious, cultural, and familial discourses that are foisted *upon* the (female) inhabitants of the domestic sphere, most often by the female inhabitants (especially the mother)" ("No Place Called Home" 111). Central to discourses on Sri Lankan diasporic women is the seemingly organic transition from daughters to wives and mothers, which is integral to replicating the homes left behind in Sri Lanka. In her analysis of Lokugé's *If the Moon Smiled,* Tantrigoda highlights the absence of the sociocultural reinforcements that provide the necessary conditions for the protagonist to perform the roles of replicating and transmitting the cultural values of Sri Lankan Sinhala Buddhist identity to her daughter (69). Tantrigoda maintains that within the social and cultural order in the West, which is at odds with the artificial environment constructed in order to instill "authentic" Sinhala Buddhist ideals in her children, the Sri Lankan diasporic woman is ill-equipped to persevere in her duties as a mother in preserving and perpetuating these traditions (ibid.).

The absence of the required or adequate space to reproduce or replicate "home" is felt more acutely among Sri Lankan Tamil diasporic women, whose sense of identity is derived from their capacity to ensure the seamless transition into homes in their diasporic contexts, against the unprecedented loss of homes in Sri Lanka. In Ganeshananthan's *Love Marriage,* Yalini ruminates on how "Sri Lankan women are always trying and failing to bring order to a world of men" (93). She observes how her mother, Vani, who during their stay in Toronto, despite her personal reservations regarding her brother's involvement in the LTTE and the potential marriage of his daughter, Janani, to one of its stalwarts, continues to recreate the affective and cultural ambiance of the family and community left behind in Sri Lanka. As such, Vani attempts to quell the heightening tension between her husband, Murali, and their visitors, Janani's prospective groom, Suthan, and his father, Vijendran, by preparing tea and familiar dishes reminiscent of their home in Jaffna, including "deep fried noodles, spicy nuts, and lentils" and "crispy *vadai,* the savoury snack that my father liked and that my mother had refused to prepare for him, because it was so unhealthy" (ibid.). Similarly, despite her unease at the presence of those who supported her brother's past with the LTTE, Vani takes great pains to transform the room to which he is restricted in Toronto, into a space that resembles the home of their shared childhood, as "she changed his sheets, made his favourite curries, read to him, and played the Tamil music that he loved" (ibid., 43).

(UN)INHABITABLE SPACES

The embodied acts in which Sri Lankan Tamil diasporic women engage, and the cultural and affective dimensions involved in reimagining home, are made intelligible, as Sivamohan (2005) opines, within the framework in which women are perceived as equivalent to the passivity of the land they have inhabited in the past and are expected to reproduce ("The Middle Passage" 15). In *Love Marriage,* Yalini observes the taciturn nature of her mother, Vani, who having left Sri Lanka for the US with the prospect of returning, is unable to do so due to the war being waged in her "home": "my mother will not show fear, because then it counts; she will not betray anger, knowing how it could come back to hurt her later; she will put your needs before hers without ever letting you know she has done this, because her mother did this, and her mother before her, and her mother before that" (Ganeshananthan 29). Central to the relationship between mothers and daughters in the Sri Lankan Tamil diaspora is the transmission and inheritance of motherhood, and thereby womanhood, that years of war, displacement and reproducing "home" have shaped into passive acceptance and subordination. However, Yalini observes that despite how her mother, Vani, "guards her expression," to "think that she feels nothing—that would be a mistake" (ibid.). In a diary entry in *Bodies in Motion,* Lakshmi, addressing her daughter, Chaya, attempts to rationalize the past while grappling with her own silence on the subject of the death of Raksha, Chaya's father: "I did what I thought was best; I did it for myself, but also for you" (120). In *Love Marriage,* Vani's inaccessible nature, her impenetrable exterior, shields both Vani and Yalini from a trauma that transcends the spatial and temporal location that they inhabit in the present but continuously shapes the relationship they share as mother and daughter.

Dwelling on the premature death of her mother, Rajani Thiranagama, Sharika Thiranagama speculates that her own "interrupted transmission" possibly influences her attempts to address the inadequate research conducted on the relationship between mothers and daughters, which she argues is integral to discourse on kinship among Muslims and Tamils in the northeast, communities that share close-knit bonds across families (interview). Thiranagama also opines that "even without war, the question of transmission becomes a central one in any family—from the material to the immaterial" and the "interrupted transmission" that occurs as a result of war is accentuated by the fact that "for those in the diaspora it is hard to share those things because there is also something about shared collective trauma" (interview). In *Love Marriage,* Vani rarely provides insight into her past, which is steeped in the monumental loss of both family and community, so deeply intertwined that the resurrection of one invariably involves the unearthing of the other. Thus Vani's silence on the topic of her past in Sri Lanka is eventually addressed through the entrance of her prodigal brother, Kumaran, into Yalini's life, as he is "the one who emerged years later, bringing Vani's daughter a war and a country from which her mother had shielded her" (Ganeshananthan 14).

Vani's relationship with her daughter is subsumed in that which is no longer accessible, the "home" that she desires to inhabit of the family and community of her childhood and youth in Jaffna. The im/possibility of inhabiting "home" is thus mediated primarily through the birth of her daughter, Yalini, in the US: "my mother, a teacher, took great pains in reading to me every night. And she saw her aunts in my many sides. She had not seen them for so long, and to see them now in this small person, this small person who was hers, was very strange. It had been a very long time since she had lived in Jaffna, she realized" (ibid. 232). Ahmed states that "if we think of home as an outer skin, then we can also consider how migration involves, not only spatial dislocation, but also temporal dislocation: 'the past' becomes associated with a home that is impossible to inhabit, and be inhabited by, in the present" (91). While Yalini's birth marks the watershed event of Black July, her name, rooted firmly in the very soil of the land from which her parents have been displaced, straddles the spatial and temporal contours of their revered "home": "my parents named me Yalini, after the part of their home that they loved the most. It is a Tamil name, with a Tamil home: a name that means, in part, *Jaffna, Sri Lanka,* the place from which they came" (Ganeshananthan 19). Yalini's birth also presents a semblance of hope for her parents, signifying the emerging "new world" (ibid.) among the diaspora in which, however, "new forms also contained within them the forms of their loss, whether directly experienced or inherited" (Thiranagama, *In My Mother's House* 10).

The making of new ways of living are characterized by a profound sense of loss for the diaspora. Discussing the issue of transmission among displaced communities in Sri Lanka, Thiranagama writes, "I use inheritance to think of how families and individuals perpetuate themselves, how parents and children imagine, transmit, and inherit (or not) not just marital wealth, but social positions, desires, and recognition" (*In My Mother's House* 94). In *Love Marriage* the "pure, clear Ceylonese diamonds" adorned by Yalini's predecessors, "daughters of Jaffna Tamils" (Ganeshananthan 239), are gifted to her, signaling the role Yalini performs in embodying the enduring traditions of her community and thereby ensuring its generational continuity, as "across oceans a grandmother long gone reached out to hand an heirloom to her granddaughter" (ibid.). As depicted through the title, the narrative of *Love Marriage* is woven around the motif of marriage, which is a central point of transmission for the Sri Lankan Tamil community, as "the rule is that all families begin with a marriage. And the other way around" (ibid., 2). However, Yalini's relationship with her parents' "home," also involves a far deeper engagement with the fragments that she inherits from her mother, whose silence and tears are as critical to forming Yalini's sense of belonging as the family heirlooms passed down the generations.

INHERITING "SPACES": PHOTOGRAPHS, BODIES AND JOURNALS

Yalini raises a question that marks the collective trauma of the Sri Lankan Tamil diaspora to posit that the inheritance of a collective identity is determined by the community in which one is located, as "when the conflict begins must depend, like everything else, on the memory you acquire" (ibid., 120). This process of acquiring memories for the second-generation Sri Lankan Tamil diaspora, therefore, is hardly an isolated one, as Halbwachs highlights, "it is in society that people normally acquire their memories. It is also in society that they recall, recognize, and localise their memories" (8). The transmission of a collective memory of "home" among the diaspora is primarily premised on the superior position endowed to Jaffna, as a point of origin and thereby a space of "memory preservation" (Gerharz 52), the inheritance of which is marked by the violent uprooting from this space.

In his *Anthropology of Violence,* which generates from the events of 1983 in Sri Lanka, Daniel dwells on those "whose participation in the ongoing process of being human has been stifled by the threat of silence, by semeiosic paralysis and by the inescapable presence of violence" (123). This pervading presence of violence, as Daniel notes, or the "continuing presence of the present" in the lives of victims of violence is "a present that has yet to be inferentially appropriated into the flow of time, a present that—if only it could be redeemed from its self-imprisonment—could play a nonstochastic part in determining future conduct, conduct guided by purpose" (127). The seamless shift into the present tense, therefore, when describing the trauma of violence that they have undergone is telling of "the presence of violence in their lives, an indication that the foaming, eddying presence of the past has yet to be fully delivered from the present into the flow of the future" (ibid.). Unbeknownst to Yalini, her own sense of belonging is formed in her mother's grief, in Vani's response to the memory of "home": "if my mother walked into a room and saw me watching the news, she turned away. I knew about the war and could guess what it had taken away from my parents. But I had never thought it could take anything from me" (Ganeshananthan 36). In Mohanraj's *Bodies in Motion,* Lakshmi, who has been a victim of abuse at the hands of her drunken husband, upon witnessing the possibility of a similar fate befalling her older daughter, Chaya, murders him while she is pregnant with Savitha. As a child, Savitha craned to hear hushed references that were made to her father, in the midst of conversations on war-torn Sri Lanka, "a land which Savitha had never seen" (Mohanraj 257). Despite the absence of direct contact with the circumstances that led to the death of her father, Savitha's own life is haunted by what remains "unsaid": "there was more to her father's story, Savitha knew. When she was growing up, there was always something unsaid, something that hovered in the air around her ... her mother often smothered her against her large breasts, sometimes bursting into tears for no reason" (ibid., 260). Similar to Yalini in *Love Marriage*, Savitha's relationship with her mother and their past is shaped by the space created at the absence of a family member, a void that is acutely felt in the inaccessible grief of her mother.

As Thiranagama opines, "you just inherit a family with certain gaps" (interview), suggesting that this space or absence is gradually integrated into the narrative of "home" through its unconscious transmission across generations among the Sri Lankan Tamil diaspora. Rose outlines the concept of "transgenerational haunting" as "forms of remembrance—most often of hidden and shameful family secrets—which hover in the space between social and psychic history, forcing and making it impossible for the one who unconsciously carries them to make the link" (5). The significance of these multidirectional hauntings, according to Rose, is that they function between and across generations and families, "creating a monstrous family of reluctant belonging" (31). This is evident in Yalini's first introduction to Rajinie (who, like Yalini, is a member of the second-generation Tamil diaspora),[8] where she acknowledges the indecipherable yet pervasive presence of a shared inheritance of collective trauma: "Rajinie looked at me, and I looked back at her. We were already friends, united in the desire to protect our parents from this, whatever this was" (Ganeshananthan 145). Yalini's words gesture at the crippling presence of trauma that culminates in the insurmountable void between parents and their offspring. Thiranagma opines that it is the magnitude of the loss "that happens to bring to parents the difficulty of conveying—what can for you be an experience—to your children—it can never happen as an experience" (interview).

In *Love Marriage,* Yalini observes, "for the rest of her life my mother will be racing to replace the irreplaceable: the photographs of her family that burned with her sister's house in 1983 in Sri Lanka. Ask my mother what she would take with her if the house was on fire, and she will not take a minute to consider the question: she would take the photographs. Of course" (Ganeshananthan 240). In *Song of the Sun God,* in preparation to migrate to Australia, "that night Nala sat on her bed" and sifted through her personal items that bore traces of a life prior to the 1983 riots, "as she looked at the camphorwood box and started a list: photographs, diaries, her wedding sari, and the portrait she had done of Rajan" (Chandran 215). In *Love Marriage,* the centrality of photographic evidence of a past prior to the loss of homes is felt acutely by Vani in its absence, in the empty frames with which she is left: "many of the photographs of her younger days, before she came to America, are missing; she did not bring very many of them to America when she came. There are perhaps ten pictures of my mother and her brother and sister. Once there were three of them. Now there are two" (Ganeshananthan 240).

Focusing on the inheritance of collective trauma, Hirsch states that "photographs in their enduring 'umbilical' connection to life are precisely the medium connecting first- and second-generation remembrance, memory, and postmemory,"[9] specifically because "they affirm the past's existence and in their flat two-dimensionality, they signal its unbridgeable distance" (*Family Frames* 23). The photographs act as a space that acknowledges what appears to be an idyllic past for Vani, while reinstating the impossibility of inhabiting that past, and thereby mediating a process of grieving that has not been afforded her. Yalini's relationship with her mother in the present is thus formed in the unprocessed grief of her mother. In such a context, the question that Stratton poses in his introspective and retrospective reading of growing up in England in the 1950s and 1960s as the child of a Jewish mother, becomes a defining one for second-generation Sri Lankan Tamil diaspora: "how has all this, my mother's unrecognized trauma, manifested in my life?" (259)

In the interstices of untold stories are those that depict the brutal violence mapped out on bodies of Tamil women, an inheritance to which even diasporic Tamil women lay claim, as "Smrithi remembered fragments of a moment" (Chandran 371) of the 1983 riots that she witnessed as a toddler in Sri Lanka. Similarly, Smrithi's birth mother, Dhara, recalls witnessing the sexual violation of her own mother, when Dhara herself is approached with the same brute force by soldiers. Fearful of the possibility that the same fate that befell her and her mother would become her daughter's predicament, Dhara pleads with Nala's daughter, Priya, to adopt Smrithi, determined to ensure that she would not "allow her daughter to grow and suffer and die in the earth of her country": "I can't raise her *acca*.[10] I can't, at least, not yet. Please take her. Take her for me—take her away from here" (ibid., 164–165). The disruption of their relationship is rooted in Dhara's frantic attempts to sever ties between her daughter and the space that they both relate to as 'home.' The silence therefore that inhibits and inhabits Dhara throughout her childhood, as she was brought up by her parents' friends, Nala and Rajan, is transmitted to her daughter Smrithi, who while developing a strong bond with Dhara, only learns that Dhara is her birth mother upon Dhara's death. However, the "shard of a broken mirror" (ibid., 145) through which Dhara recollects her past trauma, remains lodged in Smrithi's memory, in the image of her grandmother Nala's body set ablaze during the 1983 riots as they travel to the airport to hand Smrithi to her mother, Priya, to fly to Australia. Singed deep in Smrithi's memory is how the "skin on her grandmother's arm, slid away, like a runny egg" (ibid., 371), amid her grandfather's desperate appeal to his daughter, Priya, as he handed Smrithi to her at the airport, "go home, get away while you can—don't bring her back here" (ibid., 372). Smrithi recollects this "nightmare" while she dwells on her feelings of being abandoned by her birth mother and her own current reality as a Sri Lankan Tamil diasporic mother living in Australia (ibid.). Despite being far removed from the devastation of the "final months of the war" in Sri Lanka, the crippling awareness of "mothers hiding their children, using their bodies as sandbags, as shells rained down," as "mothers will do anything" (ibid., 371), torments her in the present moment while she spends time with her children on a beach in Australia, thus evoking the innocent queries of her 7-year-old daughter, Ahalya, "why are you crying, Mummy?" (ibid.).

The intergenerational transmission of memories of the trauma of physical and sexual violence, strung together, forge maternal bonds that are not constrained by familial ties. This is captured poignantly as Nala, whose own body bears scars of the 1983 riots, tends to the bruised body of Dhara whom she has raised as her own. While Dhara converses with Nala on the possibility of revealing the truth to Smrithi about Dhara being her birth mother, Nala "ran the comb through the younger woman's hair" and "poured sesame oil slowly onto her head and massaged her" attempting to arrange "Dhara's hair to cover the barren, scarred skin" where her hair "had been ripped out, not from the root but with the scalp" (ibid., 237). As the relationships between mothers and their daughters are devoured and detonated in the overarching narrative of war, the collective trauma of Sri Lankan Tamil women yields maternal bonds that cut across families and generations, culminating in a community, that like Nala's body, "was a patchwork of skin grafts: pieces borrowed from her thighs and buttocks to replace the pieces that would not re-grow" (ibid., 229). As Dhara writes in her correspondence with Priya, of the rape and murder of a young schoolgirl, Krishanthi Kumaraswamy,[11] whose body was found with those of her mother, brother and a family friend who had gone in search of her to the army base: "I don't know her at all, and yet I feel I know her well" (ibid., 369).

The sense of belonging derived through community is best portrayed through the stories that women share, which tend to be woven around the trajectories of their families and communities. As Walker observes of her participant, "weaving stories together, Meena revealed a rich tapestry of daily life, which reflected not only her own but many other women's lives in the east" (98). In *Love Marriage*, Yalini perceptively urges her mother to relate stories of her family, fully aware that a means of drawing information from her reticent mother is to "ask her about other people" (Ganeshananthan 122). Yalini thus hopes to "extract her character, piece by piece, because even the most self-effacing person can only remain an innocent bystander for so long before conceding to the past of her own presence" (ibid.). Vani's stories are peppered with recurring motifs of the loss of homes in Jaffna, and Sri Lanka, in general, contributing to the growing body of stories on the critical issue of belonging for minorities, as "the struggle of the individual" to "find a place to live is both a personal story and a collective story" (Thiranagama, *In My Mother's House* 88–89). These stories that Yalini records on a journal gifted to her by her father, are not merely about a lost past but are crucial to forming new communities beyond the geographical contours of Jaffna and Sri Lanka, in different localities, including the US and Canada. As Ahmed opines, migration does not merely involve "complex acts of narration through which families imagine a mythic past," but significantly, the "telling of stories is bound with—touched by—the forming of new communities." Subsequently, memory "can be understood as a collective act which produces its object (the 'we'), rather than reflect on it" (90–91).

While her father hesitates when he sees Yalini copiously recording his words, her mother "outright stops" sharing her stories "noting what she says about an old rift between two branches of the family" (Ganeshananthan 246). The question Vani poses to Yalini about her objective in recording these memories resonates across the political landscapes of war-torn Sri Lanka and Sri Lankan Tamil diaspora across the globe: "why are you writing that down?" (ibid., 247). Ranasinha, commenting on Sorayya Khan's *Noor*, which explores the political causes and psychological impact of the 1971 secession, elaborates on how Noor's paintings of her mother's dreams, in particular, are "central to the transmission of traumatic memory, with its silences, gaps, elisions and reliance upon the group to communicate the full horrors of collective trauma" (105). In *Love Marriage*, the journal in which Yalini records her parents' stories and her act of writing, function as the space and process, respectively, through which memories are archived and transmitted across generations. Later, in the privacy of her room, Yalini records her mother's stories, surmising that her parents "do not understand this: history" or that it is important to "cure the future by knowing the past" even when it involves a rift between their families (Ganeshananthan 247). Yalini's interpretations of the fragments of her mother's past, the trauma that Vani refuses to revisit, are woven around collective formations of families and communities. Similar to Noor's drawings that facilitate a process through which her family members explore their repressed individual and collective memories of the 1971 secession (Ranasinha 105), Yalini's act of writing, constructs a space, not just for her mother, but for members of her family who are integral to her mother's sense of belonging, to grieve that which has been unacknowledged and deemed inconsequential. In some ways, therefore, the fragments that Yalini collates and records are reflections and manifestations of the general repression of individual narratives of war-torn Sri Lanka. In this light, Yalini's writing, similar to Noor's drawings, depicts a "legacy of violence and its psychological impact on individuals, families and communities" (ibid., 102–105) and therein a legacy of inherited silences.

As Yalini inhabits the stories that she collates, her interaction with her mother's past is not based on nostalgic recollection but involves an active engagement with the snapshots of her mother's life, infused with the pathos that is transmitted through her family members in the narration of these stories. Yalini's endeavors to understand her familial relationships, which are encased within the overarching narrative of war, are prompted by her attempts to locate herself within those collective formations of family and community. Yalini contemplates on her inherent desire, as a child and an adolescent, to absorb "every story" (Ganeshananthan 243), which eventually translates into the act of writing stories of an inherited past of her parents' "home," to negotiate her own sense of belonging. As Yalini reminds her readers, 'I told you a story about that place, about their leaving it, but how do I know it? I am not the end of my parents' story, but I am the reason for its telling" (ibid., 15).

In *Bodies in Motion,* through the records she makes on her diary, Lakshmi attempts to address the silence that haunts her daughters and their relationship with her: "I stole away your father, and you have never seemed the same. Silent instead of laughing. So serious" (Mohanraj 120). The residue of an undisclosed past permeates Chaya's relationships, translating into an impenetrable silence, as evinced through the agitations of her lover, Daniel, "all we do is have sex. I want you to talk to me. Tell me about your family, your childhood. Tell me your dreams—or hell, your nightmares. Anything! This silence—it's driving me crazy. Don't you get it?" (ibid., 217). Lakshmi attempts to directly address the unintelligible void that characterizes the relationship she shares with her oldest daughter, who as a child was attached to Raksha, Lakshmi's husband: "What more is there to say? I didn't write in this journal again. I took the guilt on willingly. My life since then has been entirely for my daughters" (ibid., 120). In rooting herself firmly in her capacity as a mother, directly addressing her daughter, Lakshmi also ensures that her lost narrative, silenced by her desire to fulfill her role as a devoted mother, does not remain unheard. Cohen-Cruz explores how telling stories in the Theatre of the Oppressed, and similar practices, becomes significant, as the "political potential of personal story is grounded not in particular subject matter but rather in storytelling's capacity to position even the least powerful individual in the proactive, subject position" (103). Similarly, the intentional move to centralize the storyteller in *Love Marriage,* including Yalini and the voices of the women captured in her stories, is a politically charged, agentive act that shifts the lens from one that is saturated by nationalist propaganda, to one that includes individual stories that are rarely acknowledged. Thiranagama reiterates that the "teller lays claim to interpreting the frames by which future action and interpretation of the position of Tamils in Sri Lanka can be understood" (*In My Mother's House* 81).

Critical to Lakshmi in *Bodies in Motion* is the future potential for reconciliation with Chaya and the possible restoration of their fractured relationship. In her study on *Funny Boy,* Jayawickrama refers to the chapter titled "Riot Journals" where the protagonist, Arjie, confined to his home, records the events of the 1983 riots in a journal, which in turn, becomes a fraught space in an atmosphere of heightened communal violence. Through assuming the position of a diarist, Jayawickrama suggests that Arjie enters a liminal space, as the journal entries record his subjective experiences in a critical moment of transition, negotiating between his childhood in the past of Sri Lanka and his future as an adult in Canada (56). In a similar vein, in *Bodies in Motion*, the liminality that the journal affords Lakshmi, as a point of transition, is central to the relationship that she hopes to restore with Chaya through a common understanding of loss, both personally in their respective relationships to Raksha, and collectively, in relation to their Sri Lankan Tamil diasporic community. It is with this intention that she requests that Chaya return to her, upon perusing the journal, to help unravel Lakshmi's own unresolved trauma, "now, shall I live for myself? Or should I turn myself in, pay for my crime? Chaya, when you read this, come and tell me what you think" (Mohanraj 120). Similar to Yalini's endeavors to seek belonging through interacting with her mother's past, Lakshmi's commitment to restoring the relationship with her daughter is central to her own healing. The liminality provided through the space of the journal, which is simultaneously a private and public space, enables the continuous transactions and negotiations that must take place between mothers and daughters against the backdrop of their shared narrative of loss of family and community. Thiranagama reiterates the importance of approaching the relationship between mothers and daughters not "as some kind of static, eternal, inevitable factor" but within the volatile "context of war and politics, secrets" (interview).

In *Love Marriage,* while Yalini carries traces of the past of her mother's sense of displacement, and Chaya and Savitha, in *Bodies in Motion,* inherit the silence that pervades the narratives surrounding the death of their father against the backdrop of immense loss for their mother's community, it is impossible for them to return to that original site with which the trauma is associated. As Tucker elucidates with reference to her own practice of painting, in which she "unconsciously repeated a ritual of dislocation that goes back at least a generation" as her mother and grandmother were refugees from Germany arriving in Britain in 1939 after Kristallnacht (64): "however, I feel that what I do by implication when using paint to remake/create a landscape/place is to say that it is not possible, let alone desirable, to wish to return to it, to that original experience. Rather we are here clearly in the present with the painting/place which has been shaped by the past" (69).

As I conclude, I cannot help but revisit my own location, straddling boundaries of culture and ethnicity, that influenced my approach to the questions of belonging that framed this chapter. Writing in a post-covid milieu, however, in which we are confronted with the deepening and unraveling of societal divisions, demands a reconfiguration of the parameters that frame such issues of displacement and belonging in Sri Lanka. The boundaries we tread, the contours that shape our work, now locate us on the precipice of un/belonging. I am thus compelled to acknowledge, not merely the impossibility of returning to a space or location prior to that of the pandemic, but the sense of perpetual displacement that I now inhabit and that in turn, inhabits my writing.

(RE)CLAIMING "HOME"

In *Love Marriage,* Yalini recalls her trip to Sri Lanka as a toddler, a visit which also signals the impossibility of her parents returning to their "home" again, given the intensifying conditions of the war in the northeast. She thus contemplates on the process of leaving and losing "home," a physical space, vibrant with their family and community ties and the incomparable feeling of "belonging again" for her parents: "but after all, how does one say goodbye to a place?" (Ganeshananthan 233). Yalini mulls over her own hope of revisiting the space that her parents once called "home": "someday, I will be able to walk into that country again, because they walked out of it. When I do it will be a different place than the one they knew" (ibid., 289). Yalini's journey to her mother's "home" will be marked by the grief, loss and silence that haunt their relationship. The desire to return "home" too will be kindled by the relationship she shares with her mother and the searing loss and collective trauma that Yalini inherits both consciously and indirectly from her mother. In her introduction to *In my Mother's House,* Thiranagama writes, "this book is about returning to my mother's house, but through a glass darkly, for I have put away childish things indeed" (2). While Thiranagama's return, as she elucidates, is marked by approaching war as a social condition (ibid.), the experience of Jaffna as "home" is one that she as a child has shared with her mother. However, for the women who are daughters of this "globe-scattered Sri Lankan family" (Ganeshananthan 1), who were born and bred outside the contours of the "home" their mothers once inhabited, whose understanding of Jaffna and Sri Lanka as "home" is mediated primarily through their mothers, the "home" of their mothers will not be the same, as it will be marked by the transformations that have occurred over the course of time and their own diasporic experiences. In *Love Marriage,* Yalini notes that the earrings that she inherits from her grandmother are now "very old diamonds in a new setting," once her aunt Kalyani gets them remade to fit Yalini's piercings (ibid., 238). Similarly, the return of daughters to their mothers' "home," a journey prompted by the bonds they share with their mothers, which are integral to defining their own sense of belonging and identity, will involve a process of reclaiming their mothers' "home," one which once became uninhabitable for their mothers.

In *Song of the Sun God,* Nala makes a proposition to Smirithi,

> "Smrithi, I have an idea. I want you to go back to Ceylon. I want you to go back to our home and remember Dhara. Remember her and your mother. Do this for me darling. Your grandfather would have wanted it too." Her voice shook when she mentioned Rajan.
> "I'll start calling people to tell them you're coming."
> She put the phone down after a long conversation with Smrithi and several follow-up calls to Priya, Siva and Prashanth.
> "Memory Smrithi, memory," she whispered to her empty kitchen. (Chandran 390)

WORKS CITED

Ahmed, Sarah. *Strange Encounters: Embodied Others in Post–Coloniality.* Routledge, 2000.
Chandran, Shankari. *Song of the Sun God.* Perera-Hussein Publishing House, 2017.
Cohen-Cruz, Jan. "Storytelling: Redefining the Private: From Personal Storytelling to Political Act." *A Boal Companion: Dialogues on Theatre and Cultural Politics,* edited by Jan Cohen-Cruz and Mady Schutzman, 2006. pp. 103–113.
Coomaraswamy, Radhika, and Nimanthi Perera-Rajasingham. "Being Tamil in a Different Way: A Feminist Critique of the Tamil Nation." *Pathways of Dissent: Tamil Nationalism in Sri Lanka,* edited by Cheran Rudhramoorthy. Sage Publications, 2009, pp. 107–138.
Daniel, Errol Valentine. *Charred Lullabies: Chapters in an Anthropography of Violence.* Princeton University Press, 1996.
Ganeshananthan, Vasugi V. *Love Marriage.* Weidenfeld & Nicolson, 2008.
Gedalof, Irene. "Taking (a) Place: Female Embodiment and the Re-grounding of Community." *Uprootings/Regroundings: Questions of Home and Migration,* edited by Sarah Ahmed, et al. Berg. 2003. pp. 91–112.
Gerharz, Eva. *The Politics of Reconstruction and Development in Sri Lanka: Transnational Commitments to Social Change.* Routledge, 2014.
Halbwachs, Maurice. *On Collective Memory.* Translated by Lewis A. Coser. University of Chicago, 1992.
Hirsch, Marianne. *Family Frames: Photography, Narrative and Postmemory.* Harvard University Press, 1997.
———. "Projected Memory: Holocaust Photographs in Personal and Public Fantasy." *Acts of Memory: Cultural Recall in the Present,* edited by Mieke Bal et al. University Press of New England, 1999, pp. 3–23.
Jayasuriya, Maryse. "Terror, Trauma, Transitions: Representing Violence in Sri Lankan Literature." *Indialogs,* vol. 3, 2016, pp. 195–209, doi:10.5565/rev/indialogs.48.
Jayawickrama, Sharanya. "At Home in the Nation? Negotiating Identity in Shyam Selvadurai's *Funny Boy.*" *Interpreting Homes in South Asian Literature,* edited by Malashri Lal et al. Pearson Longman, 2007, pp. 45–60.
Jazeel, Tariq. "Because Pigs Can Fly: Sexuality, Race and the Geographies of Difference in Shyam Selvadurai's *Funny Boy.*" *Gender, Place & Culture,* vol. 12, no. 2, 2005, pp. 231–249, doi:10.1080/09663690500094922.
Mohanraj, Mary Anne. *Bodies in Motion.* HarperCollins Publishers, 2005.
No More Tears Sister. Directed by Helene Klodawsky, National Film Board of Canada Production. 2006.
Orjuela, Camila. "Distant Warriors, Distant Peace Workers? Multiple Diaspora Roles in Sri Lanka's Violent Conflict." *Global Networks,* vol. 8, no. 4, 2008, pp. 436–452. doi:10.1111/j.1471-0374.2008.00233.
Ranasinha, Ruvani. *Contemporary Diasporic South Asian Women's Fiction: Gender, Narration and Globalisation.* Palgrave Macmillan Publishers, 2016.
Rose, Jacqueline. *States of Fantasy.* Oxford University Press, 1996.

Rudhramoorthy, Cheran. "Poetry after Libricide and Genocide." *Indialogs*, vol. 3, 2016, pp. 211-doi: 10.5565/rev/indialogs.49.

Shanaathanan, T. *The Incomplete Thombu.* Raking Leaves, 2011.

Silva, Neluka. *The Gendered Nation: Contemporary Writings from South Asia.* Sage Publications, 2004.

Silva, Neluka. "No Place Called Home?": Representations of Home in Chandani Lokugé's *If the Moon Smiled* and Roshi Fernando's *Homesick.*" *South Asian Review: Sri Lankan Anglophone Literature,* vol. 3, no. 1, 2012, pp. 109–123. doi:1 0.1080/02759527.2012.11932898

Sivamohan, Sumathy, "The Middle Passage: Migration and Displacement of Sri Lankan Tamil Women of the Diaspora." *Socio-Legal Reviews,* vol. 1, no. 1, 2005, pp. 11–29. National Law School of India University, ISSN No: 0973-5216.

Sivamohan, Sumathy. "Is There a War in Your 'Ur'? Jaffna Is in the Heart." *Continuities/Departures: Essays on Postcolonial Sri Lankan Women's Creative Writing in English,* edited by Dinith Karunanayake and Selvy Thiruchandran, Vijitha Yapa, 2011, pp.116–136.

Sriskandarajah, Dhananjayan. "Tamil Diaspora Politics." *Encyclopedia of Diasporas: Immigrant and Refugee Cultures Around the World,* edited by Melvin Ember et al., Springer, 2004, pp. 492–500. doi: 10.1007/978-0-387-29904-4_50.

Stratton, Jon. "Before Holocaust Memory: Making Sense of Trauma between Postmemory and Cultural Memory." *Journal of the Australian Critical Race & Whiteness Studies Association,* vol. 1, 2005, 241–281. doi: 10.1057/9780230612747_8.

Tantrigoda, Pavithra. "Fractured Selves/Conflicting Identities: Sri Lankan Female Migrants in Chandani Lokugé's *If the Moon Smiled.*" *Continuities/Departures: Essays on Postcolonial Sri Lankan Women's Creative Writing in English,* edited by Dinith Karunanayake and Selvy Thiruchandran, Vijitha Yapa, 2011, pp. 63–75.

Thiranagama, Sharika. *In My Mother's House: Civil War in Sri Lanka.* University of Pennsylvania Press, 2011.

Thiranagama, Sharika. "Making Tigers from Tamils: Long-Distance Nationalism and Sri Lankan Tamils in Toronto." *American Anthropologist,* vol. 116, no. 2, 2014, pp. 265–278. doi:10.1111/aman.12099.

Thiranagama, Sharika. Personal interview. 9 July 2018.

Tucker, Judith. "Painting Places: A Postmemorial Landscape?." *Essays in Migratory Aesthetics: Cultural Practices between Migration and Art-Making,* edited by Sam Durrant and Catherine M. Lord. Rodopi Press Amsterdam, 2007, pp. 59–80.

Uyangoda, Jayadeva. "Sri Lanka: Continuing Dilemmas of Peace Building and Reconciliation." Conference on Memory, Justice and Reconciliation, 13 September 2017, International Centre for Ethnic Studies, Colombo. Keynote address.

Walker, Rebecca. *Enduring Violence: Everyday Life and Conflict in Eastern Sri Lanka.* Manchester University Press, 2013.

Women in War Time. Women and Media Collective, 2002.

NOTES

1. The vast majority of those who migrated from Sri Lanka are primarily from the Jaffna peninsula (Gerharz; Thiranagama *In My Mother's House*; Thiranagama "Making Tigers from Tamils"). Sriskandarajah concurs that Tamils heralding from the northeastern part of Sri Lanka, who have formed distinct communities both within and outside the country, are popularly identified as "Sri Lankan Tamils" (493). Therefore, the present study, while acknowledging the heterogeneity and complexity of the Tamil community, refers to the members of the Tamil diaspora from Sri Lanka represented in the novels, as the Sri Lankan Tamil diaspora.

2. The war between the Government of Sri Lanka and The Liberation Tigers of Tamil Eelam (LTTE), known as one of the longest running civil wars in Asia, lasted nearly three decades. The cause for the war is often associated with the 23rd of July 1983 (also known as Black July), when the LTTE, reportedly, ambushed an army convoy that killed thirteen soldiers, triggering riots in which approximately 2,500 Tamils were killed. The burning of the Jaffna Library in 1981 and Black July are often cited as the greatest acts of violence carried out against the Tamil community (Jayasuriya; Rudhramoorthy; Sivamohan "War in Your 'Ur'").

3. The documentary *No More Tears Sister* directed by Klodawsky provides an account of the life and death of Rajani Thiranagama.

4. The LTTE was labelled one of the most powerful terrorist forces and listed as a terrorist group by several countries, including the United States (US), India and the United Kingdom (UK). It was the military reawakening of the Tamil New Tigers (TNT) group in 1976. It was founded under the leadership of Uma Maheswaran and the military command of Velupillai Prabhakaran in order to form a separate state within Sri Lanka, also known as Tamil Eelam.

5. Thiranagama writes of the *ur*, "in approaching displacement, I foreground one of the most celebrated aspects of personhood in northern Sri Lanka: the notion of *ur* (home/natal village). *Ur*, home, is an *everyday* and often used Tamil word" (*In My Mother's House* 18).

6. The defeat of the LTTE and the death of its leader Velupillai Prabhakaran in May 2009, marks the official end of the war in Sri Lanka. Uyangoda commences his keynote address titled "Sri Lanka: Continuing Dilemmas of Peace Building and Reconciliation" by highlighting that the period following 2009 can be referred to as the post-war era, as Sri Lanka is yet to become a post-conflict society. Thiranagama reiterates that the "military war may have ended [but] not the political one", suggesting that the concerns of minorities in Sri Lanka remain unaddressed (*In My Mother's House* 4). Therefore, in this chapter, the military battle from 1983–2009 is referred to as the war and the period following the official end of the war is identified as the post-war period.

7. Gerharz identifies several events that are commemorated and institutionalized by the LTTE and observed by a majority of Tamil-inhabited areas in the diaspora, including Black Tigers' Day on the 5th of July and Heroes' Day on the 27th of November (49).

8. Rajinie is from a mixed background as her mother is Sinhala and her father is Tamil.

9. The term postmemory, conceptualized by Hirsch, is "meant to convey its temporal and qualitative difference from survivor memory" to examine the haunted relationship that the subsequent generation has with the trauma experienced by the previous generation ("Projected Memory" 9). Hirsch theorizes the concept of postmemory specifically in relation to children of survivors of the Holocaust, but suggests that it could be used as a lens to explore memories of collective trauma, in general, among the second-generation ("Projected Memory").

10. Translates as elder sister from Tamil.

11. See *Women in War Time,* a trilingual poetry collection, for narratives focusing on the experiences of women engulfed in the war in Sri Lanka.

Index

Abdelrazek, Amal Talaat, 116n11; *Contemporary Arab American Women Writers*, 103–4
Abirached, Zeina, 117n15
Afkhami, Mahnaz, 100, 101
Agamben, Giorgio, *Homo Sacer*, 37–38, 41
agency, 156–58
Ahmad, Aijaz, "Jameson's Rhetoric of Otherness and the 'National Allegory,'" 115n2
Aisha (refugee child), 36–37
Al-Ali, Nadje, 155
Al-deen, Taghreed Jamal, *Motherhood, Education and Migration*, 2–3
Alex (NFE coordinator), 138
Alexandra (teacher), 139, 140
Al-Haj, Majid, "The Changing Arab Kinship Structure," 115n3
Alien Land Act (1913), 126–27
Alyan, Hala, *Salt Houses*, 3
Amir Houssein (refugee child), 32, 40–41
ancestors, 6, 83
Anthias, Flora, 47
Anthropology of Violence (Daniel), 172–73
Anzaldúa, Gloria, 5, 65, 74–75, 150
Apostolidou, Anna, 136, 139

Arab Americans: after 9/11, 98, 99, 110, 116n14; and homosocial female networks, 97; hyphenation, 116n12; in *The Inheritance of Exile*, 6, 95–97, 107–12; literature, 97–99; in *West of the Jordan*, 6, 95–96, 102–7
Asian Americans. *See* Japanese picture brides; Vietnamese Americans
Asiatic Exclusion League, 122, 126
Asma (refugee child), 39
Azize (refugee mother), 31–33, 34, 38, 40–41, 42

B., David, 117n15
Baghdad Twist (documentary), 6, 7, 150–62
Balass, Joe, *Baghdad Twist*, 7, 150–62
Balass, Valentine, 7, 150–62
les bandes dessinées comics, 112, 117n15
basket weaving motif, 110–12
beauty, as a form of resistance, 13–14, 19–23, 27–28
The Best We Could Do (Bui), 5
Black feminist theory of motherhood, 6, 63, 65, 66–70
Black Feminist Thought (Collins), 68
Bloom, Lynn Z., 67

bodies, mothers': autobiographical, 105; in *On Earth We Are Briefly Gorgeous*, 24–26; as the embodiment of home, 170–72; in *Inside Out & Back Again*, 74; violence to, 174–76
Bodies in Motion (Mohanraj), 166, 169, 170, 173, 178–79
Body Counts (Espiritu), 14, 80
borderland theory, 5, 65
braiding hair, 68, 69–70
The Buddha in the Attic (Otsuka), 7, 120, 123–30
Bui, Long, *Returns of War*, 82
Bui, Thi, 4, 19; *The Best We Could Do*, 5
Butler, Judith, 71

capitalism: effects of on refugee women, 81–82; filial piety and, 82–83
care, ethics of, 37, 41, 66
care work, of mothers, 37–38, 113, 123–27
Chandran, Shankari, 6, 8; *Song of the Sun God*, 166, 168, 174–76, 177–78, 180
"The Changing Arab Kinship Structure" (Al-Haj), 115n3
"chaste warrior" trope, 54–58, 60
child birth and rearing, by Japanese picture brides, 123–27
Cohen-Cruz, Jan, 178
Cohn, Carol, 49
Collazo, Julie Schwietert, 3
Collins, Patricia Hill, 5–6, 63, 65, 66, 70–71; *Black Feminist Thought*, 68
colonialism, 97–99
community: as an answer to militarization, 51; building, 39; expectations, and resistance to education, 140–41; "livelihood systems," 53; as a means of survival, 59–60; sense of belonging through storytelling, 176
compassion, 72–73

Contemporary Arab American Women Writers (Abdelrazek), 103–4
Coomaraswamy, Radhika, 168
COVID-19 pandemic, 1, 4, 113, 137, 179
Cox, Sandra, 73
Crew, Hilary, 63, 66, 67, 68
critical refugee narratives, 79–83, 87, 89–90; *Dragonfish*, 87–90; *Short Girls*, 83–86
Cruz, Rosayra Pablo, 3

Daneil, Marguerite, 136
Daniel, Errol Valentine, *Anthropology of Violence*, 172–73
Darraj, Susan Muaddi, 6, 98–99, 116n6; *The Inheritance of Exile*, 6, 95–97, 100–101, 107–12
daughters. *See* mother-daughter relationships
Davis, Angela, 28
Defourmantelle, Anne, 38, 41; *Of Hospitality*, 5, 33–34
denaturalization, 154
Derrida, Jacques, 36, 38, 41; *Of Hospitality*, 5, 33–34
DeWitt, John, 129
Displaced (Nguyen, ed.), 87
displaced mothers: fictional representations, 3; identity constructs, 2, 4; identity narration by, 154–62; social networks of, 143–44. *See also* refugees
displacement time, 142–43, 171
Dragonfish (Tran), 6, 79, 80, 82, 87–90, 91nn2–3

education: in *On Earth We Are Briefly Gorgeous*, 15–16; goals of mothers, 7, 138; in Greece, for refugees, 135–36, 148n3; and intergenerational differences, 141–42, 143; Japanese *risshin shusse* work ethic, 128; mothers' participation in, 2–3, 38, 139–40; mothers' resistance to,

140–41, 142; refugee mothers' relationships with, 134, 142–45
Elena (teacher), 140
Embroideries (Satrapi), 112–13
embroidering motif, 96, 102–7, 109–10, 112–13
Enloe, Cynthia, 46, 47
Espiritu, Yến Lê, 15, 16, 81, 82; *Body Counts*, 14, 80
ethics of care, 37, 41, 66
Executive Order 9066, 129

Fahs, Breanne, 25
Farhud ("Violent Dispossession"), 7, 153–54
Farish, Terry, 4; *The Good Braider*, 5, 63, 65, 66–70
Fatima (refugee mother), 32, 40
feminism: Black feminist theory of motherhood, 6, 63, 65, 66–70; matricentric, 65–66; transnational, 65, 66, 76; Western perceptions, 100–101
Feminism Without Borders (Mohanty), 100
Fernando, Roshi, *Homesick*, 169
filial piety, 82–83
Forget Baghdad (documentary), 151–52
442nd Regimental Combat Team (442nd RCT), 129–30
Funny Boy (film), 178

Galland, Antoine, 98, 99
Ganeshananthan, V. V., 6, 8; *Love Marriage*, 166, 169–72, 173, 174, 176–77, 178, 179–80
Gauch, Suzanne, *Liberating Shahrazad*, 98
Gedalof, Irene, 168
gendering of women, 47–48, 58. *See also* hyperfeminization
gender role stereotypes, 73–76
genealogies, 66–69
"A Genealogy of Refugee Writing" (Rose), 66

Gerharz, Eva, 183n7
ghost, defined, 80
ghost mother trope, 6; defined, 80; in *Dragonfish*, 79, 80, 81, 82, 87–90; in *Short Girls*, 80, 81, 82, 83–86, 89–90
Giles, Wenona, 52, 58
Glenn, Evelyn Nakano, 69, 124, 126
Golley, Nawar Al-Hassan, 157
The Good Braider (Farish), 5, 63, 65, 66–70
Gordon, Avery, 15
grandmother-mother-daughter bond, 66–69
Greece, refugees in, 133–45
Greenfield, Chase, 87, 91n3

Ha, Quan-Manh, 87, 91n3
Hala (refugee child), 133
Halaby, Laila, 6, 99; *West of the Jordan*, 6, 95–96, 100–101
Halbwachs, Maurice, 172
Hassan, Wail, 156
Held, Virginia, 37, 41
Henieh (refugee child), 32–33, 34, 38, 41
Henke, Suzette A., 156
Hirsh, Marianne, 80, 90, 116n13, 174, 184n9
Hoang, Nguyen Tan, *A View From the Bottom*, 26
home and homeland: (re)claiming, 179–80; in *Bodies in Motion*, 169, 170; collective memory of, 172; embodiment of, 170–72; in *Love Marriage*, 169–72, 176–77, 179–80; motherhood association with, 167–70; in *In My Mother's House*, 180; representations of by Sri Lankan Tamil diaspora, 165–67; in *Song of the Sun God*, 168, 180; Tamil notion of *ur*, 166, 167, 183n5; use of terms, 167
Homesick (Fernando), 169
Homo Sacer (Agamben), 37–38, 41
homosocial desire, 116n7

homosocial female networks, 6, 97, 101, 112–13, 115n1; in *The Inheritance of Exile*, 100–101; in *West of the Jordan*, 100–101. *See also* community
hospitality, 33–34, 36, 38, 41–42
Human Rights Watch Organization, 50
hyperfeminization: "chaste warrior" trope, 54–58, 60; in militarized societies, 45, 47–48, 60; "military mother" trope, 49–51, 60; "modest maiden" trope, 51–54, 60
hypermasculinization of female soldiers, 47, 54–58

Ibbett, Katherine, 65
Ichioka, Yuji, 119–20
identity: and change, 143; collective, 172; establishing/re-establishing, 161–62; familial role and, 169; language and, 150, 151; narrating, 152–53, 154–62; personal, 2; social, 2; transnational familial, 2
identity politics, 107
If the Moon Smiled (Lokugé), 169
Iman Noor (refugee child), 36–37
Immigrant Acts (Lowe), 19
immigration, Japanese, 121–23
Immigration Act (1924), 123
The Incomplete Thombu (Shanaathanan), 165
Ingratitude (Ninh), 17
The Inheritance of Exile (Darraj), 6, 95–97; basket weaving motif, 110–12; embroidering motif, 96, 109–10; homosocial female networks, 100–101; storytelling, 96, 107–12
In My Mother's House (Thiranagama), 166–67, 180
Inside Out & Back Again (Lai), 5, 63–64, 65, 69, 70–76
interdependence, 37–38, 41–42
intergenerational trauma, 6, 8; in *On Earth We Are Briefly Gorgeous*, 16–17; in *Song of the Sun God*, 174–76
Interpreting the Self (Reynolds), 156
Iraqi diaspora, 149–54. *See also Baghdad Twist* (documentary)
Iraqi Jews (Shiblak), 153
Irina (teacher), 141–42
Israel, 153–54

Jameson, Frederic, "Third-World Literature in the Era of Multinational Capitalism," 115n2
"Jameson's Rhetoric of Otherness and the 'National Allegory'" (Aijaz), 115n2
Janoff-Bulman, Ronnie, *Shattered Assumptions*, 163n8
Japanese picture brides: about, 7, 119–20, 130; child birth, 123–24; child rearing, 124–27; cultural conflicts with children, 127–28; education of children, 128; history of, 121–23; incarceration, 128–30
Jayawickrama, Sharanya, 178
Jewish Iraqis, 150–54. *See also Baghdad Twist* (documentary)
Joukhadar, Zeyn, *The Map of Salt and Stars*, 3
justice, 37–38, 41

Kadowaki, Atsushi, 128
Kahane, Claire, 83
Kahf, Mohja, 116n6
Katerina (teacher), 140–41
Khan, Sorayya, *Noor*, 176–77
kinship, 115n3
Klodawsky, Helene, *No More Tears*, 183n3
knowledge: cultural transmission of, 73–76; generational transmission of, 69–70; oral transmission of, 70–72

Lai, Thannha, 4; *Inside Out & Back Again*, 5, 63–64, 65, 69, 70–76
Lam, Andrew, 19

language, and identity, 150, 151
Layla (refugee mother), 31, 38, 39
Lee, Janet, *Women Worldwide*, 46
Lenette, Caroline, 140, 144
Levi, Meredith, 143, 145
Levy, Lital, 154; "Self and the City," 153
Liberating Shahrazad (Gauch), 98
Liberation Tigers of Tamil Eelam (LTTE), 166, 183n2, 183n4, 183nn6–7
Lieu, Nhi T., 18
life narration, 152–53, 154–62
"livelihood systems," 53
Lokugé, Chandani, *If the Moon Smiled*, 169
Long, Lisa, 73
Lorde, Audre, 25, 75; *Zami. A New Spelling of My Name*, 67
Love Marriage (Ganeshananthan), 166, 169–72, 173, 174, 176–77, 178, 179–80
Lowe, Lisa, *Immigrant Acts*, 19
Lowinsky, Naomi Ruth, *Stories from the Motherline*, 69
Lydia (coordinator), 140

MacClatcy, Valentine Stuart, 123
Maedeh (refugee child), 33, 40–41, 42
Mahilé (refugee mother), 5, 31, 32, 34, 38, 39, 40
Mahmoud, Emi, "Mama," 67
Maia (refugee child), 36
Mailhot, Terese Marie, 3
"Mama" (Mahmoud), 67
The Map of Salt and Stars (Joukhadar), 3
Martin, B., 160–61
Maruoka, Hideko, 125
maternal practice, 39
Maternal Thinking (Ruddick & O'Reilly), 34, 37
Mathers, Jennifer, 55–56
matricentric feminism, 65–66
Maxey, Roth, 120

Mehta, Brinda, 106, 111; *Rituals of Memory in Contemporary Arab Women's Writing*, 103
Meiji era (Japan), 121, 124, 125, 128, 130
Melissa (coordinator), 138
memory: in *Baghdad Twist*, 161–62; collective, 172, 177; in *On Earth We Are Briefly Gorgeous*, 14–15; historical amnesia, 19, 20; as a literary trope, 106–7; of missing/displaced mothers, 6, 79–90; poetics of displacement, 20–21; postmemory concept, 80–81, 174, 184n9
Mernissi, Fatima, 103; *Scheherazade Goes West*, 99
Mexican mothers, 2
Middle Eastern women and mothers: in *Baghdad Twist*, 150–62; collective ethos, 32; cultural gaps, 6; educational navigation by as refugees in Greece, 133–45; fictional representations, 3; gendered conduct, 31–32, 39; in *The Inheritance of Exile*, 6, 95–97, 107–12; name usage, 31–32; refugee camp experiences, 31–42; Western stereotypes, 38–39, 96, 100, 156–58; in *West of the Jordan*, 6, 95–96, 102–7. *See also* Arab Americans
migrant mothers, 2. *See also* displaced mothers; refugees
militarization: defined, 46; as a destabilizing force, 58; female community as an answer to, 51; and hyperfeminization of women, 45, 47–48, 49–51, 60; and hypermasculinization of female soldiers, 47, 54–58
"military mother" trope, 49–51, 60
Mina (refugee child), 42
model minority stereotype, 14, 18, 130
"modest maiden" trope, 51–54, 60
Mohamed, Nadifa, 4, 45; *The Orchard of Lost Souls*, 5, 45–60

Mohanraj, Mary Anne, 6, 8 *Bodies in Motion*, 166, 169, 170, 173, 178–79
Mohanty, Chandra, 101, 160–61; *Feminism Without Borders*, 100; *Third World Women and the Politics of Feminism*, 100
Morrison, Toni, 66, 83
mother-daughter relationships, 6, 8; in *Bodies in Motion*, 173, 178–79; displaced mothers and, 79–80; in *Dragonfish*, 79, 80, 82, 87–90; effects of trauma and maternal abandonment, 83, 89–90; in *The Good Braider*, 63, 65, 66–70; and homosocial female networks, 97; in *The Inheritance of Exile*, 95–97, 101, 107–12; in *Inside Out & Back Again*, 63–64, 65, 69, 70–76; in *Love Marriage*, 173, 174; in *Short Girls*, 80, 82, 83–86, 89–90; in *Song of the Sun God*, 174–76, 177–78; in the Sri Lankan Tamil diaspora, 166–67, 170–72; in *West of the Jordan*, 95–96, 101, 102–7; in young adult literature, 63, 64–65
Motherhood, Education and Migration (Al-deen), 2–3
Motherhood across Borders (Oliveira), 2
motherhood studies, 2
mothering and motherhood: Bloom's definition of, 67; borders of, 1; as a collective act, 143–44; and "home" rhetoric, 167–70; in precarity, 134; as site of negotiating gender roles, 73–76
motherly aesthetics, 13, 19, 21–22, 28
mother-son relationships, 150–62
Mugo, Mugo, "Rape in Somalia," 50
multiculturalism, American rhetoric of, 15–16, 18
multigenerational caregiving, 2
Munson, Curtis, 129
Murphy, Fiona, *Remember Baghdad*, 163n2

Nadia (cultural mediator), 141
Naghibi, Nima, 100, 116n7; *Rethinking Global Sisterhood*, 97, 101, 115n1
Nancy, Jean-Luc, 72
Narghes (refugee child), 32, 34, 40
narrating identity: establishing agency, 156–58; establishing/re-establishing identity, 161–62; reflecting on loss of home and family, 154–56; relating testimonies of trauma, 158–61; storytelling pattern, 152–53
nationalism: Arab, 154; and gendering of women, 47–48; Sri Lankan, 167–68; Zionism, 153–54
Nayeri, Dina, 3, 37, 38, 39, 41; *The Ungrateful Refugee*, 36
Naz (refugee child), 35–36, 39, 42
Nelson, Kim Park, 130
neoliberal economies, critique of, 25–26
Newfield, Christopher, 15
Nguyen, Bich Minh, 4; *Short Girls*, 6, 80, 82, 83–86, 89–90; *Stealing Buddha's Dinner*, 91n1
Nguyen, Long T., 24
Nguyen, Mimi Thi, 86
Nguyen, Viet Thanh, 19, 81; *Displaced*, 87
Nguyn, Mimi Thi, 17
Night Sky With Exit Wounds (Vuong), 14, 24
Ninh, Erin Khu, 82; *Ingratitude*, 17
Nirgina (refugee mother), 31, 35–36, 38, 39, 42
Nisei (second-generation Japanese Americans), 120, 126–30
No More Tears (documentary), 183n3
Noor (Khan), 176–77

Of Hospitality (Derrida & Defourmantelle), 5, 33–34
Oido, Gentaro, 125
Okawa, Dennis, 126
Oliveira, Gabrielle, *Motherhood across Borders*, 2

On Earth We Are Briefly Gorgeous (Vuong), 4–5, 13–29; beauty as resistance, 13–14, 19–23, 27–28; domestic violence, 25; education, 15–16; freedom, 22–23; intergenerational trauma, 16–17; memory, 14–15; motherly aesthetics, 13, 19, 21–22, 28; mother's body, 24–26; poetics of displacement, 20–21, 22, 26–27; song and singing, 17–18, 27–28; submission, as power, 26–27; war, 13–17, 19–21

The Orchard of Lost Souls (Mohamed), 5, 45–60; "chaste warrior" trope, 54–58; militarization of women, 48–49; "military mother" trope, 49–51; "modest maiden" trope, 51–54; women as public symbols, 48; women as reproducers, 48

O'Reilly, Andrea, 39, 66, 69; *Maternal Thinking*, 34; *Textual Mothers/Maternal Texts*, 64

orientalism, 97–99, 109

Otsuka, Julie, 6; *The Buddha in the Attic*, 7, 120, 123–30

Oulié (refugee mother), 40

Ozawa, Takao, 122

Palestinian basket weaving, 110–12

Palestinian History Tapestry project, 116n10

Palestinian *roza*, 102–7

Patriarchy: effects of on refugee women, 81–82; homosocial female networks and, 101; Japanese *ie* system, 125; Japanese *ryosai kenbo* ideology, 125–26; transmission of values of, 73–76

Pearl Harbor attack, 128–29

Perera-Rajasingham, Nimanthi, 168

Peterson, William, "Success Story Japanese American Style," 129

Pham, Amy, 19

picture marriages. *See* Japanese picture brides

Podnieks, Elizabeth, 69; *Textual Mothers/Maternal Texts*, 64

poetics of displacement, 20–21, 22, 26–29

postmemory concept, 80–81, 174, 184n9

Prabhakaran, Velupillai, 183n6

precarity, 134

Putnam, Robert D., 144

queer theory, 5, 65

Quong, Spencer, 14

racism: resistance to, 70–72; towards Japanese, 122, 126, 127–30

Rakia (refugee mother), 31, 33, 34–35, 38, 39

Ranasinha, Ruvani, 176–77

"Rape in Somalia" (Mugo), 50

Raven-Roberts, Angela, 46, 53

Reading Autobiography (Smith & Watson), 105

"A Refugee Again" (Tran), 87

refugees: expectations of gratitude from, 36–37; and the "gift of freedom," 17, 19, 82–83; in Greece, 133–45; identity constructs, 1; Palestinian, 103, 108, 116n11; protracted refugee situations, 58–59; social navigation by, 7, 134, 136; unassimilable, 19; use of term, 148n1; from wartime displacement, 52; young adult literary texts, 63–65. *See also* displaced mothers

Remember Baghdad (documentary), 163n2

Rethinking Global Sisterhood (Naghibi), 97, 101, 115n1

Returns of War (Bui), 82

Reynolds, Dwight F., *Interpreting the Self*, 156

Rich, Adrienne, 63, 69

Rituals of Memory in Contemporary Arab Women's Writing (Mehta), 103

Roosevelt, Franklin, 129

Rose, Arthur, "A Genealogy of Refugee Writing," 66
Rosinsky, Natalie, 64
Ruddick, Sara, 39; *Maternal Thinking*, 34, 37

Sabry, Somaya Sami, 98, 99
Safaa (refugee mother), 133, 138, 142, 145
Salaita, Steven, 116n14
Saliha (refugee mother), 31, 33, 42
Sallis, Eva, *Scheherazade Through the Looking Glass*, 99
Salt Houses (Alyan), 3
Sarikoudi, Georgia, 136, 139
Satrapi, Marjan, 117n15; *Embroideries*, 112–13
"Scheherazade and the Limits of Inclusive Politics in Arab American Literature" (Shomali), 98
Scheherazade archetype, 97–99, 109, 115–16nn4–5, 116n6
Scheherazade Goes West (Mernissi), 99
Scheherazade Through the Looking Glass (Sallis), 99
Sedgwick, Eve Kosofsky, 101, 116n7
self, and other, 33–34
"Self and the City" (Levy), 153
self-care metaphor, 28
self-sufficiency, 32, 38
sexual violence: in refugee camps, 52; wartime, 50–51, 54; within the armed forces, 56
Shanaathanan, T., *The Incomplete Thombu*, 165
Shattered Assumptions (Janoff-Bulman), 163n8
Shaw, Susan M., *Women Worldwide*, 46
Shiblak, Abbas, *Iraqi Jews*, 153
Shohat, Ellah, 152
Shomali, Mejdulene B., 116n6; "Scheherazade and the Limits of Inclusive Politics in Arab American Literature," 98

Short Girls (Nguyen), 6, 80, 82, 83–86, 89–90
Silva, Niluka, 169
Sivamohan, Sumathy, 168, 170
Six-Days War, 103, 108, 116n11
Sjoberg, Laura, 47, 54
Smith, Sidonie, *Reading Autobiography*, 105
social navigation, 7, 134, 136, 144
social networks, 143–44
Song of the Sun God (Chandran), 166, 168, 174–76, 177–78, 180
sovereignty, 37–38
"Sri Lanka" (Uyangoda), 183n6
Sri Lankan Tamil diaspora, 165–66, 183n1. *See also* home and homeland
Sriskandarajah, Dhananjayan, 183n2
Stealing Buddha's Dinner (Nguyen), 91n1
Stimson, Henry, 129
Stories from the Motherline (Lowinsky), 69
storytelling: as community building, 176; in *The Inheritance of Exile*, 96, 107–12; in *Love Marriage*, 176–77; narrating identity, 152–53, 154–62; political potential of, 178; Scheherazade archetype, 97–99, 109, 115–16nn4–5; in *West of the Jordan*, 96, 102–7
Stratton, Jon, 174
submission, as power, 26–27
"Success Story, Japanese American Style" (Peterson), 129

Takaki, Ronald, 128
Tantrigoda, Pavithra, 169
Textual Mothers/Maternal Texts (Podnieks & O'Reilly, eds.), 64
Thiranagama, Rajani, 166, 171, 183n3
Thiranagama, Sharika, 166, 171, 172, 173–74, 179, 183nn5–6; *In My Mother's House*, 166–67, 180

"Third-World Literature in the Era of Multinational Capitalism" (Jameson), 115n2
Third World Women and the Politics of Feminism (Mohanty), 100
The Thousand and One Nights, 97–98, 109
Thunder Cake (story), 20
Thuy, Le Thi Diem, 19
Torres, Justin, 22–23
Tran, Hong Kong, *Vietnamese Manicurists*, 23
Tran, Vu, 4, 8; *Dragonfish*, 6, 79, 80, 82, 87–90, 91nn2–3; "A Refugee Again," 87
transgenerational haunting, 173–74
transmaternalism, 73
transnational feminism, 65, 66, 76
Transnationalism (Vertovec), 111
trauma: collective, 83, 174, 177; as a disruption of the "rescue and liberation" myth, 80; effects of maternal abandonment, 83, 89–90; family separation policies and, 81; intergenerational, 6, 8; and postmemory concept, 80–81; in the Sri Lankan Tamil diaspora, 170–79; testimonies of in narrating identity, 158–61
Truman, Harry, 129
Tucker, Judith, 179
Tuon, Bunkong, 71
Turshen, Meridith, 46, 59

Um, Katharya, 81, 90
unassimilability, 15–16, 19, 122–23, 130
The Ungrateful Refugee (Nayeri), 36
"universal sisterhood," 100
unsettlement, 134–35, 144–45
"The Use of Traditional Vietnamese Medicine Among Vietnamese Immigrants Attending an Urban Community Health Center in the United States" (Nguyen), 24

Uyangoda, Jayadeva, "Sri Lanka," 183n6

Vertovec, Steven, *Transnationalism*, 111
Vietnamese Americans: class stratification, 18; in *Dragonfish*, 79, 80, 82, 87–90; in *On Earth We Are Briefly Gorgeous*, 4–5, 13–29; in *Inside Out & Back Again*, 5, 63–64, 70–76; literature, 14, 19, 28, 73; manicurists, 23–24; as a "model minority," 14, 18; in *Short Girls*, 80, 82, 83–86; traditional medicinal practices, 24–25
Vietnamese Manicurists (Tran), 23
A View From the Bottom (Hoang), 26
Vigh, Henrik, 134, 136, 144
violence: to mothers' bodies, 174–76; sexual, 50–51; trauma of, 172–73
voice, use of, 70–72
Vuong, Ocean, 4; *On Earth We Are Briefly Gorgeous*, 4–5, 13–29; *Night Sky With Exit Wounds*, 14, 24

Walker, Rebecca, 167, 169, 176
war and wartime: American invasion of Iraq, 149, 150–51, 158, 163n1; displacement due to, 52, 53; in *On Earth We Are Briefly Gorgeous*, 13–17, 19–21; female collectives as a means of survival during, 59–60; impacts of on women and mothers, 16–17, 46–47, 50; in *The Orchard of Lost Souls*, 45–60; sexual violence, 50–51, 54; in *Song of the Sun God*, 174–76; Sri Lankan civil war, 165, 166, 167, 183n2, 183n6, 184n11
Watson, Julia, *Reading Autobiography*, 105
West of the Jordan (Halaby), 6, 95–96; embroidering motif, 102–7, 109–10; homosocial female networks, 100–101; storytelling, 96
Whitehead, Anne, 160
Willmann Robleda, Zubia, 144

Women Worldwide (Lee & Shaw), 46

Yanagisako, Ikumi, 126
young adult literature: mother-daughter relationships in, 63, 64–65; verse novels, 64

Yuval-Davis, Nira, 47

Zami. A New Spelling of My Name (Lorde), 67
Zionism, 153–54

About the Contributors

Lamees Al Ethari is the Associate Director of the Arts First Program and a Continuing Lecturer in the Department of English Language and Literature at the University of Waterloo, where she has been teaching creative and academic writing and literature since 2015.

Through her poetry collection, *From the Wounded Banks of the Tigris* (2018) and her memoir, *Waiting for the Rain: An Iraqi Memoir* (2019), she reflects on her experiences of the 2003 American invasion of Iraq, the violent aftermath, and her migration from home. Her poems have appeared in *About Place Journal*, *The New Quarterly*, *The Malpais Review*, and the anthology *Al Mutanabbi Street Starts Here*. She is in the process of completing a monograph titled, *Patterns of Telling: Iraqi Women's Autobiography in the Diaspora*, which is a critical exploration of contemporary Iraqi women's life narratives, poetry, and prose. She is also a consulting and nonfiction editor with *The New Quarterly* and a co-coordinator for The X Page: A Storytelling Workshop for Immigrant Women.

Janet J. Graham is an Assistant Professor at the University of Nebraska at Kearney. She earned her PhD in literary studies from the University of Hawai'i at Mānoa in 2019 for her dissertation that examines Vietnamese diasporic literature through the frameworks of relationality and critical refugee studies. In addition to her work with critical refugee studies, Glissant's poetics of relationality, and Vietnamese diasporic literature, her current research interests include anti-racist education, carceral life writing, migration narratives, multiethnic American and anglophone literature, and postwar Vietnamese literature in translation.

Alison Graham-Bertolini is an Associate Professor of English and Women's Studies at North Dakota State University. Her research focuses on contemporary literature, with specializations in women's literature, ethnic literature, and literature of the southern United States. Graham-Bertolini is co-editor of *Understanding the Short Fiction of Carson McCullers* (2020) and *Carson McCullers in the Twenty-First Century* (Palgrave Macmillan, 2016). She is the author of *Vigilante Women in Contemporary American Fiction* (Palgrave Macmillan, 2011). Graham-Bertolini has published in peer-reviewed publications including the *The Journal of the Midwest Modern Language Association* and *The Southern Quarterly*, and plays bass guitar in NDSU's popular feminist collective, Aca-SHE-mia (rhymes with "academia").

Lucy Hunt teaches and researches issues at the intersection of migration and education. She is pursuing a DPhil at the University of Oxford, for which she explores young refugees' participation in post-15 education in Greece. She has an MSc in Educational Studies from the University of Leuven, Belgium.

Adrianne Kalfopoulou is the author of three collections of poetry, most recently *A History of Too Much* (Red Hen Press, 2018), two essay collections, and several chapbooks. She was the McGee Distinguished Professor of Creative Writing at Davidson College (2020–2021), and currently teaches at RIT, Dubai, where she is Associate Professor of Creative Writing.

Maria D. Lombard is an Assistant Professor in Residence at Northwestern University in Qatar where she teaches writing, rhetoric, and literature courses. Her research focuses primarily on writing studies, with interests in the stories of refugee and displaced mothers, minority and gendered voices, and postcolonial travel writing. Her work on motherhood, mobility, and migration has appeared in several anthologies.

Stella Mililli is a PhD candidate in English Literature in the Department of Teacher Education at the Norwegian University of Science and Technology (NTNU) in Trondheim. Her dissertation research examines representations of refugees in Young Adult (YA) fictional and non-fictional contemporary literature, and how this type of literature can function in the classroom to create an ethical pedagogy of English.

Sabreena Niles is a Senior Lecturer at the Department of English of the University of Kelaniya in Sri Lanka. Her work focuses on gendered memories/archiving, disability and inclusive pedagogies, and storytelling in theatre and performance art. In her teaching and research in literature and cultural studies, she approaches post/war narratives primarily from the perspectives of women, social justice, space, memory, and performance.

About the Contributors

Leila Moayeri Pazargadi is an Associate Professor of English at Nevada State College, teaching composition, postcolonial literature, life writing, ethnic American literature, and Middle Eastern literature courses. She received her Doctorate of Philosophy in Comparative Literature with a certification in Gender Studies from the University of California, Los Angeles, in 2012. Her research focuses on Middle Eastern women writers producing autobiographical material in fiction and non-fiction after 9/11, which also includes scholarship on the visual forms of comics, in addition to Persian photography of the Qajar era. In 2020, she was a Visiting Scholar at UCLA's Center for Near Eastern Studies researching Middle Eastern women's memoirs for her upcoming monograph: *Mosaics of Exiled Identity: Reading Middle Eastern Women's Memoirs from Across the Diaspora*.

Quynh H. Vo is a Professorial Lecturer of Asia, Pacific, and Diaspora Studies at American University where she teaches and researches globalization and Asian literature, Asian American interdisciplinary studies, Vietnamese American literature and culture, and neoliberalism in American transnational literature. Dr. Vo's writings have appeared in *The Los Angeles Review of Books*, *diaCRITICS*, *Journal of Literary and Cultural Studies*, *Journal of Vietnamese Studies*, *Da Mau*, *Saigoneer*, the *Peace, Land, Bread*, and other venues.

Kaori Mori Want is an Associate Professor of English at Konan Women's University, Japan. She is the author of refereed articles and book chapters on Asian Pacific Americans. She is the author of *Hapa America: The History and Culture of Multiracial Asian Pacific Americans* (Ochanomizu Shobo, 2017).

www.ingramcontent.com/pod-product-compliance
Lightning Source LLC
Chambersburg PA
CBHW020744020526
44115CB00030B/918